Business English

Writing in the Workplace

FOURTH EDITION

Blanche Ettinger, Ed. D.

Bronx Community College of the City University of New York

Edda Perfetto, Ed. D.

Educational Consultant

PEARSON

Prentice Hall

Upper Saddle River, New Jersey 07458

Library of Congress Cataloging-in-Publication Data

Ettinger, Blanche.
   Business english writing in the workplace / Blanche Ettinger, Edda Perfetto. — 4th ed.
      p. cm.
   Title of 3rd ed.: Communication for the workplace.
   Includes bibliographical references and index.
   ISBN 0-13-156570-2
1. Business communication.   2. Business writing.   I. Perfetto, Edda.   II. Ettinger, Blanche.
Communication for the workplace.   III. Title.
   HF5718.E88 2007
   808'.06665—dc22

                                                                    2006025631

Editor-in-Chief: Vernon R. Anthony
Senior Acquisitions Editor: Gary Bauer
Editorial Assistant: Dan Trudden
Marketing Manager: Leigh Ann Sims
Marketing Coordinator: Alicia Dysert
Managing Editor—Production: Mary Carnis
Manufacturing Buyer: Ilene Sanford
Production Liaison: Denise Brown
Full-Service Production and Composition: Judy Ludowitz/Carlisle Publishing Services
Manager of Media Production: Amy Peltier
Media Production Project Manager: Lisa Rinaldi
Senior Design Coordinator/Cover Design: Christopher Weigand
Cover Image: Photodisc/Getty Images
Printer/Binder: Banta Harrisonburg
Cover Printer: Phoenix Color

Pearson Education Ltd.
Pearson Education Singapore Pte. Ltd.
Pearson Education Canada, Ltd.
Pearson Education—Japan

Pearson Education Australia PTY, Limited
Pearson Education North Asia Ltd.
Pearson Educatión de Mexico, S. A. de C. V.
Pearson Education Malaysia, Pte. Ltd.

10 9 8 7 6 5 4 3 2 1
ISBN 0-13-156570-2

BRIEF CONTENTS

CONTENTS

CHAPTER 5

Lots of Commas in Real Estate 96

CHAPTER 6

Maintaining Healthy Complex Sentences   *121*

CHAPTER 7

Retailing Commas in Words, Phrases, and Clauses 148

CHAPTER 8

Check-In with the Semicolon

CHAPTER 9

Marketing Possessives   *203*

CHAPTER 10

Traveling with Colons and Pronouns

CHAPTER 11

Governing Quotations

CHAPTER 12

PREFACE

Globalization of the marketplace has required businesses to modify their strategies so that they can remain competitive. One major area that is affected is the workforce. The demand is for employees who are skilled, diverse, and literate. Communicating effectively means survival for a company. Consequently, students, many of whom have diverse cultural and socioeconomic backgrounds, are faced with the task of developing basic language skills required in both the academic and business world.

Business English: Writing in the Workplace, Fourth Edition focuses primarily on mastering the communication skills necessary for employees to possess in a multicultural environment. Following the format of the previous editions, this text workbook uses a no-frills approach to help the learner get to the core of basic problems in **written communications.** Throughout the text, changes have been made and material has been added to enhance the content of the book.

As in previous editions, students will find the text workbook user-friendly, challenging but not overwhelming. Students are involved in the learning process through a step-by-step approach in developing their writing skills. Users progress from a novice level of writing to a stage at which they are more confident in composing. Learners are encouraged to develop their critical thinking, decision-making, and problem-solving skills when faced with case studies.

One of the unique features of this text is that each chapter focuses on a **specific industry.** To broaden the student's knowledge of today's workplace, all the content in a chapter relates to the particular business.

This material includes a review of grammar, punctuation principles, vocabulary, spelling, proofreading, composing correspondence, and report writing. Throughout the book, there is information on companies, diversity, cultural customs, and potential career opportunities.

STUDENT TEXT FEATURES

Each chapter is formatted into sections that build on previous learning and develop new skills with a variety of activities:

- **Language Arts Recall** (activity A)
  Section reviews grammar, punctuation, and English usage rules followed by a short deductive-approach exercise to reinforce learning.

- **Building English Power** (activity A)
  This review exercise applies the rules learned in the Language Arts Recall section.

- **Building Word Power** (activity B)
  Vocabulary related to a particular industry is introduced; words are taken from the documents that will be completed in the chapter.

- **On the Alert**
  This segment alerts the student to troublesome words and technical keyboarding formats that appear in the chapter.

- **Industry Perspectives** (activity C)
  This exercise has a dual purpose. Students are given updated information about trends in particular industries. At the same time, students are required to

proofread and correct errors in English usage, punctuation, and formatting. Each exercise builds on principles studied in previous lessons; again, reinforcing learning.

- **Editing Power** (activity D)
Students are given more complex tasks which require editing, proofreading, and formatting rough draft copy. In keeping with the guidelines of the book, previously learned principles are incorporated into the content.

- **Writing Practicum** (activity E)
This is an important activity in each chapter. It deals with troublesome aspects of writing. Through a variety of exercises, students refine their writing skills by tackling individual areas of concern, such as correct use of verb tenses, word choices, parallelism, and concise writing.

- **Writing Power** (activity F)
All prior activities culminate in this section. Students develop their ability to compose correspondence. Within the chapter, the cases progress from easy assignments to more complex cases that require mastery of language arts and decision marking. The transition from one chapter to another is also noted by incorporating previous learning.

- **Report Writing Power** (activity G)
In later chapters, students are expected to prepare reports, proposals, news releases, and minutes of meetings.

- **Surfing the Web** (activity H)
The use of the Internet is crucial in global communications. In the latter part of the book, students are assigned tasks that involve obtaining information on the Web. This assignment gives students an opportunity to refine researching skills which they need both in academic and business environments.

- **Self-Assessment Exercises:** These exercises appear at the end of each chapter. They can be used as practice tests to assess the student's understanding of concepts or as tests for grading. **Unit tests** for formal grading are also included in the text content.

Writer's OneKey: This is an online tutorial resource site that includes grammar and punctuation review exercises, practice quizzes, research guidelines, and tutorial writing assistance. Students will be able to interact with their instructor by linking on to course documents and progress reports. Wherever applicable, Writer's OneKey is correlated with the text chapters. Access to this Web site offers students another venue for reinforcing writing skills

OTHER FEATURES OF THE TEXT

- Web exercises related to realistic research topics
- Annotated models of letters, memorandums, and reports
- Corporate snapshots featuring individual companies
- Job snapshots portraying a variety of jobs within an industry
- Notations highlighting cultural diversities pertinent to the business world

This user-friendly text workbook can be used individually, in cooperative group learning, and in traditional classroom settings. It is an excellent reference guide because it offers an abundance of information on English usage and business writing.

The goal of this book is to make each user a successful communicator in today's global, diverse workplace.

ACKNOWLEDGMENTS

We are indebted to our students who have inspired and challenged us throughout our teaching careers to search for alternative instructional strategies that encourage learning.

For our families' continued support and understanding, we extend our appreciation. We thank Marie Ruvo for volunteering her time in assisting us in the preparation of the manuscript.

Thank's to Gary Bauer, Dan Trudden, Michelle Churma, and Alicia Dysert at Pearson Prentice Hall for your confidence in us to continue to provide a professional textbook to meet the challenges of today's academic and business world. Thank's to Judy Ludowitz at Carlisle Publishing Services for all her efforts.

We also feel it is important to acknowledge the important contribution of our reviewers who made valuable suggestions which we incorporated in this edition: Sandy Boyd, Ed.D., College of Marin, San Rafael, CA; Doreen LaBlanc, Bronx Community College, Bronx, NY; Evelyn Gardner, Trident Technical College, Charleston, SC; Susan Guzman-Trevino, Temple College, Temple, TX; Henry Castillo, Temple College, Temple, TX; Gwen L. Eltz, Spokane Falls Community College, Spokane, WA; Sara Morgan, Minnesota School of Business, Minneapolis, MN.

ABOUT THE AUTHORS

Blanche Ettinger is a professor in the Department of Secretarial and Office Information Systems at Bronx Community College of The City University of New York. She received her M.S. degree from Hunter College of The City University of New York and an Ed.D. in business education from New York University. Blanche is recognized nationally for her professional contributions and involvement in business education. Among the many awards, Blanche received the prestigious Delta Pi Epsilon National Research Award for her dissertation on identifying word processing competencies to develop a curriculum at the post-secondary level. She has served on many executive boards of college and professional associations. Through the years, Blanche has been a speaker, moderator, and panelist at national and local professional seminars. Among her publications (some with co-authors) are: *Machine Transcription, Applied Language Skills, Third Edition; Medical Transcription;* career series that include *Opportunities in Secretarial Careers, Opportunities in Office Occupations, and Opportunities in Customer Service Careers; A Secretary's Reference Guide* for use at Bronx Community College.

Edda Perfetto received her Master's degree from Hunter College of the City University of New York and an Ed.D. from New York University. For over thirty-five years, Edda was a dedicated teacher, supervisor, and Dean of Students on the secondary level. She also taught secretarial studies at the community college level. Her interest in providing instructional materials that were relevant and exciting to her students motivated Edda to focus her doctoral studies in the area of curriculum and instructional design. She co-authored *Machine Transcription, Applied Language Skills, Third Edition;* conducted seminars and workshops on methods of teaching business education subjects; and was actively involved on the executive boards of professional organizations. Well-respected by her colleagues, Edda received numerous professional awards as an outstanding educator.

The authors are accessible to any colleague who seeks their support. They are willing to share their experiences in the teaching of business communications. You can get in touch with Blanche and Edda by e-mail or a simple phone call. They wish you success with the text.

CHAPTER 1

Banking on Good Sentence Structure

CORPORATE SNAPSHOT

WASHINGTON MUTUAL's belief in change for the better has been a strategy for success. The bank was formed to offer financial assistance to the Seattle community after the devastating Great Fire of 1889. From a small West Coast bank, the customer-oriented Washington Mutual has expanded to become one of the nation's largest mortgage lenders.

Washington Mutual is committed to support the communities it serves. It has been a leader in providing affordable lending to neighborhoods across the country. Such a program has been especially beneficial to lower-income families.

Employees are encouraged to give back to their communities. They can take up to four hours of paid time per month to volunteer their services. Washington Mutual is respected as a good employer and a good neighbor.

Source: *http://www.wamu.com/home.htm*

WHAT YOU WILL LEARN IN THIS CHAPTER

- To analyze basic sentence structure
- To apply correct capitalization
- To develop a business vocabulary in **BANKING**
- To proofread and edit correspondence and reports
- To acquire the skills for effective writing
- To compose an informational letter
- To compose promotional letters

Introduction

Our global economy demands accurate interchanging of ideas and information. A successful organization requires its employees to possess excellent communications skills. Employees must be able to communicate effectively with management, coworkers, customers, and the general public. Frequently, this interchange of ideas takes place among individuals of diverse cultures in different parts of the world. A miscommunication can cause a firm financial losses and even social misunderstandings. Therefore, information must be transmitted accurately, correctly, and clearly understood.

Activities in this text are designed to provide you with the skills to become a proficient communicator. With this goal in mind, each chapter presents sections that focus on those writing components that are necessary in achieving your final goal, mastering written communications.

The activities include:

- reviewing grammar and punctuation principles
- building vocabulary related to specific industries
- improving proofreading skills
- developing the writing process

Job Snapshot   Banking

LOAN OFFICER: Works for banks or mortgage companies, facilitates the lending process for a client, gathers personal information on applicant, analyzes and verifies the credit status of an individual, proposes best type of loan, executes application forms and payment schedule.

Skills: college degree in finance or economics, computer, interpersonal skills.

BANK TELLER: Represents the bank to individual clients and businesses, direct contact with customers, handles all money transactions such as deposits, withdrawals, and cashing of checks. Excellent experience for promotions.

Skills: communication, listening, math and interpersonal skills; associate degree preferred.

CUSTOMER SERVICE REPRESENTATIVE: Serves as bank consultant, problem solver, and financial counselor to individual clients; facilitates opening of new accounts, offers suggestions on bank products, such as IRAs, CDs, annuities; handles customer complaints.

Skills: two-year degree majoring in business preferable, on-the-job experience, knowledgeable in bank products, interpersonal and organizational skills.

Activity A Language Arts Recall

In each chapter, Activity A will focus on reviewing grammar and punctuation principles.

Sentence Structure

You must write in complete sentences to express your thoughts clearly and accurately. Sentences are varied from simple statements to more complex patterns. This chapter will review the basic format of a sentence. In succeeding chapters, more intricate patterns intended to enrich content will be reviewed.

> **Rule 1.1:** A **sentence** is a group of words which expresses a complete thought and makes sense grammatically. It consists of a complete subject and a complete predicate.

The **subject** is a person or thing spoken about. It is usually a *noun* or a *pronoun* (known as a simple subject). The *complete subject* includes modifiers related to the noun or pronoun.

Examples:

bank, customer, loan, we (noun, pronoun)

local bank, preferred customers, equity loan (noun plus modifiers)

The **predicate** expresses what the subject does or what is done to the subject. It may consist of a main verb or a verb with its modifiers. The *simple predicate* is the main verb or one with several helping words. The *complete predicate* includes the verb and all other related words.

Examples of simple predicate (verb):

apply, review, and approve (verb or action word)

should apply, has reviewed, will be approved (verb with helping words)

Examples of sentences that contain complete subjects and complete predicates:

simple subject / simple predicate

The bank will review immediately the mortgage application.
complete predicate

complete subject / simple predicate

The home equity loan has not been approved by the bank.
complete predicate

> **Rule 1.2:** **Sentence fragment** is a group of words which does *not* express a complete thought. Sentence fragments are grammatically incorrect.

Still Puzzled? See *Writer's OneKey* Home Page select topic: Sentence Fragments. Click on: What is a sentence fragment? How to identify sentence fragment?

Examples:
- The bank will review immediately. (does not express a complete thought; a fragment, not a sentence)
- Banks that offer many services. (*that* introduces a restrictive clause; no predicate; a fragment)
- Although the software was available. (dependent clause; cannot stand alone; a fragment)

CAPITALIZATION

Rule 1.3: The first word of a sentence is capitalized.

Example: **O**ur local bank will be closed on Labor Day.

Rule 1.4: Proper names, days of the week, and months are capitalized.

Example: The **H**artsdale **S**avings **B**ank will have extended hours beginning **M**onday, **S**eptember 1.

Rule 1.5: Abbreviations of well-known organizations and common business terms are usually capitalized.

Examples: FDIC (Federal Deposit Insurance Corporation) ATM (automated teller machine IRA (individual retirement account) CD (certificate of deposit)

Rule 1.6: Capitalize all major words in the title of complete published works, such as books, periodicals, and newspapers. Do not capitalize articles (the), conjunctions (and), or short prepositions (with) unless they begin the title. Italicize the complete title of a published work.

Examples: Our local newspaper, *Daily Review,* carries a weekly column on consumer saving.

The American Council for Banking Reform has published a booklet titled *The Consumer's Guide to Managing Income*.

Rule 1.7: Capitalize words derived from proper nouns.

Examples: American (derived from "America") Japanese (derived from "Japan")

Note: These derivatives are used as adjectives, words that describe a noun.

Example: The *Canadian* bank will open branches in Eastern Europe.

Check for Understanding

The following exercise will help you to identify a complete sentence versus a sentence fragment.

Directions: Read each of the following statements and complete the questions that follow.

1. Community Savings Bank is expanding on the West Coast.

2. The $25,000 home equity line of credit that was approved.

3. Since interest rates are rising, the demand for loans has dropped.

4. After the bank's announcement to offer a six-month CD.

QUESTIONS

a. What do statements 1 and 3 have in common relative to their sentence structure?

_____

b. How are statements 2 and 4 different from 1 and 3 in their sentence structure?

_____

c. What part of speech is missing to complete statement 2?

_____

d. Why is statement 4 not considered a sentence?

_____

Answers to "Check for Understanding"
a. complete sentence   b. sentence fragments
c. verb   d. dependent clause

Building English Power: Sentence Structure

Answers to "Building English Power" in each chapter can be found in appendix A. Complete this activity before checking answers.

EXERCISE 1 In the blanks provided on the left, indicate whether the sentences are complete (C) or incomplete (I). In the complete sentences, underline the <u>simple subject</u> with a <u>single line</u> and the <u>simple predicate</u> (verb) with a <u>double line</u>.

_____ 1. Internet banking is replacing traditional banking practices.

_____ 2. Bank mergers throughout the country.

_____ 3. Finance charges do not appear on this month's statement.

_____ **4.** To access an ATM, you need the customer's personal identification number.

_____ **5.** No annual fee for the first year.

_____ **6.** When you use a debit card.

_____ **7.** As a valued customer, you have a minimum credit line of $10,000.

_____ **8.** The bank requested collateral before issuing the loan.

_____ **9.** If you pay your credit card balance in full each month to avoid interest charges.

_____ **10.** At the end of the calendar year, the bank will inform you of the total interest accrued on all accounts.

_____ **11.** Direct deposit is encouraged.

_____ **12.** Banks require that you provide identification when cashing a check.

_____ **13.** The local bank offers investment plans to its customers.

_____ **14.** The penalty charge for insufficient funds in your checking account.

_____ **15.** Because ATMs are available 24 hours a day.

_____ **16.** Banking on the Internet.

_____ **17.** The bank credit card can be used as a cash card when making purchases.

_____ **18.** The financial advisor suggested opening an IRA account.

_____ **19.** A popular banking service is direct payments of utility bills.

_____ **20.** Some bank credit cards offer frequent flyer bonus points.

Need more practice? See *One Writer's Key* Go to toolbar and click on Practice & Assess, then click on Exercises.

Complete exercises 1 and 2 on Sentence Fragments.

EXERCISE 2 Rewrite each incomplete sentence which you identified in Exercise 1 to make it a complete sentence. Add words if necessary. (See appendix A for sample answers.)

Note: Writing tasks may be completed on a computer.

_____

_____

_____

_____

_____

_____

Building English Power: Capitalization

Directions: In the following sentences, (circle) each lowercase letter that should be capitalized. Indicate italics by <u>underlining</u>. Corresponding rules follow each sentence.

1. you must reply by september 1 to receive the promotional rate for the cd. (1.3, 1.4, 1.5)

2. the monthly newsletter, the bank forum, gives investment advice to the employees. (1.3, 1.6)

3. new york bank will be closed on saturdays during july and august. (1.3, 1.4)

4. most savings accounts are insured by the fdic, a government agency known as the federal deposit insurance corporation. (1.3, 1.5)

5. what did you think of mr. baker's speech in san francisco on banking reforms? (1.3, 1.4)

6. the federal home loan mortgage corporation announced that mortgage rates are on the rise. (1.3, 1.4)

7. eastern trust offers an ira that has no annual fee. (1.3, 1.4)

8. a cd account offers the investor a higher rate of interest. (1.3, 1.5)

9. the new computer software, known as bank express, will allow users to keep personal and financial records up to date. (1.3, 1.4)

10. on thursday, december 1, the royal bank will introduce its new service for investors. (1.3, 1.4)

11. dr. alan smith will speak on global investments at the orlando convention center in florida on saturday, july 8. (1.4)

12. atms are located in many shopping malls in the united states. (1.3, 1.4, 1.5)

13. the american bank will sponsor the next world cup usa. (1.3, 1.4)

14. pathways to financial security made the new york times best-seller booklist. (1.3, 1.4, 1.6)

15. the european bank will expand its offices to singapore and hong kong. (1.3, 1.4, 1.7)

16. the banking institute of america publishes a spanish edition of its pamphlet on ira's. (1.3, 1.4, 1.5, 1.7)

17. the weekly newspaper, *financial review*, publishes the popular column, "world banking." (1.3, 1.6)

18. bank savings and ira accounts are fdic insured. (1.3, 1.5)

19. The bank will be closed on monday, presidents' day. (1.3, 1.4)

20. The union bank of new york has appointed jane pastor chairperson of the health benefits task force. (1.3, 1.4)

Activity B   Building Word Power

A rich vocabulary gives an individual superior communication skills. Such an individual is a valuable asset to a company that strives to portray a positive image in the marketplace.

A well-written letter or report reflects the strong use of words. In this activity throughout the text, you will be able to increase your vocabulary of particular industries.

Directions: The words that follow are commonly used in the banking industry. From this list, select the word or phrase that correctly completes each statement. Before completing the vocabulary exercise in each chapter refer to the Personal Dictionary in Appendix F for the meaning of each word.

As a new employee, watch, listen, and learn.

accrued
ATM
authorization
electronic banking
CDs
co-applicant
collateral
debit card
equity line of credit

FDIC
global
insufficient funds
IRAs
mortgage
network
specialists
transactions

_____ 1. The depositor had _____ in the account to pay the bill.

_____ 2. With _____, customers can use computers, telephones, or teller machines to conduct banking business.

_____ 3. To meet _____ competition, business is required to understand the needs of foreign markets.

_____ 4. A(n) _____ is a long-term loan obtained by an individual to purchase a home; the debt is repaid to the bank on a monthly basis.

_____ 5. The client gave written _____ to his lawyer to sell his property.

_____ 6. Banking _____ frequently involve the transfer of money.

_____ 7. _____ are experts who are consulted in specific areas, such as home mortgages, foreign investments, and bonds.

_____ 8. How much interest has _____ on my CD account?

_____ 9. His sister was willing to be a(n) _____ in assuming the financial responsibility for repayment of the loan.

_____ **10.** The firm's computer _____ links the main office with its branches throughout the country.

_____ **11.** Banks offer specialized savings accounts, known as _____, that cannot be withdrawn without a penalty until the depositor reaches retirement age.

_____ **12.** The greatest advantage of a(n) _____ is the opportunity to withdraw cash 24 hours a day without interacting with a bank employee.

_____ **13.** Individuals can pledge as _____ their automobiles, jewelry, bank accounts, and stocks to guarantee a loan.

_____ **14.** The government agency, the _____, insures savings accounts to a maximum of $100,000.

_____ **15.** Savings banks offer _____ for one, two, and three years. Although these investments generally offer a higher interest rate, they carry a penalty for early withdrawal.

_____ **16.** I use my _____ when paying for the grocery bill at the supermarket.

_____ **17.** I pledged my house as security to obtain a $25,000 _____.

(Answers to "Building Word Power" in each chapter can be found in appendix A.)

 On the Alert

This section will highlight troublesome words, grammar, and number rules that apply to the proofreading and editing documents that appear in each chapter. The items mentioned in this section have not been covered in previous chapters. Read this information carefully before completing activities C and D.

■ A sentence that makes a statement or gives information is a *declarative sentence* and *ends with a period*.

Example: U.S. banks invest in foreign countries.

■ A sentence that begins with the words *who, what, where, when, why,* or *how* is a question and ends with a question mark (?).

Example: Who is the new bank manager?

■ Common business abbreviations are acceptable when understood by the reader. Plurals of abbreviations that are two or more letters are formed without an apostrophe.

Examples: ATM, IRA, ATMs, IRAs

■ Periods are generally omitted in abbreviations that are all capitalized.

    Examples: FDIC, CD (certificate of deposit)

■ access (noun)—means of entry, approach

    Example: John had *access* to the bank vault.

■ excess (noun)—surplus, extra

    Example: The *excess* profits will be distributed to the stockholders.

EDITING AND PROOFREADING

After the initial draft of a document is completed, editing and proof-reading become the next stage in the writing process. The completed document should meet the criteria of the six Cs: clear, complete, concise, consistent, correct, and courteous. Editing is the final review of the written document. The message must be checked to be certain that it is effective in its structure and readability. The writer should consider the following:

• Sentences do not begin with the same word.

• Words in the document are not overused.

• Sentences should flow and be interconnected, rather than choppy.

• Avoid slang or informal language.

• Quality of the message is powerful yet attractive to the reader.

Proofreading focuses on correcting mechanical errors in spelling, punctuation, capitalization, grammar, and word usage. A document needs to be error-free. It is suggested that you proofread the hard copy by reading each word. This will slow you down to catch errors. If you read the screen copy, scroll down slowly so that you read for meaning. If a document is very important, two individuals should proofread the material together. Feel free to use the spell-and-grammar checks provided by the software programs. This is an added way of proof-reading copy. However, these programs do not always catch errors. The writer must decide on the choice of words and clarity of the message.

    Checklist for Effective Writing

_____ Content focused on main idea of the document

_____ Correct sentence structure; no run-on or incomplete sentences

_____ Even flow of sentences for smooth reading

_____ Varied use of words rather than repetitive use; ex. I

_____ Correct spelling, grammar, punctuation

    Activities C and D in each chapter will help you refine the important skills of proofreading and editing.

TRENDS

Activity C   Industry Perspectives: Banking Trends

In this section of each chapter, new trends of a particular industry are discussed. "Industry Perspectives" is presented as a report that requires you to proofread for English usage, spelling, punctuation, and typographical errors.

Directions: Using appropriate revision marks, proofread, correct, and key the following report. (See appendix E for explanation of proofreaders' marks.)

Rule Reference	
	Electronic banking service has become very popular in
1.4	banking transactions in america. This is also true in
1.7	european and asian countries. You may us an automated
	teller machine to make deposits or withdrawals without
1.3	interacting with a bank employee. in automated systems,
	you may withdraw cash immediately from your checking or
	savings account. Deposits can also be made to these
	accounts, and funds between accounts can be exchanged
	easily. You simply insert a card with your personal
1.5, 1.2	identification code number at at an atm station. Which
	is available at most banks.
1.2	You can do your banking. In any part of the country
1.3	and at any time through a computer networking system.
1.4	Electronic banking service is expanding to include
	direct payroll deposits, retail store purchase
	transactions, and personal bankking transactions from a
	home computer.
1.3	for individuals with busy schedules, electronic
1.4	banking is available seven days a week, monday through
	sunday.

Did you find these errors?

8 capitalization errors
2 sentence fragments
3 typographical/spelling

(See Appendix B for models of letter format. You have the option of choosing your preferred style for the inside address.)

Activity D   Editing Power

Introduction

When editing correspondence, you should read carefully for correct English usage, punctuation, content, and clarity. "Editing Power" has two tasks that will help you refine your proofreading skill to produce error-free copy.

    After you have completed Task A, compare your copy with the answer in Appendix A. At this stage, it is important that you analyze your errors and review any rules that pertain to the errors. Task B is a more challenging assignment in which you are expected to submit a mailable copy to your instructor.

Task A: Edit, format, and proofread the following letter for errors. Use proofreaders' symbols to mark the errors; then key the letter correctly. Answers to Task A can be found in Appendix A.

Errors

- Sentence fragments
- Capitalization
- Typographical
- Italicize published work

```
Date

Mr. Joseph Robinson
131 Post Road
Duluth, MN 55803-5122

Dear Mr. Robinson

Thank you for choosing fidelity savings bank for your

banking needs. We are confident you will be happy doing

business with us.

    we are enclosing our latet brochure, banking made

easy for the consumer. Which describes teh many services

we offer customers. These services include free checking

with interest, direct deposits, iras, cds, and life

insurance.
```

Our bank is open six days a week monday to friday, from 9 a.m. to 3 p.m. and on saturday until noon. For your convenience, we have evening banking hours on tuesday and thursday. We are also expanding our canadian services by opening branches on october 10 in montreal and quebec.

You will benefit from the many services offered by fidelity savings bank, a member of the federal deposit insurance corporation.

Cordially yours,

Peter Gerena
Manager
ri
Enclosure

Challenge Task B: Edit, format, and proofread the following unarranged letter for all errors, then key it correctly. (See Appendix B for model of letter format.)

International Electronics Company, 14 Central Avenue, Indianapolis, IN 46204-1352 Ladies and Gentlemen: american trust company is happy to announce the formation of a of a new department to serve ourr international clients. we will be able to serve corporations and financial institutions with branch offices in europe and asia.

Global Services, the name of this department, will be staffed by specialists who understaand the foreign market and can supply you with information to help you make profitable business decisions.

You may contact us at our main office on 56 river road to open an account. So that we may assist your firm in meeting international competition. Yours truly, Frank

Jarcho, Vice President.

Activity E   Writing Practicum

Introduction

The ability to write well involves multitasks. The focal point of a message is to convey accurately to the reader the thoughts of the writer. The writer needs to recognize correct organizational and grammatical aspects involved in good writing.

The exercises in this writing practicum will enhance your writing skills by focusing on specific areas of composing that a writer must know when preparing correspondence or documents.

EXERCISE 1   WRITING IN COMPLETE THOUGHTS

A common writing problem is sentence fragments. As you learned, a sentence fragment is an incomplete thought. The focus of this writing practicum is to recognize sentence fragments and to revise each one into a complete sentence that has a subject and a verb and that expresses a complete thought.

Either begin or end each sentence with a complete thought. Use the blank space provided to complete each sentence.

1. When a small Midwestern bank failed, the FDIC assured depositors _____.

2. Banking online allows depositors _____.

3. Bank USA, a global bank, offer its clients _____.

4. One of the restrictions in a CD account is _____.

5. As interest rates dropped, many customers of the bank chose _____.

6. _____ is one of the ways in which banks make money.

7. The benefit of using an ATM account _____

8. If mortgage rates continue to increase, _____.

9. The letter from Mr. Robinson, the bank president, explained _____.

10. An IRA is an important way for an individual_____.

(Answers to writing practicum in each chapter are in Appendix A.)

EXERCISE 2 COMBINING SENTENCES

Sentences should not be wordy, choppy, or fragmented; they should flow for clarity and easy reading. Your goal is to combine each set of sentences into one meaningful sentence that expresses the main idea. You may add, delete, or rephrase words.

Example

National Trust is a bank.

It has opened a branch office in our neighborhood.

It has Saturday banking hours.

Combined Sentence: National Trust Bank opened a branch office in our neighborhood that has Saturday banking hours.

1. ATMs are convenient.

    Busy persons who conduct banking transactions 24 hours a day.

    ATMs are open 24 hours a day.

    Combined Sentence: _____

2. The bank has a special loan rate.

    The loan rate for a car is 7 percent.

    It must be an American-made car.

    Combined Sentence: _____

3. A certificate of deposit is a term savings account.

    It pays a higher rate of interest.

    That carries a penalty for early withdrawal of money.

    Combined Sentence: _____

4. The Internet is used for banking transactions.

    Many depositors have online accounts.

    Depositors can download statements and pay their bills.

    Combined Sentence: _____

5. The bank offers a basic checking account.

    With a basic checking account, you can open the account for as little as $250.

    With a basic checking account, you do not need to maintain a minimum balance.

    Combined Sentence: _____

6. Some individuals choose an equity line of credit. They choose equity loans to make large purchases. Use an equity loan for a down payment on a house.

    Combined Sentence: _____

EXERCISE 3 DEVELOPING MEANINGFUL PARAGRAPHS

The following passage needs to be rewritten for correctness of expression and logical flow of thoughts.

You may change any sentence that you believe is incorrect. Examine each sentence and decide whether you agree to keep the original sentence or rewrite it. In the blank space provided after each sentence, indicate whether you will keep (K) or rewrite (R) the sentence.

Rearrange the order of the sentences so that the ideas are related and there is a logical flow of thought forming meaningful paragraphs, then key the passage.

1. Banking in America has changed dramatically over the past decade. _____

2. Banks have responded to changing needs of the consumer in the local communities. _____

3. The electronic age has introduced ATMs, direct deposits, and computer transactions, which improved banking services. _____

4. Customers now receive fast, without long waiting lines, efficient service. _____

5. Also, with electronic banking systems, customers can transact their financial business from any area of the country. _____

6. Also, a large number of banks have merged to offer additional services that facilitate handling global transactions. _____

7. They are open some evenings, Saturdays, and Sunday mornings. _____

8. Banks are prepared to meet the challenges of the next millennium with these changes. _____

   ■ List in order of preference the sentence numbers, and then key the passage.

   ____ ____ ____ ____ ____ ____ ____ ____

EXERCISE 4   WRITING OPENING AND CLOSING SENTENCES IN LETTERS

INTRODUCTION

Correspondence in the workplace needs to be clear, specific, and positive. The tone of a letter or memo is very important; it reflects the feelings of an individual or an organization. To attract the reader's attention, the message should convey favorable information. It should avoid the use of negative words or gender-related language.

OPENING SENTENCES

A reader's reaction is formed immediately with the opening statement in a firm's correspondence; therefore, it is important that the introductory sentence attracts the reader to continue reading the message.

In preparation for composing business letters, this exercise will help you focus on writing good opening sentences. From each group, choose the best sentence that would appear in correspondence from a bank. Write your answer, A or B, in the space provided.

_____ **1. a.** Some banks charge fees. Does yours?

b. Are you paying a fee for your bank credit card?

_____ **2. a.** We want you as a Webb customer, and to prove it we're offering you many free banking services.

b. At Webb we are offering many free banking services.

_____ **3. a.** North Branch Bank is expanding into Westchester County.

b. North Branch Bank, with more than $10 billion in assets, is now building branches to serve Westchester County.

_____ **4. a.** The Money Master Debit Card from Suburban Bank is convenient and fast.

b. At Suburban Bank, we understand your busy life and are offering the Money Master Debit Card.

CLOSING SENTENCES

Closings in correspondence should end with a courteous, positive statement. A favorable impression should be left with the reader. In order to maintain goodwill, it is suggested that the writer offer any required action when needed.

Directions: From each group choose the best closing sentence that would appear in letters from a bank. Write your answer, A or B, in the space provided.

_____ **5. a.** Feel free to talk to our bank counselors at 800-465-2000.

b. Our bank counselors are available to help you. We invite you to call us at 800-465-2000 or visit us at any of our branches.

_____ **6. a.** Call now and protect your future.

b. Call now to protect your future; open an IRA with us.

_____ **7. a.** We invite you to take advantage of this special offer.

b. Come in and take advantage of this special offer.

_____ **8. a.** Our retirement plan is important to your future. We are confident that we shall hear from you soon.

b. Our retirement plan is important to your future so see us soon.

INTRODUCTION: GOOD LETTER WRITING

Effective business correspondence is essential for an organization to maintain a positive image with customers and to obtain the desired results. Business letters are used primarily to communicate formal messages to persons outside the organization. There are various reasons for writing business letters. They may provide information, respond to requests, order goods and services, or give notifications.

A good communicator must use the six Cs of writing. The correspondence should be:

- *Clear*—understood easily by the receiver
- *Complete*—give all the necessary facts or data
- *Concise*—present information to the point; avoid wordiness
- *Correct*—provide accurate information without grammatical or formatting errors
- *Consistent*—write in a logical manner to include an opening, body, closing
- *Courteous*—convey a friendly, helpful tone

The following guidelines will help you write an effective business letter:

■ State purpose of letter (to inform, to respond, to request, to persuade, to express a feeling).

■ Focus on a specific audience (global, local, or internal audience).

■ Gather accurate information.

■ Organize information (opening, middle, closing).

■ Use correct format and attractive appearance.

■ Communicate a friendly tone.

■ Use courteous closing.

In each chapter, "Writing Pointers" highlight essential items that need to be considered before writing a specific type of business correspondence effectively. These pointers give helpful suggestions to aid you in composing your response to the case studies in activity F. Study "Writing Pointers" before composing the correspondence.

The "Model Letters" that appear in each chapter offer another opportunity to review good letter writing. The models refer to specific types of business letters discussed in the chapter.

Writing Pointers

INFORMATIONAL LETTER

■ Focus on the information to be disseminated.
■ Write to the point.
■ State main idea immediately.
■ Give specific facts and details.
■ End with a courteous, positive tone.

PROMOTIONAL LETTER

■ Attract attention with a strong opening statement.
■ Build up the reader's curiosity to react to the promotion.
■ State the objectives of the promotional offer.
■ Appeal to reader's needs.
■ Be specific when indicating benefits.
■ Use appealing language.
■ Close with action statement; motivate customers to act.

A *form letter* is used to:
■ Reply to frequent requests for information.
■ Communicate information to a large number of people.

Model Informational Letter

Date

Mr. and Mrs. James Stevens
14 Maple Drive
Dobbs Ferry, NY 10532–1600

Dear Mr. and Mrs. Stevens:

Opening focuses on message

Appeals to specific reader's needs

Gives specific facts

Positive ending

Today's high cost of a college education often poses a financial hardship on the family. County Trust Bank is offering a special educational loan to its depositors.

For a limited time only, you will be able to obtain a loan at a special rate of 5 percent per annum. A loan kit explains in detail the specific benefits and affordable options. Fill out the enclosed card for your complimentary copy or call us at 800-623-5000.

If you wish to discuss this loan offer with one of our representatives, stop in at any one of our branch offices. We will be happy to help you get a loan.

Sincerely yours,

Ruth Marlowe
Financial Officer
ri
Enclosure

Activity F   Writing Power: Composing Correspondence

Now that you have reviewed the elements of English, expanded your business terminology, developed your editing and proofreading skills, and sharpened your ability to compose, you are ready to prepare correspondence based on practical business and personal business situations.

In each chapter, activity F presents case studies. In chapters 1, 2, and 3, case studies 1 and 2 are given as exercises to help you to organize your ideas in composing a letter that is simple, logical, and to the point.

Date

Dear Depositor:

Question attracts
attention

Are you facing the dilemma of the high cost of sending your child to
college?

Appeals to
specific reader's
needs
Gives specific
facts

County Trust Bank is introducing a new educational loan plan to help you
meet the rising cost of a college education. Our plan is geared to families
whose income falls below $50,000, and the introductory rate for the loan is
only 5 percent. If you act immediately, you will receive a loan kit that
explains in detail the specific benefits and affordable options.

Positive ending

Our representatives will gladly help you to apply for this outstanding offer.
Call us at 800-623-5000 and start saving money immediately.

Sincerely yours,

Ruth Marlowe
Financial Officer

ri

Case Study 1: Promotional Letter

Read Case Study 1. Then read options A, B, and C for each section of
the letter. Select the option that you believe is most appropriate for the
opening, body, and closing statements. Then key the entire letter
based on the options you selected.

Case: You are asked to draft a promotional letter to inform customers
of a new premium credit card. Key the letter based on your
options. Do not include an inside address or salutation.

Opening sentence:

a. As a customer, you have the opportunity of getting a premium
   credit card from us.

b. As our customer, we invite you to consider choosing our new premium card.

c. As one of our valued customers, we are offering you the opportunity to choose our premium credit card.

   Option A, B, or C_____

Sentences in body of letter

Sentence 1:

a. The card provides superior benefits and services without an annual fee.

b. Our card provides superior benefits and service. There is no annual fee.

c. The card gives you, the cardholder, benefits and services. No annual fee is charged.

Option A, B, or C_____

Sentence 2:

a. If you have a monthly balance, you will be charged a rate that is below the average of other financial institutions.

b. Our finance charge for unpaid balances is below the average rate required by other financial institutions.

c. Our charge for unpaid balances is below the average rate charged by other financial institutions.

Option A, B, or C_____

Sentence 3:

a. The card also offers a 90-day protection on purchases against theft or damage.

b. It also offers 90 days of protection on purchases against theft or damage.

c. It offers 90-day protection against theft or damage of merchandise.

Option A, B, or C _____

Sentence 4:

a. If you decide you want more cash, you can get the cash at an ATM.

b. You will be able to get cash at any ATM when you need it.

c. ATMs offer cash.

Option A, B, or C_____

Closing statement:

a. Call our toll-free customer service for your valued card.

b. We hope to hear from you soon.

c. There is 24-hour customer service at 800-255-5000. Complete the enclosed application form or call one of our representatives to receive your valued card.

Option A, B or C _____

Case Study 2: Informational Letter

Read case study 2. Then read Options A or B for each section of the letter. Select the option that you believe is most appropriate for the opening, body, and closing statements. Then key the entire letter based on the options you selected. At this time, do not include an inside address or salutation.

Case: You are asked to draft an informational letter that will be sent to depositors of County Trust Bank. The bank is expanding its financial services. A financial advisor will be available to offer investment plans to meet the needs of the individual depositor.

Opening sentences

Sentence 1:

a. County Trust Bank is announcing expansion of its financial services.

b. In response to many of our depositors, County Trust Bank is expanding its financial services.

Option A or B _____

Sentence 2:

a. In your branch, a financial advisor will be available to offer an investment plan to meet your needs.

b. We will provide a financial advisor to help with an investment plan.

Option A or B _____

Sentences in body of letter

Sentence 1:

a. The financial plan will be prepared by an advisor with experience.

b. The financial plan designed for you will be prepared by an advisor who has experience in this field.

Option A or B _____

Sentences 2/3:

a. You will be able to choose among a number of options. Long term investments include IRAs, CDs, mutual funds, and bonds.

b. You will be able to choose a number of long term options.

Option A or B _____

Body of letter continued with new paragraph

Sentences 4 and 5:

a. We are committed to offer you high quality investments with low risks. Planning now for a secure future is the advice we give to our depositors.

b. Plan now for a secure future by investing in high quality securities is our motto.

Option A or B _____

Closing statement:

a. Plan to meet with our financial advisor.

b. We invite you to make an appointment with the financial advisor at your branch in the near future.

Option A or B _____

Case Study 3: Informational Form Letter

Read case study 3, then respond to the questions that follow to help you organize your ideas before beginning to compose the correspondence. After you have completed the questions, compose the correspondence. Do not copy sentences as presented in any of the case studies. Remember when composing correspondence in any chapter use the correct format. Be creative and remember to add a closing line to retain the goodwill of the customer.

Case: Customers have been complaining that the banking hours are inadequate. Therefore, the County Trust Bank is adding hours on Thursday until 6 p.m. and on Saturdays from 9 a.m. until 1 p.m. Full banking services will be available to customers in the loan, investment, and insurance departments. Draft a *form letter* to bank customers notifying them of this added service. Use "Dear Depositor:" for the salutation.

Note: The following case study should be written as a form letter that is used when the same message is sent to many addresses. Inside addresses may be merged to personalize a form letter. (See letter format in the appendix.)

ORGANIZE YOUR IDEAS

1. What is the most important point you want to make to the bank's customers?

_____

_____

_____

2. What should you include in the opening statement?

_____

_____

_____

3. What specific details should you include in the body?

_____

_____

_____

4. What should you include in your closing statement to demonstrate the bank's goodwill toward its customers?

_____

_____

_____

Case Study 4: Promotional Form Letter

Case Study 4 will _not_ present a series of questions to guide you in your writing assignment. It will be challenging for you to compose correspondence without any prompts. If you feel that you need to have an outline of questions to help you draft the letter, feel free to refer back to case study 3, "Organize Your Ideas." Then compose the correspondence. (see letter format in Appendix B.)

You are reminded that good writing often requires revising the original draft. Do not hesitate to edit, proofread, and rewrite a draft for the final version of the correspondence.

Case: Draft a promotional form letter that will attract new depositors to Union Bank. Two types of CDs are being offered by the bank. One is a 12-month CD, minimum deposit $500, paying 4 percent. A two-year CD with a minimum of $1,000 is offered at 5 percent.

In addition, there are no fees for use of the ATM card. Also, for new depositors the bank is offering a free consultation with the bank's financial advisor. Encourage readers to open an account soon so they can take advantage of this limited offer. Use "Dear Depositor:" as salutation. The letter should be signed by Mario Lopez, Bank Manager.

Challenge Level Case

Case Study 5: Promotional Letter

To challenge you further, case study 5 in each chapter will present a case for which you will prepare the correspondence.

Case: The Empire State Bank wants to announce a limited-time offer for automobile loans at a low interest rate of $7\frac{1}{2}$ percent. This loan will be available only for the month of May. Ms. Laureen Ramos, your manager, has asked you to draft a form letter to be mailed to bank customers encouraging them to consider applying for such a loan. Individuals who want more information may contact their local branch office or call the toll-free number, 800-433-5000. (See letter format in Appendix B.)

➤ Cultural Communication

Culture is behavior patterns and values shared by a group of people. Culture influences people's way of life within a social group; that is, behavior, etiquette, and protocol.

American businesses are involved globally with multicultural societies. Both clients and employees come from diverse environments. Therefore, there is a need that we in America become familiar with and appreciate various cultures. We then can be more understanding and tolerant of individuals with different ethnic and social backgrounds. The challenge of American industry will be to communicate effectively with others on a global level.

Throughout the text, we have presented interesting facts about some countries that do business with Americans. We hope that you will continue to learn and communicate with diverse people in the United States and abroad who share other beliefs.

"Leadership and learning are indispensable to each other."

—John F. Kennedy

Self-Assessment
English Power

Directions: In the following sentences insert correct capitalization where needed.

1. executives at american bank will hold their meeting in salt lake city.

2. what effect will the federal reserve bank's increase in interest rates have on the economy?

3. in october my brother in minneapolis applied for a home equity loan at the century bank.

4. the main offices of southeast bank will move from atlanta to jacksonville.

5. atm accounts are convenient for individuals who travel throughout the united states, europe, and asia.

Directions: Choose which statements are complete. In the space provided, write the letter of the correct answer.

_____ 6. a. The increase in the CD rate.
   b. The increase in the CD rate will take effect immediately.

_____ 7. a. When customers open new accounts, they will receive the $50 cash bonus.
   b. When customers open new accounts.

_____ 8. a. One of the advantages of ATMs is the quick availability of funds.
   b. An advantage of an ATM.

_____ 9. a. While traveling in Europe, the client cashed.
   b. While traveling in Europe, the client cashed a traveler's check.

_____ 10. a. When the home equity line of credit is issued.
   b. When the home equity line of credit is issued, you will be able to refurnish your home.

Editing Power

Directions: Edit the following form letter for errors in capitalization, sentence structure and word usage; then key it correctly.

```
Dear Depositor:

we welcome you as a new depositor at franklin national

bank. As the largest american bank with branches in
```

europe, we can offer our customers a wide variety of financial services.

Besides the regular consumer savings and money market accounts. We provide loans, mortgages, and home equity line of credit accounts at excellent rates. you can borrow from $10,000 to $500,000 and become a new homeowner.

For your convenience, we offer a credit card that can be used as a debit card so that wherever you are, you are sure that money is always available. This versatile card will give you excess to atm's throughout the world.

If you are interested in a retirement savings plan. A financial advisor will gladly recommend an investment program for you.

We look forward to serving all your bank needs.

Sincerely yours,

James Hopkins

Customer Services

ri

Writing Power

Directions: After reading the case below, draft the *body* of an informational letter.

Case: Your employer, Western Bank, is adding a new service for its business clients. The new program will offer an efficient way of processing credit card and debit card purchases. Transactions will be recorded at a rapid rate and stored into the individual merchant's database. A merchant can retrieve all business transactions at the end of the day.

Inform the merchants that the new system has security measures to avoid mistakes. Remind them that mistakes are costly to a business. Remember to end the letter in a positive tone by inviting the merchants to make an appointment to discuss the system with one of the representatives at the bank's Business Services Department. Telephone no. 800-600-5500.

CHAPTER 2

Ensuring Subject-Verb Agreement

WHAT YOU WILL LEARN IN THIS CHAPTER

- To apply correct subject-verb agreement principles in business correspondence
- To develop the skill of writing concisely
- To develop a business vocabulary in **INSURANCE**
- To proofread and edit correspondence and reports
- To compose a sales letter
- To compose letters of notification

CLAIMS ADJUSTER: Handles claims of property damage and bodily injury, investigates claims by interviewing claimant, visually inspects damages for insurance companies.

Skills*:* continuing education to stay abreast of laws and court decisions, in-house training, may need experience in specialized area (auto repair), communication.

ACTUARY: Assembles and analyzes data to estimate the probability and cost of certain events, such as death, disabilities, or property losses. These facts determine the insurance premiums.

Skills: professional status available through series of exams, two- or four-year degree with strong math background, computer.

SALES AGENT: Works for a specific insurance company or is an independent insurance agent representing a number of companies, sells all types of insurance policies, advises clients on best insurance coverage based on individual needs.

Skills: state license may be required, specialized courses in insurance field, interpersonal skills.

Activity A   *Language Arts Recall*

Subject–Verb Agreement

A verb must agree with its subject in number and person.

> A **subject** is a noun or pronoun that identifies what is being discussed. The subject is a person, a place, a thing, or an idea.

> A **verb** expresses action or a state of being. A verb tells what the subject is *doing* or how the subject is *feeling*.

Rule 2.1: A singular subject takes a singular verb; a plural subject takes a plural verb.

> Examples: The ***agent is*** planning a seminar on life insurance. (singular subject, singular verb)

> The two insurance ***plans offer*** similar benefits. (plural subject, plural verb)

> Note: An "s" after a regular verb indicates a singular number. Example: An employee requests. (singular)

> The employees request. (plural)

> **Rule 2.2:** A subject that has two nouns joined by "and" takes a plural verb. (compound subject)

Example: **Kevin** and **Maria are submitting** a claims form for their property damage. (compound subject, plural verb)

> **Rule 2.3:** A collective noun (a group of individuals acting as a whole) takes a singular verb.

Example: The **committee is revising** automobile insurance policies.

> **Rule 2.4:** The pronoun "you" takes the same verb as a plural subject.

Example: **You are** eligible for a discount on your homeowner's policy.

 ## Check for Understanding

The following exercise will help you to better understand subject-verb agreement.

Directions: In the spaces provided, indicate the subject and verb in each of the following sentences. Also identify whether each is singular (S) or plural (P).

1. Our policy offers a comprehensive health plan.

2. The agent and his client have accepted the terms of the insurance policy.

3. Your insurance plan requires a second opinion for surgery coverage.

4. Management expects to offer dental insurance next month.

5. Auto insurance premiums increase with a rise in the number of accidents.

6. The research department authorizes any change in insurance rates.

7. You always receive a rebate on your insurance premium if you enroll in a defensive driving course.

8. The insurance company and the policyholder have agreed on the amount of financial settlement.

9. The union members decide to pay 10 percent of the health insurance premiums.

10. A committee has been formed to review the building's liability insurance coverage.

Subject	Verb	S or P
1. _____	_____	_____
2. _____	_____	_____
3. _____	_____	_____
4. _____	_____	_____
5. _____	_____	_____
6. _____	_____	_____
7. _____	_____	_____
8. _____	_____	_____
9. _____	_____	_____
10. _____	_____	_____

Question: Summarize the subject-verb rule that applies to your answers in the above exercise. _____

(Answers are given below.)

Building English Power: Subject-Verb Agreement

Directions: In each of the sentences, (circle) the subject; underline the correct form of the verb that agrees with the subject. (Check your answers in Appendix A.)

1. The insurance plan (protect, protects) you against personal damages. (2.1)

2. These cost-cutting procedures (help, helps) to lower premiums. (2.1)

3. Your automobile club (has, have) been able to increase services without additional costs. (2.1)

4. You (ask, asks) your insurance agent about the new 24-hour claim service. (2.4)

5. Union and management (disagree, disagrees) on cost-cutting procedures to lower the company's insurance expenses. (2.1)

6. After a natural disaster, the insurance industry often (face, faces) an excessive number of property damage claims. (2.3)

7. A $1-million umbrella insurance policy (was, were) available to the policyholders. (2.1)

8. The car rental contract (include, includes) property damage insurance. (2.1)

9. Michael and his friend (pay, pays) paying high premiums for their automobile insurance. (2.2)

10. The safe-driving course usually (qualify, qualifies) the driver for a decrease in auto insurance. (2.1)

11. Under the contract, you (become, becomes) eligible for benefits after three months of employment. (2.4)

12. Flood damage and theft (is, are) not covered under your basic automobile insurance plan. (2.2)

13. Our records (indicate, indicates) that the above balance is outstanding. (2.1)

14. The employees' negotiating team (has, have) presented management with a comprehensive health plan. (2.3)

15. Dental insurance and optical coverage (is, are) fringe benefits offered to employees by some companies. (2.2)

16. According to the insurance policy, you (is, are) eligible for a reimbursement. (2.4)

17. The faculty (agree, agrees) that the proposed medical insurance plan is satisfactory. (2.3)

18. The automobile insurance rates (has, have) decreased for safe drivers. (2.1)

19. The company (was, were) advised to increase its fire insurance coverage. (2.3)

20. The insurance representative and the manager (plans, plan) to hold a workshop on the revised employee benefits package. (2.2)

Still Puzzled? See *One Writer's Key* Home Page: Subject-verb Agreement. Click on: What is subject-verb agreement? How do verbs work when subjects are connected by *and*?

Activity B Building Word Power

Show leadership qualities by volunteering for projects, meeting deadlines, and being a team player.

Directions: The words that follow are commonly used in the insurance industry. From this list, select the word or phrase that correctly completes each statement. Refer to the personal dictionary if you are uncertain of the meaning of a word. (Check your answers in Appendix A.)

accelerate, accelerated	liability insurance
alternative	option
bodily injury insurance	phasing out
cafeteria-type medical insurance	premium
catastrophic insurance	property damage insurance
deductible	subsidized
escalate, escalating	umbrella insurance

_____ 1. To protect yourself against excessive financial claims or expenses, _____ is available to you. A(n) _____ policy covers you above the basic insurance terms.

_____ 2. Because of a reorganization, the XYZ Company needs to eliminate departments; therefore, it will be _____ its claims department.

_____ 3. In an attempt to reduce the _____ number of automobile accidents, some insurance companies are giving a discount for safe driving records.

_____ 4. _____, which is very much like a restaurant menu, gives employees the _____ of selecting insurance benefits that meet their needs.

_____ 5. The driver's _____ covered the medical costs of the injured pedestrian who was hit by the car.

_____ 6. I will sue John Smith under the _____ clause for the damages that occurred to my car when his van hit it.

_____ 7. Most insurance policies have a _____ clause that requires the insured to pay a minimum amount when claims are settled.

_____ 8. You will notice a higher _____ for your insurance due to a rate increase of 10 percent.

_____ 9. When a company cafeteria is _____, employees pay less for their meals.

_____ 10. To pass a truck on the hill, the motorist _____ his speed.

_____ 11. The judge gave the young offender the option of performing community service as a(n) _____ to paying a fine.

_____ 12. _____ protects the insured against injury or property damages suffered by another person.

On the Alert

■ *their (possessive)*—belonging to them

   Example: We mailed **their** insurance policy yesterday.

■ *there (adverb)*—in or at that place

   Example: **There** are several changes in the policy.

- *titles*—Italicize the title of a complete published work, such as a book, periodical, newspaper, pamphlet, or brochure. (Do not capitalize articles, conjunctions, or short prepositions [the, and, with] unless they are the first word of a title.)

    Example: The ABCs of Auto Insurance

- *million*—Amounts of money in millions are expressed partially in numbers. When using the $ sign, do not write out the word *dollar* at the end of the phrase.

    Example: $1 million

Activity C   *Industry Perspectives: Insurance Programs*

Directions: Using appropriate revision marks, proofread, correct, and key the following report.

Rule Reference	
1.4, 2.2	In the united states, corporations and individual households is concerned with increasing costs of insurance. Companies that are faced with escalating expenses are reexamining employee insurance benefits.
2.1	One alternative is to offer cafeteria-type medical insurance plans to employees. Under these plans,
2.1	employees has the option of choosing the best medical
1.3	coverage for there needs. in one firm, vacation days can be earned by those employees who select a plan that does not include every type of coverage or that has a higher deductable. The trend is away from a uniform medical plan for all of the company employees.
2.1	For retirees, health costs has accelerated so much that some companies are phasing out health insurance subsidies for future employees. In some instances, a
2.1	special stock ownership plan for employees have been

introduced. The acumulated value of the stock can be
used to pay for medical costs at some later date.

2.3   Business find these changes to be financialy
beneficial; however, employees may be affected in their
personal insurance protection. Experts in teh insurance
2.1, 2.4   field recommends that you reviews the type of insurance
that meets your personal needs.

Did you find these errors?

7 subject-verb agreement
1 confusing word
4 typographical/spelling errors
3 capitalization problems

Activity D   *Editing Power*

Task A: Edit, format, and proofread the following letter. Use proofreaders' symbols to mark the errors; then key the letter correctly.

Errors

■ Subject-verb
  agreement
■ Sentence
  fragments
■ Spelling
■ Capitalization
■ Typographical

MR. William Simms
10 Maple Avenue
Toledo OH 43692-9987

Dear Mr. Simms:

We are happy to enclose a renewal for your automobile
insurance policy for the coming year. Please review you
policy carefully so that you are fully protected.

Our brochure, The ABCs of auto insurance, is
enclosed. To help you determine whether your present
policy is meeting your needs. This brochure list in
detail the features we offer automobile owners. Our
policy offer discounts to drivers with good safety
records. For full protection, you should have adequate
bodily injury and property damage coverage.

If you agree with the limits of liability and coverge included in the enclosed policy, detach the premium statement and mail it with your payment. If you have any questions, our representative are available 24 hours a day at 800-841-9000. After doing business with us, you will agree that our reliability and customer services is superior to those of our competitors.

Our firm value policyholders like you, and we sincerly appreciate the opportunity to serve you.

Sincerely yours,

David Knight
Vice President
ri
Enclosures

Challenge Task B: Edit, format, and proofread the following unarranged letter for all errors; then key it correctly.

Ms. Sandra Davis, 32 Leeds Place, Boston, MA 02155-2199

Dear Ms. Davis:

Our company invite you, a valued customer, to consider our Plus Insurance Policy.

This umbrella policy insure you to a maxmum of $1 million dollars against catastrophic financail loses from unexpected lawsuits. The cost of this umbrela insurance policy are only a few cent a day. You and your family enjoys peace of mind knowing that your assets are protected.

Our expereinced representatives are available 24 hours a day to answer any questions you may have.

Sincerely yours, William Snyder, Vice President

Activity E — *Writing Practicum*

Conciseness

One of the six Cs of good writing is correspondence that is concise. Sentences should not be wordy, that is, contain unnecessary words that are not important to the meaning of the sentence.

Examples:

Wordy	Concise
at the present time	now
for the purpose of	to
final outcome	outcome
my personal opinion	I believe or my opinion
in the event that	if
in order to	so

EXERCISE 1 REWRITE SENTENCES TO MAKE THEM CONCISE. ELIMINATE UNNECESSARY WORDS.

1. The pamphlet on health insurance options was published for the purpose of explaining in detail the benefits.

   _____

   _____

2. This is to let you know that there will be a 10 percent increase in automobile insurance premiums effective immediately.

   _____

   _____

3. After the storm, needless to say, there were hundreds of claims by homeowners.

   _____

   _____

4. As you can imagine, the injured motorist, no doubt, will sue the other driver.

   _____

   _____

Still Puzzled? See *Writer's OneKey* Home Page select topic: Conciseness
Click on: How can I write concisely? How can I avoid redundant writing? How can I avoid wordy sentence structures?

Need more practice? Go to toolbar and click on Practice & Assess, and then click on Exercises.

Complete exercises on Conciseness.

5. As it turned out, it was decided that the firm will offer its employees a life insurance policy.

   _____

   _____

6. In the event that you would like to increase your liability insurance, feel free to give me a call.

   _____

   _____

7. The final completion of the study showed that auto insurance rates were on the increase because of fraudulent claims.

   _____

   _____

8. We are happy to say, you will receive a gift free of charge if you attend our seminar to be held at the Americana Hotel.

   _____

   _____

9. There is no doubt, in my opinion, that there should be a federally funded insurance program for catastrophic disasters.

   _____

   _____

RUN-ON SENTENCES

Run-on sentences are made up of two or more independent clauses that have no punctuation or conjunction.

Example

Run-on Sentence:

Our automobile insurance policy offers many options in fact you need to choose the best coverage for you. (punctuation missing, wordy ending)

Revised sentence options:

Our automobile insurance policy offers many **options. You** need to choose the best coverage. (period)

Our automobile insurance policy offers many **options, but** you need to choose the best coverage. (comma, coordinating conjunction)

Our automobile insurance policy offers many **options; you** need to choose the best coverage. (semicolon)

Our automobile insurance policy offers many **options; however**, you need to choose the best coverage. (semicolon and transitional word)

Tip: To avoid run-on sentences connect with a comma and conjunction; semicolon, or a period.

EXERCISE 2   REWRITE RUN-ON SENTENCES

1. We offer insurance specifically on small businesses they often have difficulty finding insurance rates that are affordable.

   _____

   _____

2. The judge ruled in favor of the plaintiff's lawsuit the defendant was found negligent and fined $1,000.

   _____

   _____

3. In most states insurance companies do not offer flood insurance to individual homeowners they must apply through a federal program.

   _____

   _____

4. Shana completed the safe driving program she will receive a discount on her automobile insurance premium.

   _____

   _____

5. Most insurance policies have a deductible clause the insured is required to pay a minimum amount before claims will be processed.

   _____

   _____

6. The bottom line was that the building was underinsured the claims of the tenants could not be met.

   _____

   _____

EXERCISE 3   WRITING OPENING AND CLOSING SENTENCES

Directions: For each group, choose the best opening and closing sentences that were taken from letters sent to an insurance company. Be aware that some sentences have built-in grammatical errors. You are reminded that the sentences should be written clearly, state a purpose, and not be wordy. Write your answer (a, b, c) in the blank space provided.

OPENING SENTENCES

_____ 1. **a.** Our firm, Computex, Inc., is seeking insurance coverage for its electronic equipment.

           b. Computex, Inc., would like to find a suitable insurance policy to cover its electronic equipment.

           c. We have electronic equipment of Computex, Inc., that need to be insured.

_____ 2. **a.** This is to inform you that our clients James Roberts and Mary Simms has taken legal action against the Atlas Health Club for injuries sustained from a ceiling collapse.

           b. Sustaining injuries when the ceiling collapsed, our clients James Roberts and Mary Simms have decided to take legal action against the Atlas Health Club.

           c. James Roberts and Mary Simms, our clients, have taken legal action against the Atlas Health Club for injuries sustained from a ceiling collapse.

_____ 3. **a.** I would like to inform you that your company has not sent me my insurance settlement.

           b. I am writing to say that your company delayed in sending me my insurance settlement for many months.

           c. For the past two months, your company has delayed sending me my insurance settlement payment.

_____ 4. **a.** For tax purposes, my accountant needs to know if the Metro Insurance Company and its affiliates are controlled by individual state laws.

           b. We would like to know if Metro Insurance Company is governed by laws of each state.

           c. I am writing to inquire if the Metro Insurance Company and its affiliates are regulated by individual state laws.

_____ 5. **a.** In response to your request, we are enclosing a brochure explaining all the services available to our clients.

b. We are pleased to send you the brochure you requested that describes our services.

   c. A brochure has been enclosed describing our services.

CLOSING SENTENCES

_____ **6. a.** We appreciate your prompt settlement of our claim.

   b. We appreciate your firm's prompt action to make a settlement of our claim.

   c. We express our appreciation of your prompt settlement.

_____ **7. a.** If we can be of further help, feel free to contact our office.

   b. We shall be happy to help you and be of further assistance.

   c. Feel free to contact your insurance representative with any problems or questions you may have.

_____ **8. a.** We look forward to the pleasure of serving you, and we hope you continue to do business with us.

   b. We look forward to your continuing business.

   c. We enjoy having you as a customer, and hope we can be of further service to you in the future.

EXERCISE 4   WRITING FOR CORRECT SENTENCE STRUCTURE

The body of the sales letter that follows has flaws, such as wordiness, run-on sentences, and fragments. Rewrite the paragraphs for clarity, conciseness, and correct sentence structure.

```
    You could save hundreds of dollars. By insuring
your automobile with us this could mean savings for
you. Our operating expenses are among the lowest
in the industry and savings are then passed on to you,
our customers.
    We have additional money-saving discounts safe
drivers, security systems, multi-car coverage. Along
with our quality service which includes 24-hour access
to our auto insurance specialists.
    Call us free no obligation to get a rate quote.
```

Writing Pointers

SALES LETTERS

- ■ Identify your potential customers.
- ■ Capture reader's attention in the first paragraph.
- ■ Use a question to get reader's attention.
- ■ Specify details of a service or product.
- ■ Give source for further information.
- ■ Offer specific suggestions or recommendations for reader to act.
- ■ Conclude on a positive note to promote goodwill.

NOTIFICATION LETTERS TO CUSTOMERS

- ■ State specific change (price increase, new location).
- ■ State reason for change.
- ■ Indicate benefit of change.
- ■ Express sympathetic attitude toward hardships that might be created.

Model Sales Letter

Date

Ms. Laura Jacobson
11 Thornwood Drive
Paramus, NJ 07652-3146

Dear Ms. Jacobson:

Question to arouse curiosity

Are you getting the best insurance rate for your safe driving record? Many companies insure drivers of all ages and levels of experience; they do not acknowledge good drivers. Costs of insurance claims are passed on to the insured.

Stresses benefits

Logical appeal to save money

Our insurance program is different. We, at Apex Insurance Company, primarily insure safe, experienced drivers with excellent driving records. As a result, we are able to keep our claim costs down and pass the savings to our customers. We have the lowest rates in the country. At the same time, our insurance package includes extra benefits not usually found in the industry.

Source for more information

Builds goodwill

Look at the enclosed brochure and learn more about our excellent coverage. Our, experienced representatives will gladly answer any questions. We hope you will join our other subscribers with safe driving records and save hundreds of dollars a year.

Cordially Yours,

Larry Ward
Vice President, Marketing

ri
Enclosure

Date

Mr. Edward Carney
141 Ft Washington Avenue
Albany, NY 12200-3541

Dear Mr. Carney:

SUBJECT: PREMIUM NOTIFICATION

Addresses
specific issue

Gives facts

According to our records, you have not responded to our premium notification to continue your group life insurance policy. If payment of $73.50 is not received within ten days from the above date, we shall be forced to terminate your insurance. The insurance period covered under your renewal will be from July 1, 2007 to June 30, 2008.

Expresses
sympathy

States benefit

We are confident that this is an oversight on your part since this type of coverage is essential to your financial security and peace of mind. It is important to realize that the issue of money is not a concern during a crisis. You should be aware that you will be unable to re-enroll in this program if there is a lapse in the policy.

Willingness to
help

If you have any further questions or concerns, please feel free to contact our customer service department at 518-793-3000.

Sincerely yours,

Irene Dorsay
Customer Service Representative

ri

Activity F *Writing Power: Composing Correspondence*

Case Study 1: *Notification Letter*

Read Case Study 1. Then read Options A and B for each section of the letter. Select the option that you believe is most appropriate for the opening, body, and closing statements. Then key the entire letter based on the options you selected. (see letter format in Appendix B.)

Case: A letter addressed to Mr. Richard Hodge from your insurance firm, General Casualty Corporation, tells him of an increase in his automobile premiums. Costs of auto repairs, legal fees, and medical care are on the rise; therefore, an increase of 5 percent is necessary. Explain that your company attempts to keep costs down. Ask the policyholder to cooperate by being a safe driver. The increase will take place when the insurance policy is renewed. Mr. Hodge's address is 22 Gates Street, New City, NY 10962–2245.

Opening Sentences:

a. General Casualty Corporation is committed to keeping your automobile insurance premiums low.

b. We at General Casualty Corporation are finding it hard to keep our costs low.

Option A or B _____

Body of letter giving specifics of situation:

a. We are faced with increasing costs from auto repair claims, legal fees, and medical expenses. Therefore, we have no choice but to impose a 5 percent increase on your premiums. This increase will take effect upon renewal of your policy.

b. When we reviewed our expenses, we found that claims from auto repairs, legal fees, and medical expenses are high and are going up even more. Therefore, we have no choice but to raise your premiums by 5 percent upon renewal of your policy.

Option A or B _____

Body of letter indicating company action, using positive tone:

a. We keep looking for new ways in our attempt to be efficient and to be able to keep our premiums at a reasonable cost to you. Please try and be a safe driver.

b. Our firm continuously studies ways to offer you efficient service at a reasonable cost. We ask that you assist by being a safe driver.

Option A or B _____

Closing statement to maintain goodwill:

a. Upon due date, you will receive your policy renewal.

b. For further information about your policy renewal, call us at 800-750-3000. We value your continued patronage.

Option A or B _____

Case Study 2: Sales Letter

Read Case Study 2. Then read Options A or B for each section of the letter. Select the option that you believe is most appropriate for the opening, body, and closing statements of a sales letter. Be sure to review the guidelines given in Writing Pointers. Then key the entire letter based on the options you selected. Address the letter to Ms. Rita Lorenzo, 10 Kings Plaza, Hastings, NY 10562-0530. Closing: Ned Hall, Sales Director

Opening sentences:

a. Does your automobile insurer recognize motorists with safe driving records? Optimum Insurance Company rewards the safe driver with a 15 percent decrease on the premiums.

b. Safe driving deserves to be rewarded. We, at Optimum Insurance Company, recognize a safe driver by decreasing the premiums.

Option A or B _____

Body of letter

Sentences 1 and 2:

a. Safe driving not only saves lives, but it decreases the amount of money our insurance company needs to pay to accident victims. These savings are then passed on to you.

b. Safe driving saves lives. At the same time, we pay out less to accident victims. These savings show up in lower premiums.

Option A or B: _____

Sentences 3 and 4:

a. We offer a comprehensive insurance plan at the lowest rate in the country. We promise to match any lower rates offered by our competitors.

b. Optimum Insurance Company offers a comprehensive insurance plan which includes bodily injury protection, property damage liability, collision coverage, and work loss benefits at the lowest rate in the country. We promise to match any lower rates offered by our competitors.

Option A or B: _____

Closing:

a. We shall be happy to answer any questions you may have. Visit our Web site www.optinsurance.com or call at 800-733.2000.

b. For more information visit our Web site, www.optinsurance.com or call us at 800-733-2000. We look forward to serving your insurance needs.

Option A or B: _____

Case Study 3: Notification Letter

Read Case Study 3 and respond to the questions that follow the case study. Based on your responses, compose the letter to Mr. Steven Morris, 267 South Central Avenue, White Plains, NY 10602–9999.

Case: Your local office of the National Insurance Company is relocating to 2 Main Street, Tarrytown, New York 10591–4926. Draft a letter to your clients informing them of a change of address, which is a more convenient location and has parking facilities. You should also mention in your letter that a new service has been added at this new location. Insurance claims can be submitted here.

ORGANIZE YOUR IDEAS

1. Indicate the most important point you want to make to your readers.

   _____

   _____

   _____

2. What should you include in the opening sentence?

   _____

   _____

   _____

3. What specific details should you include in the body of the letter?

   _____

   _____

   _____

4. What should you include in your closing statement that expresses a desire for a continued business relationship?

   _____

   _____

   _____

Case Study 4: Sales Letter

Read Case Study 4, then compose the letter. If you need to have an outline of questions to help you draft the letter, refer to Organize Your Ideas section in Case Study 3.

Case: National Insurance Company is now offering a homeowner's policy to individuals who rent apartments. A form letter announcing this new type of coverage will be mailed to local residents. For the first year, the premium will be only $200 for all household contents up to $10,000 and will include $100,000 personal liability. If more coverage is needed, it can be obtained. Anyone interested in more information should complete the enclosed postage-paid card and return it to the office located at 2 Main Street, Tarrytown, New York 10591–4926. Use "Dear Neighbor:" for the salutation.

Challenge Level Case

Case Study 5: Notification Letter

Read Case Study 5; then compose the letter.

Case: Draft a letter to be sent to the policyholders who are renewing their automobile insurance. Inform them that there will be a 10 percent increase in their insurance rate. This increase is necessary because of the rise in claims on automobile accidents. Mention that one of the major causes of accidents is driving under the influence of alcohol. Remind the policyholders to be responsible drivers so that insurance rates will not continue to increase. Suggest the convenience of direct payment through their checking account. Conclude on a positive note by thanking them for choosing your firm, ABC Insurance Company. Your Web site is http://www.abcinsure.com. For the salutation, use "Dear Policyholder:" For the closing, use David Franke, Vice President of Operations.

Cultural Communication

English is the language of business; however, it is a second language to foreigners. Tips in writing to foreign individuals:

- Avoid complex or long sentences.

- Avoid slang or colloquial terms.

- Use formal language and format style.

- Summarize or repeat important points of the correspondence.

Self-Assessment
English Power

Directions: In each of the following sentences, underline the correct form of the verb so that it agrees with the subject.

1. You (qualify, qualifies) for a discount on your automobile insurance.

2. The proposed plan (outline, outlines) the catastrophic insurance coverage.

3. Management (disagree, disagrees) with the newly adopted budget.

4. Our study (show, shows) that home insurance rates are rising throughout the country.

5. The condominium (carry, carries) high liability insurance.

6. To qualify for disability insurance, you (need, needs) to submit a medical note.

7. We (has, have) informed the claimant that the request was denied.

8. Business owners (understand, understands) the need for adequate fire and theft insurance.

9. Each year insurance premiums (increase, increases) by 5 percent.

10. The policyholder (dispute, disputes) the settlement offer.

Editing Power

Directions: Edit, proofread, and format the following letter for all errors in grammar and sentence structure. The letter should be addressed to Mr. Roy Salinger, 44 Green Acres Avenue, Columbus, OH 43288-1005, from Dennis O'Malley, Manager.

Your renewal homeowner's insurance policy are enclosed. We ask that you review the package to make sure that you are satisfied with your present coverage. Any home improvements or additions. May affect the terms of your policy. It is important to carry adequate insurance. So that you is protected against unforeseen losses.

Have you tried our new automated billing service? It is an easy way to make payments. this plan is designed for you to pay in four equal installments with no added fees. The payments will be made directly to us from your checking account. no longer do you need to worry about premium payment deadlines. This system further provide policyholders with information on last payment made and balance due.

If you have any questions or wish to make changes on your policy, speak to one of our specialists at 800-733-2000. We appreciate your business. liberty insurance company is committed to offering the low-est possible rates.

Writing Power

Directions: After reading the case that follows, draft a form letter to the policyholders of Liberty Insurance Company. Use "Dear Policy-holders" for the salutation and closing, Chad Freeman, Vice President.

Inform the policyholders of the two new added services that are available. They will be able to file claims, renew policies, or seek infor-mation 24 hours a day on a new hotline, 800-721-3200. Also, policy-holders can choose the new Electronic Billing Option to pay the premiums automatically from the individual's checking account. For details of this plan, they need to check the Web site www.liberty.com

You are reminded to appeal to the policyholders that Liberty In-surance Company is committed to high-quality service. Also, include a positive closing statement.

> "Coming together is a beginning, staying together is progress,
>
> and working together is success."
>
> —Henry Ford

CHAPTER 3

Investing in Subject-Verb Agreement

CORPORATE SNAPSHOT

MURIEL SIEBERT & CO., INC., bears the name of its founder. Although Muriel Siebert never graduated from college, she rose to partnership in a leading Wall Street brokerage firm. In a male-dominated industry, Ms. Siebert was willing to take risks and pursue her goals. In 1967, after many challenges, she was elected as the first woman member of the New York Stock Exchange. She spearheaded the drive to make her company a discount brokerage firm. Today Muriel Siebert & Co. is a successful and respected discount broker.

Acknowledging the financial needs of women, the firm began the Women's Financial Institute. This was the first organization within a brokerage house established to meet the growing demands of this segment of the population.

For Ms. Siebert, the secret of making a difference is to "take stands, take risks, take responsibility—and care deeply about how America's big institutions affect the lives of individual people." In keeping with this philosophy, the firm is involved in many philanthropic and educational programs.

Source: *http://www.msiebert.com*

WHAT YOU WILL LEARN IN THIS CHAPTER

- ☛ To apply correct subject-verb agreement principles in business correspondence

- ☛ To develop a business vocabulary in **FINANCE/INVESTMENTS**

- ☛ To proofread and edit correspondence and reports

- ☛ To compose a letter of request

- ☛ To compose a letter of response to request

- ☛ To write a memorandum

STOCKBROKER (SECURITIES SALES AGENTS):   Serves individual investors with purchase and sale of stocks, bonds, mutual funds, etc.; offers advice on purchases of particular securities, keeps abreast of the financial market.

Skills: college degree in business administration, economics, or finance; state license, in-house training, sales experience, interpersonal skills.

BROKERAGE CLERK: Handles the day-to-day operations of brokerage firms, computes and records data pertaining to securities transactions. Good entry-level job for career with brokerage firm.

Skills: on-the-job training, computer, communication, attention to details, associate degree preferred.

FINANCIAL ADVISOR: Assesses financial needs of individuals and recommends investment options, manages client's portfolio of mutual funds, stocks, bonds, etc., keeps abreast of the financial market.

Skills: certification recommended, state license required to buy/sell securities, college degree in business administration or finance, computer and problem-solving skills.

Activity A   Language Arts Recall

Subject–Verb Agreement (continued from Chapter 2)

Rule 3.1: A phrase between the subject and verb does not affect agreement. The subject must agree with the verb.

Examples: The new ***booklet*** on financial opportunities ***is*** available.

Management, as well as the employees, ***is*** eligible for the stock-sharing plan.

Rule 3.2: If both of the subjects are singular and are joined by "either/or" or "neither/nor," the verb is singular.

Example: ***Either*** a savings account ***or*** a treasury bill ***is*** a good investment.

If both of the subjects are plural and are joined by "either/or" or "neither/nor," the verb is plural.

Example: **Either** savings accounts **or** treasury bills **are** good investments.

Rule 3.3: If one subject is singular and the other is plural, and the subjects are joined by "either/or" or "neither/nor," the verb agrees with the subject nearer the verb.

Examples: **Neither** the stockholders **nor** the Executive Board **agrees** with their financing plan.

Are you sure **either** the controller **or** at least two members of the Board of Directors **plan** to attend the meeting?

Rule 3.4: Indefinite pronouns (each, every, anyone, everyone, someone, one, it) always require a singular verb.

Examples: **Everyone agrees** that U.S. bonds are a safe investment.

One of the analysts **speaks** frequently on the TV show.

Rule 3.5: When the word *there* begins the sentence, it is never the subject. The subject appears after the verb.

Examples: There **are** many **types** of investment plans.

There **is** a new investment **plan.**

Rule 3.6: "The number" is a singular subject and takes a singular verb; "a number" is a plural subject and takes a plural verb.

Examples: **The number** of people investing in stocks **is** growing.

A number of banks **have** merged.

Check for Understanding

Directions: In the spaces that follow, indicate the subject with which the verb must agree and the verb in each of the following sentences. Also identify whether each subject is singular (S) or plural (P).

1. A glossary of financial terms appears in the back of the booklet. (3.1)

2. There are many advantages to an investment fund. (3.5)

3. According to reports, the number of investors in mutual funds is increasing every day. (3.6)

4. Either management or the employees are expected to attend the monthly meeting. (3.3)

5. Everyone on the research committee was asked to review the annual report. (3.4)

6. Each of us agrees that financial planning is important. (3.4)

7. Either savings bonds or a certificate of deposit is a wise choice. (3.3)

8. A growing number of employees have enrolled in company stock plans. (3.6)

9. Neither the stockbroker nor the financial advisor recommends a change in the client's investment portfolio. (3.2)

10. The number of firms offering employees stock option plans is increasing. (3.6)

Subject	Verb	S or P
1. _____	_____	_____
2. _____	_____	_____
3. _____	_____	_____
4. _____	_____	_____
5. _____	_____	_____
6. _____	_____	_____
7. _____	_____	_____
8. _____	_____	_____
9. _____	_____	_____
10. _____	_____	_____

(Answers are given below.)

Answers to "Check for Understanding"

1. glossary, appears, S
2. advantages, are, P
3. (the) number, is, S
4. employees, are expected, P
5. Everyone, was asked, S
6. Each, agrees, S
7. certificate of deposit, is, S
8. A (growing) number, have, P
9. advisor, recommends, S
10. (The) number, is increasing, S

Building English Power: Subject-Verb Agreement

EXERCISE 1 Review

Directions: This exercise will review *all* the subject-verb agreement rules. Decide whether the subject and verb agree in the following sentences. If the verb agrees with the subject, write C; otherwise, write the correct form.

_____ 1. The annual report and the proxy statement are ready for distribution. (2.2)

_____ 2. Our comprehensive guide on retirement options explain the 401(k) plan. (3.1, 2.1)

Still Puzzled? See *Writer's OneKey* Home Page: Subject-Verb Agreement. Click on: Can I ignore words between a subject and its verb? How do verbs work when subjects are connected by or? How do verbs work with indefinite pronouns?

Need more practice? Go to toolbar and click on. Practice & Assess.

Complete subject-verb agreement additional exercise

_____ 3. Neither she nor her colleagues appears dissatisfied with the staff reorganization. (3.3)

_____ 4. The number of people investing for retirement are growing. (3.6)

_____ 5. The president and the board of directors of Acme Electric always attend the shareowners' annual meeting. (2.2, 3.1)

_____ 6. The Securities and Exchange Commission review new stock offerings of firms. (2.3)

_____ 7. Each one chooses the team partner in the stock-picking game.

_____ 8. You always encourage small investors to choose mutual funds. (2.4)

_____ 9. Either staff or management always attend the president's monthly conference. (3.2)

_____ 10. There is many reasons for the decline in stock prices. (3.5)

Building English Power: Subject-Verb Agreement

EXERCISE 2 Directions: In each of the following sentences, underline the <u>subject</u> with a single line and underline the <u>verb</u> with a double line; in the space provided, change the subject and verb to plural form.

1. Foreign demand for American technology is increasing. (3.1)

   Plural Form: _____

   _____

2. The number of stockholders is demanding more communication from corporate executives. (3.6)

   Plural Form: _____

   _____

3. Neither the employee nor the manager agrees with the arbitrator's decision. (3.2)

   Plural Form: _____

   _____

4. There is a concern about the company's financial condition. (3.5)

   Plural Form: _____

   _____

5. The report in which we compare multinational corporations appears in several business magazines. (3.1)

    Plural Form: _____

    _____

6. The enclosed pamphlet from the brokerage firm gives information on a variety of mutual funds. (3.1)

    Plural Form: _____

    _____

Still Puzzled? See *Writer's OneKey* Home Page: Subject-Verb Agreement. Click on: Can I ignore words between a subject and its verb? How do verbs work when subjects are connected by or? How do verbs work with indefinite pronouns?

Need more practice? Go to toolbar and click on Practice & Assess.

Complete subject-verb agreement additional exercise.

7. Each of the brokers predicts an upswing in the stock market. (3.4)

    Plural Form: _____

    _____

8. A seminar on financial planning is offered by the local bank. (3.1)

    Plural Form: _____

    _____

9. There is a tax-free municipal bond that pays a high dividend. (3.5)

    Plural Form: _____

    _____

10. Everyone agrees that individuals should have a savings plan. (3.4)

    Plural Form: _____

    _____

11. Either a U.S. savings bond or a treasury note is a secure investment. (3.2)

    Plural Form: _____

    _____

12. Each financial decision impacts your net worth. (3.4)

    Plural Form: _____

    _____

13. The stock price of the electronics company has increased during the past year. (3.1)

    Plural Form: _____

    _____

14. The fund, which invests in diversified stocks, has a high rate of performance. (3.1)

Plural Form: _____

_____

15. Neither the bank nor the investment firm was willing to underwrite the project. (3.2)

Plural Form: _____

_____

Activity B   Building Word Power

Directions: The words that follow are commonly used in the finance/investment industry. From this list, select the word or phrase that correctly completes each statement. Refer to the personal dictionary if you are uncertain of the meaning of a word.

blue chip stock(s)   prospectus
bonds   proxy
glossary   securities
investment portfolio   stockbroker
investments   stocks
multinational   Web site
mutual fund

_____ **1.** Companies often borrow money by issuing _____, which are loans to be repaid on a certain date, including interest.

_____ **2.** _____ is another term used for stocks and bonds.

_____ **3.** _____ are shares that individuals own as an investment in companies. These shares are sold by companies to raise capital.

_____ **4.** An investor usually refers to a(n) _____ to examine the detailed financial background of a proposed investment in a firm.

_____ **5.** Individuals attempt to make more money through _____ in securities, savings, and real estate.

_____ **6.** An investor has a(n) _____ that lists the securities owned by the individual.

_____ **7.** An individual investor may buy shares in diversified securities offered by an investment group. This type of investment is known as a _____.

_____ 8. _____ people who want to buy or sell securities contact a(n) _____ who is a registered sales representative of a member firm in the stock exchange.

_____ 9. To understand the terms used in the financial pages of a newspaper, refer to a(n) _____ for an explanation of the words.

_____ 10. Corporations that do business in foreign countries are known as _____ firms.

_____ 11. The shareholder was unable to attend the annual meeting and voted by _____ for the proposal on performance-based compensation.

_____ 12. For the latest stock information, visit the _____ http://www.dailystocks.com.

_____ 13. IBM, General Electric, and Exxon Mobil are examples of _____.

On the Alert

- *a/an (indefinite article)*—"An" is used before all words beginning with a vowel. It is also used before the silent "h." "A" is used before all other words.

    Examples: *a* number; *an* individual; *an* hour

- *advice (noun)*—recommendation

    Example: The financial advisor gave her clients *advice* on municipal bonds.

- *advise (verb)*—to recommend or give counsel

    Example: The broker will *advise* his investors to attend the seminar on the new stock offering.

- *personal (adjective)*—individual, private

    Example: The bank approved a *personal* loan to purchase the car.

- *personnel (noun)*—staff, employees

    Example: All *personnel* in the accounting department are being trained to use the new software program.

Activity C   Industry Perspectives: Investments

Directions: Using appropriate revision marks, proofread and key the following report.

Rule Reference	
	A successful investor need to be well informed about
2.1	financial issues. There is many ways to obtain relevant
3.5	information and advise about investing in securities.
3.1	The financial sections of a newspaper offers its
	readers valuable data on current economic conditions and
2.1	investment opportunities. Investment columns often
	appears in newspapers and magazines written by experts
3.6	who offer money management suggestions. A number of
	television programs focuses on stock market news,
	securities investments, and industry information.
2.1	Internet systems offers subscribers up-to-the-minute
	stock informationa, and daily trading activities of
2.2	securities and mutual funds is available
	instantaneously.
	In a marketplace enviromnent, known as the stock
2.2	exchange, the buyng and selling of securities occurs.
	Only registered brokers can trade on the stock exchange.
	A individual who is interested in investing in stocks
	and bonds should have a knowledgeable broker.
	The most popular and largest exchange is known as the
1.4, 1.7	New york stock Exchange. Every leading american
3.4	industrial, financial, and service corporation trade its
1.5	stock on the NYse.
3.6	The number of individuals investing in securities are
3.2	growing. Neither a stockbroker nor a financial advisor
	are solely responsible for an individual's investment
	decisions. Choices must be based on personnel financial
2.2	goals and information that has been researched.

Did you find these errors?

10 subject-verb agreement
3 typographical/spelling
4 capitalization
3 confusing words
1 grammar

Activity D Editing Power

Task A: Edit, format, and proofread the following letter. Use proof-readers' symbols to mark the errors, then key it correctly.

Ms. Barbara Simmons
One Park Road
Kansas City, MO 64141-6202

Dear Ms. Simons:

A growing number of americans is using financial

planning to manage there money better. Everyone agree

that investors should be well informed of market trends.

We invite you to send for a free copy of our

Financial planning Guide. it is written in an easy,

understandable manner. Ten experts in the investment

field offers suggestions on how to invest money. A

glossary of financial terms appear in the back of the

booklet for reference.

There is many types of investments. We suggest that

you carefully read what the recognized authorities in

the financail field have to say. Then you will be able

to make wise decisions.

Why not send for your copy today?

Sincerely yours,

Suzanne Rudman
Vice President
ri

Errors
- Subject-verb agreement
- Capitalization
- Typographical
- Confusing word

Challenge Task B: Edit, format, and proofread the following unarranged letter for all errors and missing notations, then key it correctly.

Mr. Troy Johnson, 22 Cara Lane, Cincinnati OH 45230-7214

Dear Mr. Johnson:

We have enclosed a copy of our current prospectus which serve as your reference for information about the World Fund.

The primary objective of our money fund is to invest in foreign companies that have a potential for capital growth. This fund focuses on the emerging asian market. Everyone agree that this is a promising area for business expansion.

World fund is recognized for its quality service. Our financial consultants are always ready to provide you with the personnel attention and advise you deserve. Neither institutions nor a small investor are excluded from participating in the fund to receive more information or to open a account, call us at 800-567-9000 or visit our web site http://www.worldfund.com.

Sincerely yours, Fred Rodriguez, Account Executive

Activity E   Writing Practicum

Good writing involves the flowing of ideas so that the thought in the first sentence leads to the very next idea in the sentence that follows. In essence, ideas are interconnected within a reading passage.

EXERCISE 1 REARRANGING SENTENCES FOR CONTINUITY OF IDEAS

Directions: In problems 1 through 5, rearrange the sentences in a logical order, list the sentence order in the spaces provided, and then key each passage.

1. **a.** The use of computers to keep abreast of financial information is becoming increasingly popular.

   b. Online computer networks are making conventional ways of researching information as obsolete as using a typewriter.

   c. With the Internet, an investor can communicate with investment specialists, retrieve securities information, and refer to financial databases.

   d. All you need are a personal computer, a modem, and Internet access to keep the information superhighway at your fingertips.

   List in order of preference _____ _____ _____ _____

2. **a.** Last summer, I had experience working as an intern for a small investment firm in my hometown.

   b. In response to your advertisement placed in the summer job mart at River Community College, I would like to apply for the position.

   c. I was fascinated by the challenges of the brokerage field.

   d. Please send me an application for your management trainee program.

   List in order of preference _____ _____ _____ _____

3. **a.** There are no fees for this service, and you can terminate the plan at any time.

   b. If you have any further questions, please call your account representative.

   c. With this plan, you authorize us to transfer a fixed amount each month from your bank account to your mutual fund account.

   d. You will be pleased to know that we are introducing an automatic monthly investment plan.

   List in order of preference _____ _____ _____ _____

4. **a.** We have enclosed a brochure that explains our services; feel free to contact one of our experienced representatives for further help.

   b. All of our investment consultants are professionals who are knowledgeable in the securities market.

   c. Our firm offers a wide range of investment plans tailored to the needs of our clients.

   d. Thank you for contacting Investment Services Corporation.

   List in order of preference _____ _____ _____ _____

5. **a.** As an experienced investor, you will find this monthly newsletter an incredible source of information on all types of investments.

   b. We have enclosed your free copy of *Financial Review*.

    c. Each month a prominent business professional writes about a financial topic of interest to our readers.

    d. Please take time to read this valuable pamphlet and don't hesitate to send in your subscription.

List in order of preference _____ _____ _____ _____

EXERCISE 2 INAPPROPRIATE AND OUTDATED PHRASES

Sometimes we use slang or informal phrases in our everyday speech. However, when more formal communication is used, as in business correspondence, some words and phrases are unacceptable. Furthermore, some phrases used in the past are no longer accepted; they have become outdated in our present form of communications. The following chart lists some examples of such wording.

Inappropriate/outdated words and phrases	Acceptable words and phrases
as per your request	at your request, as you requested
at this point in time	now
being that	because
due to the fact that	because
got to	must
hadn't ought to	should not
I trust that	I believe, I know
kind of	somewhat
lots of	many
on account of	since
per	according
should of	should have
thanking you in advance	thank you
under separate cover	separately

Unacceptable slang in business vocabulary

It's cool
It's neat
Chill out

Directions: Substitute the correct word(s) for each of the underlined inappropriate phrases.

1. There are <u>lots of</u> good investment opportunities for individuals who do careful research of the financial market.

2. <u>Per</u> your telephone conversation, the investors' meeting will be held next month.

3. <u>At this point in time</u>, you are able to purchase stock on the Internet.

4. <u>Due to the fact that</u> you have an excellent credit rating, we are increasing your cash limit to $10,000.

5. The manager <u>should of</u> discussed the stock option plan with the staff beforehand.

6. <u>Being that</u> you have been with the firm for one year, you are eligible to join its investment plan.

7. <u>On account</u> of the company's high earnings for the year, the stock has increased in value.

8. The president of the company <u>hadn't ought to</u> announce his successor until the board of directors meets next week.

9. When you go for the interview, you <u>got to</u> know the company's history.

10. We were <u>kind of</u> disappointed with the seminar on investments.

11. <u>I trust that</u> you will do some research before investing in a company stock.

12. We <u>are thanking you in advance</u> for accepting our invitation to be our main speaker.

13. <u>As per your request</u>, we are sending you our annual report.

14. <u>Being that</u> I have my broker's license, my promotion will take place immediately.

15. After a stressful day, <u>it's cool to chill out</u>.

INTRODUCTION: MEMORANDUMS

Memorandums are written communications to inform individuals within a business organization. They are easy, informal means of sending written messages internally to colleagues, supervisors, or other departments. Although the format is simpler than a letter, the purpose of transmitting information or data in hard copy is that it becomes a valuable written record.

The following are some guidelines when writing a memo:

- When addressing a memo to a number of individuals, list names according to position in organization and alphabetical.

- State the purpose of memo clearly on the subject line.

- Convey the facts, ideas, or statistics clearly and to the point.

- Omit salutation and closing.

Writing Pointers

LETTER OF REQUEST

- Be specific in your request—date, place, item.
- Get to the point; ask for specific information.
- Give reason for request.
- Address the letter to an individual whenever possible.
- Request specific action in a courteous tone.
- Show appreciation.

LETTER OF RESPONSE TO A REQUEST

- Consider the individual making the request as a prospective customer.

- Acknowledge appreciation for interest in product or service.
- Give information pertinent to the request; don't give needless information.
- Indicate action to be taken.
- Offer further assistance to the reader, which can build goodwill.

LETTER FORMAT

- Subject line is double spaced after the salutation (see model in Appendix).
- *Salutation*—when inside address is to an organization, salutation reads "Ladies and Gentlemen:"

MEMORANDUM

- Use for internal communications.
- Make it brief and specific.
- State purpose of memorandum in opening paragraph.
- Provide a clear, informative subject line.
- See appendix B for memorandum format.

Model Letter of Request

Date

Mr. Richard Barnes
Portfolio Manager
Asset Management Funds
1170 Pikes Peak Road
Boulder, CO 80323-5400

Dear Mr. Barnes:

Positive opening

Praises reader

Your speech at the Investors' Convention in Salt Lake City was most informative. I found the booklet, *Cybermarket for Investors*, which you distributed at the conference, an invaluable reference guide.

Reason for request

Specific request

This guide would be an excellent resource for my staff to share with their clients. Is it possible to receive 50 copies? If there is a charge, please let me know.

Positive appeal to reader

Since this reference guide is an extremely valuable book for investment specialists, I hope you will be able to fulfill this request.

Sincerely yours,

Lisa Willis
Vice President

ri

Date

Ms. Lisa Willis
Parker Financial Group
55 Thornwood Road
Des Moines, IA 50392-4150

Dear Ms. Willis:

Acknowledge
appreciation

Positive comments
about convention

Thank you for your thoughtful comments regarding my recent presentation in Salt Lake City. I, too, found the convention both enjoyable and informative. All the sessions were most professional.

Indicates action

Yes, we will honor your request and ship the 50 copies of *Cybermarket for Investors* next week. It has been a very successful booklet, and I am sure your staff will find that it is an excellent guide when dealing with clients.

Gives pertinent
information about
positive response

Although the booklet is free, we will bill you for the shipping charges. If there are any further questions, please feel free to contact me.

Offers assistance

Sincerely yours,

Richard Barnes
Portfolio Manager

ri

Internal
communication

To: Members of the Planning Committee

From: Edith Boswell, Chairperson Investor Relations

Date: September 15, 200x

States purpose
clearly

Subject: Investor Conference in Orlando

Purpose of memo

Specific
Instructions

The date for the Investor Conference to be held in Orlando is fast approaching. We need to finalize the program and the speakers for each session. I am requesting that the Planning Committee submits to me by next Thursday an outline of the activities of this two-day conference. In the following week, we will have an all-day meeting to make the final decisions on the organization of the conference.

Offers assistance

Positive tone

If you have any questions, feel free to contact me at any time. From the preliminary reports, I am confident that this conference will be a success

ri

Activity F **Writing Power: Composing Correspondence**

Case Study 1: Letter of Request

Read Case Study 1. Then read Options A and B for each section of the letter. Select the option that you believe is most appropriate for the opening, body, and closing statements. Then key the entire letter based on the options you selected. (See letter format in Appendix B)

Case: You have seen an advertisement in the magazine *Smart Investing* to open an IRA mutual fund account with the American Investment Group. The ad invites the reader to contact one of its specialists to discuss this type of investment. Address the letter to Investor Relations Manager, Investment Services, American Investment Group. One Broad Street, Baltimore, MD 21298-9391. Salutation should read "Ladies and Gentlemen:" Use your name for the closing.

Opening sentence:

a. I read with interest your ad about investing an IRA in mutual funds.

b. I read the American Investment Group advertisement in *Smart Investing* about opening an IRA mutual fund.

Option A or B _____

Body of letter:

a. The information in your ad was of interest to me. At present I do not have any investment accounts. I believe that I need to make some wise financial decisions for the future.

b. Your ad was interesting. I do not have any investment accounts and need to invest for the future.

Option A or B _____

Closing:

a. I would like to speak to one of your specialists about opening an account with your company. I can be reached at 865-230-8182.

b. I look forward to speaking to one of your specialists regarding my situation and the possibility of opening an account with your firm. My home phone number is 865-230-8182.

Option A or B _____

Case Study 2: Letter of Response to a Request

Read Case Study 2. Then read Options A and B for each section of the letter. Select the option that you believe is most appropriate for the opening, body, and closing statements. Then key the entire letter based on the options you selected.

Case: The Investment Department of American Investment Group received a request for information about mutual funds from Sarah Preston, 65 Circle Run, Reston, VA 20191-5000. One of the investment specialists, Greg Alvaro, is responding to Sarah's letter and sending a mutual fund information kit. The letter mentions the firm's excellent long-term returns on its mutual funds. They also have low costs and no sales charges. Suggest to Sarah to read the enclosed material. A specialist will be in touch with her. The company also has a Web site www.aminvest.com that gives investors additional information.

Opening sentence:

a. Thank you for your request.

b. Our Investment Department received your request for information about our mutual funds.

Option A or B _____

Body of letter

Sentences 1 and 2:

a. We offer our investors a large selection of mutual funds. We keep our costs low, have no sales charges, and give good returns on your investments.

b. American Investment Group offers a broad selection of funds with a history of excellent long-term returns. We also keep costs low and have no sales charges.

Option A or B _____

Sentences 3, 4 and 5:

a. An investment kit which explains each of our funds is enclosed. We suggest that you read the information carefully. One of our investment specialists will contact you shortly.

b. Our investment kit on mutual funds is enclosed. Read it; it contains helpful information. One of our investment specialists will contact you.

Option A or B _____

  a. Thank you for your interest in American Investment Group. Our Web site aminvest.com also has additional investment information.

  b. We look forward to assisting you in making the right financial decision. You can visit our Web site aminvest.com for additional investment advice.

  Option A or B _____

Case Study 3: Response to a Request

After reading the case, respond to the questions that follow to help organize your ideas before beginning to compose the letter. Then draft the letter to:

Mr. Michael Gibson
85 Byron Place
New Haven, CT 06515–2281

Case: Mr. Gibson has called your office requesting information on one of your mutual funds, the Select Fund. Prepare a cover letter to send with the literature and prospectus that describe this fund. You may want to mention to Mr. Gibson the advantages of this fund, which has had an average growth rate of 5 percent annually. Also, there are no sales commissions. State that there is a toll-free number for further information about our services, 800-531-5575.

ORGANIZE YOUR IDEAS

  1. Indicate the most important point you want to make to Mr. Gibson.

  _____

  _____

  2. What should you include in the opening sentence?

  _____

  _____

  3. What specific details should you include in the body?

  _____

  _____

  _____

4. What should you include in your closing statement that would get a response from your reader?

_____

_____

Case Study 4: Memorandum

Read Case Study 4. Then prepare the memorandum to Joseph Peluso, Regional Manager, from Alex Rice, Vice President, on the subject of the Annual Investment Expo. Use correct memorandum format.

Case: Alex Rice believes that some of the investment analysts should attend the informative show, Annual Investment Expo. It will be held at the Convention Center in Dallas on March 16 and 17. Mr. Rice is asking his regional manager, Joseph Peluso, to forward the names of staff members who would be eligible to attend. Mr. Rice plans to hold a meeting within a week of the individuals who have been recommended.

Challenge Level Case

Case Study 5: Request Letter

Read Case Study 5; then compose the letter.

The investment firm of Brooks and Carney plans to expand its financial services. To determine which services are important, the firm has designed a survey questionnaire to be sent to its clients.

You have been assigned the task of composing a letter for your boss, Daniel Brooks, president, in which you ask clients to complete the survey.

To get a good response, you will have to explain the importance of the survey and the need for clients' participation. Include a subject line referring to the Important Client Survey.

Address the letter to Mr. Alan Barnett, 83 Cimarron Drive, Oklahoma City, OK 73100–2290.

⟩ Cultural Communication

Australia:

■ Maintain a conservative attitude and dress in business.

■ Establish rapport in business dealings.

■ Don't engage in aggressive sales techniques; keep presentation "to-the-point."

■ Refrain from discussing personal issues; don't brag about achievements.

See www.executiveplanet.com

Self-Assessment
English Power

Directions: In each of the following sentences, choose the correct form of the verb so that it agrees with the subject.

_____ 1. There (is, are) increasing use of Web sites for investment information.

_____ 2. The government publication on IRA investments (explain, explains) clearly the features of this type of saving.

_____ 3. Neither the manager nor the brokers (was, were) responsible for the misleading analysis.

_____ 4. You (is, are) able to make a stock transaction quickly on the Internet.

_____ 5. The number of employees investing in 401(k) plans (has, have) increased.

_____ 6. One of the investment newsletters (recommend, recommends) mutual funds.

_____ 7. The new database, sponsored by Value Associates, (contain, contains) extensive information on global companies.

_____ 8. Wise investing (require, requires) serious research of companies.

_____ 9. The efforts by the firm to increase sales (make, makes) the stock an attractive buy.

_____ 10. The nation's economy (appear, appears) to be very strong.

Editing Power

Directions: Edit, proofread, and correct the following form letter. Key it correctly.

```
Dear Prospective Client:

Are your investments financially secure with a good

return? The Price Fund offer the investor a mutual fund.

That has outperformed in the past five years. You can

feel confident that your money is well invested.

    Our staff are committed to a conservative approach

towards investing in stocks, bonds, and mutual funds.
```

The financial analysts will advice you in choosing the
investment that best meets your personnel needs.

The enclosed booklet present details of The price fund
as well as our other broad range of investments. We
invite you to contact our representative at 800-620-2000.

Sincerely yours,

Maria Salina

Chief Marketing Officer

Writing Power

Directions: After reading the case that follows, draft a letter to
Mr. Raymond Staples, One Railroad Avenue, Essex, CT 06426-7900,
sent by Doug Polinsky, Regional Vice President.

Raymond Staples requested information from United Investment
Services about its investment plans. This letter is in response to that request. Inform Mr. Staples that Ms. Annette Stark, an experienced financial counselor with the firm, has been assigned to him. She will be
in contact with him soon to explain the investment options that are
available. Also, inform Mr. Staples that United Investment Services is
a well-respected firm. The research department investigates any investment suggestions given to the client, whether it be stocks, bonds,
or mutual funds. The main goal of the staff is to recommend the best
investment to meet the client's needs.

> "Leadership has a harder job to do than just choose sides. It
> must bring sides together."
>
> —Jesse Jackson

CHAPTER 4

Telecommunicating with Verbs

*C*ORPORATE SNAPSHOT

INTEL ® Corporation is the world's largest chip maker, supplying advanced technology solutions for the computing, networking, and communications industries. Intel's chips can be found in everything from PCs to servers, cell phones, and telecommunications equipment.

Through Intel Involved, the company's worldwide volunteer program, employees focus their energies on being an asset to the communities where they live and work. The company has a strong commitment to education. The Intel Innovation in Education initiative contributes more than $100 million annually in more than 30 countries around the world to strengthen mathematics and science education, the foundation for the high technology industry and for much of the global economy.

Source: Intel Corporation, Corporate Affairs, Media Relations

WHAT YOU WILL LEARN IN THIS CHAPTER

- To use correct verb tense in business correspondence
- To develop a business vocabulary in **TELECOMMUNICATIONS**
- To proofread and edit correspondence and reports
- To rewrite a poorly written letter of apology
- To compose a memorandum
- To compose a letter of complaint
- To write e-mail correspondence

CUSTOMER SERVICE REPRESENTATIVE: Represents the firm to clients and outside business associates, direct contact with customers, responds and handles telephone, e-mail, and face-to-face inquiries and complaints, provides product and service information to clients.

Skills: communication, listening, and interpersonal skills, knowledge of firm's products and services; associate degree desirable.

SYSTEMS ANALYST: Solves computer problems, applies computer technology to meet the needs of an organization, develops systems for a firm's operations.

Skills: may work on a contract basis, minimum B.A. degree in computer science or information technology, problem-solving and analytical skills, internship.

COMPUTER SUPPORT SPECIALIST: Provides technical assistance, support, and advice to users of a particular computer system or network; troubleshooting is done through the Internet or by telephone.

Skills: extensive knowledge of the particular system, interpersonal, oral communications, associate degree in computer science.

Activity A   *Language Arts Recall*

Verb Tense

Verb tense refers to time. The verb in a sentence indicates when the action occurred.

> **Rule 4.1:** simple present—actions that are happening now.
>
> **Rule 4.2:** simple past—actions that happened in the past and were completed.
>
> **Rule 4.3:** simple future—actions that will happen.

Simple Present Tense	Simple Past Tense	Simple Future Tense
(verb)	(verb + "d" or "ed")	("will" or "shall" + verb)
invite	invited	will invite

Perfect tense indicates an activity that happened in the past, either before the present or before another time in the past, or an activity that will have been completed before a time in the future. The perfect tense uses the auxiliary (helping) verb "to have" plus a special form of the main verb, known as the past participle, usually formed by adding "d" or "ed" to the regular verb. The three perfect tenses are present perfect, past perfect, and future perfect.

> **Rule 4.4:** present perfect—action began in the past but was completed either before the present or at some unspecified time in the past; when used with "since" or "for," the action is continuing.

continued

Present Perfect Tense	Past Perfect Tense	Future Perfect Tense

Active voice: subject performs the action

have, has, had, will have, shall have—helping verb used in perfect tenses

has, have	had	will have, shall have
has, have invited	had invited	will have invited
has, have reviewed	had reviewed	will have reviewed
has, have chosen*	had chosen	will have chosen

*irregular verb "chose"

4.6a *Passive voice: subject is acted upon; it receives the action of the verb*
    Often the helping verb form "to be" is used

has been invited	had been invited	will have been invited
is presented	was presented	will be presented
has been presented	had been presented	will have been presented

Examples:
  The final report has been presented by the manager. (passive, subject receives action)
  The final report was presented by the manager. (passive)

Change to active voice:
  The manager has presented the final report. (subject performs action)
  The manager presented the final report.

Note: Avoid the use of passive voice in business writing.

Present	Past	Past Participle	Perfect Tense (helping verb + participle)
is, are	was, were	been	(has, have, had) been
begin	began	begun	(has, have, had) begun
bring	brought	brought	
choose	chose	chosen	
drive	drove	driven	
eat	ate	eaten	
give	gave	given	
grow	grew	grown	
have	had	had	
know	knew	known	
lead	led	led	
say	said	said	
see	saw	seen	
speak	spoke	spoken	
spend	spent	spent	
take	took	taken	
teach	taught	taught	
tell	told	told	
think	thought	thought	
wear	wore	worn	
write	wrote	written	

Check for Understanding

Directions: Compare each set of the verbs in Column A and Column B; then answer the questions that follow:

Column A	Column B
invite	has invited
discuss	have discussed
produce	will have produced
analyze	had analyzed
speak	had spoken

QUESTIONS

1. What do all of the verb forms in column B have in common?

   _____

2. Which verb does not end in *d* or *ed?* Why? _____

Conclusion: Complete the following sentence.

To form the perfect tense of regular verbs, _____

   _____

(Answers are given below.)

Answers to "Check for Understanding"

1. Consist of auxiliary verb (has, have, had) plus main verb
2. spoken, irregular verb

   Conclusion to form the perfect tense of regular verbs, use the auxiliary verb with the past participle of the main verb.

Building English Power: Verb Tense

Directions: In the spaces provided on page 76–77, indicate the subject and verb in each of the following sentences. Also identify the tense of each verb.

1. Last year, our office introduced electronic mail for speedier communications. (4.2)

2. Fax machines have decreased in price over the past year. (4.4)

3. During the past decade, consumer interest in cellular phones has increased. (4.4)

4. The corporation will have introduced videoconferencing by next year. (4.6)

5. The editor of the magazine has used desktop publishing for the past year. (4.4)

6. The new subscriber took the two-year contract. (4.7)

7. The control of computer viruses has been discussed at our staff meetings. (4.6a)

8. With a CD-ROM, you have the opportunity to listen to music and study the composition. (4.1)

9. A task force of advertisers has been organized to study how high-tech media can reshape ads. (4.6a)

10. The popular TV personality has been invited to speak at the opening session. (4.6a)

11. The company had planned to upgrade its computer capabilities to include high-speed data networking. (4.5)

12. Many executives carry a notebook computer when traveling in business. (4.1)

13. I chose the latest cellphone model. (4.7)

14. The electronic firm has given the college $25,000 to purchase laptop computers. (4.4, 4.7)

15. At last month's meeting, the personnel directors had discussed the difficulties in hiring qualified technicians. (4.5)

16. We had demonstrated our graphics software at the trade show before our competitor announced a similar product. (4.5)

17. The bank has encouraged its customers to use the Internet for onscreen checking transactions. (4.4)

18. I wrote to the president of the company describing the poor quality of the equipment. (4.7)

19. We will drive to the trade show. (4.3)

20. The popularity of the iPod has risen over the past year. (4.4, 4.7)

	Subject	Verb	Verb Tense
1.			
2.			
3.			
4.			
5.			
6.			
7.			
8.			
9.			
10.			

11. _____ _____ _____

12. _____ _____ _____

13. _____ _____ _____

14. _____ _____ _____

15. _____ _____ _____

16. _____ _____ _____

17. _____ _____ _____

18. _____ _____ _____

19. _____ _____ _____

20. _____ _____ _____

Activity B   Building Word Power

Good telephone etiquette starts with a good tone of voice. A pleasant, helpful attitude is communicated through one's voice.

Directions: The words that follow are commonly used in the telecommunications industry. From this list, select the word or phrase that correctly completes each statement. Refer to the Personal Dictionary if you are uncertain of the meaning of a word.

configuration	mouse
electronic mail (e-mail)	networking
facsimile equipment (FAX)	notebook
Internet	protocols
laptop computer(s)	software
modem	telecommunications
monitor	videoconferencing

_____ **1.** A popular method of holding face-to-face meetings between locations by using video equipment is known as _____.

_____ **2.** With the need to send printed copy instantaneously, the _____ is replacing conventional mail deliveries.

_____ **3.** To receive up-to-date stock information, you can add a(n) _____ to connect a PC to a telephone to transmit information.

_____ **4.** When traveling, business executives carry portable computers that are called _____.

_____ **5.** _____ is the term used to describe the transfer of data from one place to another over communication lines.

_____ **6.** _____ allows businesses to send, receive, and store messages over telecommunications facilities.

_____ 7. A more compact, lightweight computer than a laptop is known as a(n) _____.

_____ 8. The computer _____, which is the display screen, may produce a glare that is disturbing to the user.

_____ 9. Many computer users prefer to use a(n) _____ to move the cursor around the screen freely without using a keyboard.

_____ 10. The engineer is studying the _____ of the office before submitting a new design plan.

_____ 11. A new _____ program allows you to do your banking by computer.

_____ 12. Through the _____, an individual can communicate electronically worldwide on many subjects and draw information from databases.

_____ 13. To communicate successfully on the Internet, standardized procedures and regulations, known as _____, need to be used.

_____ 14. _____ systems can connect computers within an office and throughout the world.

On the Alert

■ *its (possessive pronoun)*—belonging to

Example: The computer in my office is useless because **its** monitor is broken.

it's (contraction)—it is

Example: **It's** a high priority for a business to subscribe to an Internet service.

■ *past (noun)*—the time before the present

Example: In the **past**, electronic games did not exist.

past (adjective)—no longer current

Example: The firm is studying its **past** sales records in the Northeast.

passed (past tense of verb)—moved on; accomplished

Example: Most of the students **passed** the course.

■ *affect (verb)*—to influence

Example: Advances in telecommunications **affect** people's daily lives.

effect (noun)—result

> Example: One of the **effects** of the computer has been a need to retrain employees.

effect (verb)—to bring about change

> Example: The law that was passed in Congress **effects** a change in taxes.

■ *assistance (noun)*—help, aid

> Example: **assistance** was provided to the fire victims.

assistants (plural noun)—an individual who assists someone in a managerial position

> Example: The office **assistants** will provide you with the necessary data on mobile phones.

■ *site (noun)*—location

> Example: The **site** of the new building is a popular tourist attraction.

sight (noun)—1. the ability to see

> Example: He lost his **sight** after the accident.

2. (noun) something worth seeing

> Example: The lake in the winter was a beautiful **sight**.

sight (verb)—to see or observe

> Example: Columbus **sighted** land in 1492.

cite (verb)—to quote or mention

> Example: When you do research, **cite** the source of quoted material.

■ percent—Express percentages in figures; write out the word "percent."

> Example: 5 percent

Activity C   *Industry Perspectives: Telecommunications*

Directions: Using appropriate revision marks, proofread and key the following report.

2.1

The fast-paced telecommunications industry have affected

every aspect of our lives both at home and in business.

What is telecommunications? Its the process of

1.3   transmitting information over long distances through a
          communication line such as telephone, cable, microwaves,
          and satellites. this information may take the form of
          voice, data, image, or message.

3.1, 2.1   Expedient transmission of information and data on a
          global scale are crucial in today's business markets.
          Whether a firm's offices are located in the United
1.4   States, europe, or asia, business transactions can take
          place anywhere and at any time. With telecommunications,
          business is less dependent on face-to-face interactions.
          Business dealings can be accomplished through networking
2.1   systems. Within minutes, a sender connect with the
          receiver to share information and data. This new
2.1   technology also enable employees to interact with there
          coworkers anywhere in the world. Therefore, it is
3.4   essential that everyone respect different cultures and
          customs of individuals in foreign countries.

4.6   On a personnel level, individuals become more
          dependent on telecommunications. The cell phone today is
          viewed as a necessity to keep in touch with family and
3.6, 2.1 friends. The number of people surfing the web for the
          latest information on consumer goods, medical data, and
3.4   financial news are constantly growing. Everyone agree
          that in this Digital Era technological advances will
          continue to effect the way we live and do business.

Did you find these errors?
4 subject-verb agreement
4 word usage
3 capitalization
1 perfect tense

Activity D   Editing Power

Task A: Edit, format, and proofread the following letter for verb tense, subject–verb agreement, and other errors. Use proofreaders' symbols to mark the errors, then key it correctly.

Errors

- subject-verb agreement
- verb tense
- confusing words
- typographical

Mr. Edward Burke, Jr.
1100 Broad Street
Cleveland, OH 44190-8030

Dear Mr. Burke:

Thank you for your inquiry about our computer product line. The authorized dealer nearest you is Computer Mart, 5 Metro Office Park, Cleveland, OH 44190-3598. Computer Marte offer a complete line of products from laptop computers to network systems. For businesses, custom configurations and on-sight installations are available. You may want to consider Computer Mart's excellent leasing program, which has been popular for for many years.

Our dealer has maintain it's efficient and reliable service for the passed 20 years. The sales representatives has received training on our equipment. Therefore, they will be able to discuss your needs and recomend equipment best suited for your business.

Feel free to visit the showroom; you will find everyone most helpful.

Sincerely yours,

Lloyd Pearson
Sales Manager

Challenge Task B: Edit, format, and proofread the following memorandum for all errors, especially verb tense, then key it correctly. (See Appendix B for memorandum format.)

This memorandum is being sent from Inez Santos, manager of the Marketing Division, to the Sales Staff. The subject is New Product.

```
(P) Our latest upgraded computer, Bell SX25, is

available on December 1. As we have discuss at previous

sales meetings, this product will have consumer appeal.

It has been equipped with a CD-ROM storage device and

multimedia software. It also has been preload with

several computer programs. Enclosed you will find a

booklet describing the the new product. (P) The next

sales meeting held in the Main Building Conference Room

on october 10 at 9:15 a.m. The sales approach to

introduce this new product will have been discussed at

this meeting. (P) If you are unable to attend, please

call my office to arrange for a video conferencing

session.
```

Activity E Writing Practicum

EXERCISE 1   CORRECT VERB TENSE, SUBJECT-VERB AGREEMENT, CORRECT WORD USAGE

Directions: Rewrite the following paragraphs to reflect the verb tense requested, subject-verb agreement, and correct word usage.

a. (Use simple present tense)

Casual games is very popular online. Sights on the Internet offered hundreds of games free. To test one's knowledge, there was online versions of Scrabble and Jeopardy. Today's cell phones allowed individuals to download the games. The future promised to join the mobile phone and personal computer to offer games interchangeably.

b. (Use present perfect tense)

The trend in technology is toward easier excess and ease of communications for small business and the individual proprietor.

Computer networks and online sources give the entrepreneur the opportunity to retrieve valuable information related to a particular industry or market. Reports on consumer trends, product innovations, and sales analyses helped small business compete in the marketplace.

c. (Use simple past)

Last year mobile technology had expanded rapidly. A number of innovations had added new features to cell phones such as built-in cameras and text imaging. Companies had offered to download films and music for a small fee. Consumer demand has grown for these new phones.

d. (Use simple future tense)

A popular online innovation is the practice of blogging. Web sites on which the writer posts messages for anyone to read show up on the Internet. On such Web sites, individuals interchange ideas on any subject. The interaction occurs immediately with high-speed Internet access.

EXERCISE 2   CHANGING VERB TENSE FROM PRESENT TO PAST

Directions: The following fax was sent to every branch office of a large corporation. The message was written in the present tense. Rewrite the fax and change all of the verbs to the simple past tense. Use correct format.

```
Date: (Current Date)

To: Branch Offices

R. J. Tompkins Corporation

From: Ray Dejesus

Subject: Telenetwork System

    We want to alert all of our branch offices that we

are converting our telephone lines to a new computerized

system on September 5.

    This allows for several improvements over our old

system. Each new desk unit consists of a modular console

that includes fax, voice mail, and three-way

conferencing features. Executive offices have hookups

for videoconferencing and taping facilities. We are
```

confident that our interoffice communications benefit
from this change.

The plan is to install the system over the Labor Day
weekend so that the business day has few interruptions.

We appreciate your cooperation in this matter.

EXERCISE 3 CHANGING VERB TENSE FROM PRESENT TO PRESENT PERFECT

Directions: In the following paragraphs that will be published in a magazine column, change the verb tense from simple present to present perfect tense.

The Internet introduces a new era in communications.
Through a computer network, friends, business
colleagues, and customers interact and share information
instantly with one another. The Internet is as popular
as using a cellular phone or faxing a message. It is the
focus of the computing world.

Computer networks change the way business handles its
transactions. Information is globalized and resources
are available from all over the world. The following
services are available to the Internet user: online
shopping, banking transactions, checking status of
orders, researching databases, voice messaging, and
exchanging e-mail.

The Internet is growing rapidly. Protocols for this
online computer network do not limit the type of users.
An increasing number of large corporations, small
businesses, and individual subscribers join the Internet
for their means of communication.

Writing Pointers

LETTER OF COMPLAINT BY CUSTOMER LETTER

- Avoid starting letter in a negative tone.
- Acknowledge past service or good product.
- Describe specifically the item or model.
- State the problem clearly and reasonably; do not be wordy.
- Avoid using offensive or unnecessary words.
- Indicate your suggestion for resolving the problem.
- Avoid threats and demands.

LETTER OF APOLOGY

- Explain reason for delay or error.
- State action taken.
- Express empathy.
- Offer assistance or an alternative solution.
- Avoid negative words that suggest blame (regret, unfortunately, fault).
- End with goodwill statement.

Model Letter of Complaint

Date

Mr. Roy Folsom
President
Central Technology Company
881 Central Avenue
Akron, OH 44321-1452

Dear Mr. Folsom:

Positive
Opening praise
past service

Your firm has always given us excellent service. This is the reason why I am perplexed at the present situation regarding the backlog order.

Problem stated
clearly

One month ago, I ordered ten mobile phones from your firm, which still have not arrived. Your salesperson promised delivery within two weeks. When I spoke to your customer representative about this problem, I was told that the delay was a backlog of orders on this item.

Polite approach
Expresses
concern
regarding
delivery

This excuse is unsatisfactory. I can understand a delay; however, no attempt has been made to explain when the order will be filled. These mobile phones are essential to my business; without them, I cannot contact my employees to service my customers.

Requested action	Please let me know the status of this order and how you intend to resolve this matter.

Sincerely yours,

Kenneth Murdoch
Manager

ri

Model Letter of Apology

Date

Mr. Kenneth Murdock
Manager
The Electronic Store
224 Clearview Parkway
Richmond, VA 23234-5512

Dear Mr. Murdock:

Apology for delay Opening shows empathy Explanation given	We are sorry that your shipment of ten mobile phones has been delayed. An unexpected equipment failure has caused a backlog of this item. Since this particular model is not readily available from other manufacturers, we are unable to fill the order. Our representative should have explained the situation to you.
States action to be taken	We understand your frustration and will make every attempt to special handle the order when we receive the mobile phones. A shipment is expected next week.
Positive tone Gesture of goodwill	Please accept our apologies. A 10 percent deduction will be credited to your account; we hope this meets with your approval. You may contact me at any time.

Sincerely yours,

Roy Folsom
President

ri

 Activity F   *Writing Power: Composing Correspondence*

In chapters 4 through 7, Case Study 1 will consist of a poorly written letter. After reading the case study, critique the letter by responding to the questions. This will guide you in writing an effective letter by adding, rewording, or deleting words or phrases that do not demonstrate good writing techniques. Remember to use the six Cs of writing a good letter: **Clarity, Correctness, Conciseness, Completeness, Consistency,** and **Courteousness.** Review the "Writing Pointers" in each chapter to help you improve your writing skills.

Case Study 1: Rewrite a Poorly Written Letter of Apology

After reading the poorly written letter addressed to one of your customers, Cyber Mart, Inc., 11 Elwood Drive, Portland, ME 04101-3190, your supervisor, James Winter, requested that you rewrite the letter. To help you complete this task, (a) answer the questions that follow; (b) rephrase sentences, if needed; and (c) rewrite the letter for mailing.

Case:

Dear Mr. Ruiz:

Our company is sorry to say that we have had problems in our company and cannot ship at the present time the five laser-jet printers you ordered.

Unfortunately, the reason for this delay was due to a job slowdown at the manufacturing plant. We recognize that the delay will be an inconvenience to you. However, this situation was beyond our control.

Once again, we are sorry. We hope to serve you in the future.

QUESTIONS

1. In this letter of apology, what is the first statement you should make to your customer?

   _____

   _____

2. What is wrong with the second sentence?

   _____

   _____

3. How can you improve the third and fourth sentences to reflect a caring attitude and to show empathy for the customer?

   _____

   _____

4. What is missing in this letter that should be included?

_____

5. What is wrong with the closing sentence?

_____

_____

Case Study 2: Memorandum on Price Increase

After reading the case that follows respond to the questions that follow, which will help you organize your ideas. Then prepare a memorandum to the sales force from Glen Chase, marketing vice president, on the price increase. Use correct memorandum format.

Case: Glen Chase, marketing vice president, has been asked to notify his sales force that a 5 percent increase in price on the entire line of electronic equipment will become effective on June 1. The price increase is the result of rising manufacturing costs. A revised price list has been attached to this memo. Inform the salespeople that they should contact their managers if they have any questions.

ORGANIZE YOUR IDEAS

1. What is the most important point you want to make to your sales force?

_____

_____

2. What would you include in the opening sentence?

_____

_____

_____

3. What specific details would you include in the body of the memorandum?

_____

_____

4. What would you say in your closing statement that would get a positive reaction from your sales force?

_____

_____

Case Study 3: Letter of Complaint

Read Case Study 3; Organize your ideas before composing the letter.

Case: You purchased a cellular telephone five months ago from CompuMax, an authorized dealer of Cellular Systems. The model you bought, XL95, has a one-year warranty from Cellular Systems, the manufacturer. Recently, you began to hear a high-frequency hum when using the phone. This is distracting and interferes with your conversation. Notify the manufacturer that you are returning the phone for a replacement. The manufacturer's address is 17 Grand Avenue, Des Moines, IA 50312–9526.

Case Study 4: Letter of Apology

Read Case Study 4; then complete the letter.

As a customer representative, you have the responsibility of answering complaint letters. Ms. Esther Reynolds of 21 Magnolia Boulevard, Savannah, Georgia 31504–5213, is complaining that her recent telephone bill shows charges for long-distance calls that she did not make. She feels that there must be some mistake and asked you to check her records. You reviewed this matter and found Ms. Reynolds is correct. Write a letter explaining the situation and apologizing for the error.

Challenge Level Case

Case Study 5: Letter of Complaint

Read Case Study 5; then complete the letter.

Sid Kantor, manager of operations, has asked that you draft a letter to Frank Ambrosio, vice president of sales, on a matter of the unsatisfactory operation of new printers Tech 2005. Five printers were purchased last month; three of them are not producing quality prints. After 100 copies, the colors fade so that the photo is no longer bright or sharp. In your business, these prints are unacceptable. The service person who inspected the three printers concluded that there was nothing mechanically wrong. You depend on good equipment to get satisfactory results. This is a serious matter for your firm. Request that the printers be replaced. You expect a prompt solution to the problem. Address the letter to Mr. Frank Ambrosio, Vice President of Sales, Tech, Inc., 3211 Office Park, Cincinnati, OH 45200.

INTRODUCTION: E-MAIL CORRESPONDENCE

One of the most widely used features of the Internet is electronic mail. It has become a cost-effective means of communication within an organization as well as with customers. E-mail facilitates the flow of information among correspondents at various locations and time zones. Individuals receive messages more quickly than the printed document and are able to respond immediately.

An advantage of electronic mail is that you can communicate with an individual halfway around the world. The person may be from a different culture, have different customs, and speak a different language. You need to be sure that your message is understood so that no misinterpretations occur.

E-mails are replacing the use of paper memos within a company. E-mail memos offer several advantages:

- Correspondence can be sent quickly for an immediate reply.

- Memorandums frequently are written in an informal manner suitable for e-mail.

- Correspondence can be sent at any time. The mail is held in an electronic mailbox until the recipient opens it.

- Messages can be sent to several people in the organization at one time.

- Reports and other documents from other programs can be attached.

Although e-mails may be informal among friends, in business correspondence e-mails must be correct, clear, concise, and easy to understand. They should basically follow the same rules of good writing as in traditionally written correspondence.

Basic rules in e-mail correspondence:

- Subject line is important in an e-mail; it should inform the reader of the content. Avoid a general statement that may be interpreted as junk mail.

- Message should be focused, concise, and clear.

- Message needs to be error-free (correct grammar, punctuation, and spelling).

- Message should be proofread. In minutes an error can be forwarded to a large audience.

- Correspondence should not be long (recommended maximum 250 words).

- E-mails are not confidential; do not send security-sensitive information without protective measures.

- The use of attachments is not encouraged—people are reluctant to open attachments; however, there are times when it is necessary to attach a report.

- The script of an e-mail should not be in all capital letters.

- Slang and sarcasm should be avoided.

Note: Because e-mails are not confidential, be aware of sending sensitive materials that can be retrieved easily by anyone. To solve this problem, some firms are adopting other types of software tools, such as workplace wikis that allow only authorized individuals to communicate with one another on secured sites.

E-Mail Format (may vary depending on the software)

To:	The receiver's e-mail address (some individuals prefer to add their names to the e-mail address; place it in angle brackets)
From:	The sender's e-mail address (may be omitted)
Cc:	Copy sent to other receivers
Salutation:	Optional; e-mail outside company is more formal
Subject:	Heading should give reader immediate information related to the content
Closing:	May be optional; however, in some e-mails it is unclear who the sender is. Therefore, individuals may prefer to include their name, title, company e-mail address, and phone number
Body of e-mail:	For easier readability use bullets, listings, and double space between paragraphs

Model E-mail Correspondence

Subject of E-mail

File	Edit	View	Tools	Message	Help	
Reply	Reply All	Forward	Print	Delete	Previous	Next

Receiver's
e-mail address

Purpose of
message

To: cruz@aol.com
Cc:
Subject: Subscription Renewal
Attachments: none

Salutation
included:
message sent
outside
company

Message is
concise and
clear

Contact
information

Dear Ms. Cruz:

We acknowledge your subscription renewal to Money Matters.
Every Friday online you will receive a weekly update of financial news.

Thank you for renewing.

Laura Crawford
Subscription Manager
lcrawford@aol.com

Model E-mail Memorandum within a Company					
Subject of E-mail					
File	**Edit**	**View**	**Tools**	**Message**	**Help**
Reply	**Reply All**	**Forward**	**Print**	**Delete**	**Previous**	**Next**

To: O'Brien.sue@packards.com
Cc:
Subject: Meeting for Sales Staff
Attachments: none

Informal style

Salutation and
closing optional

Hi Sue:

Just a reminder that Wednesday's meeting to discuss the sales
promotional campaign for the Notethink laptop is scheduled for 10 a.m.
See you then.

Case Study 6: E-Mail Correspondence

Note: In each chapter use the following format when writing the heading of an e-mail

To: (receiver's e-mail address)

Cc: (optional; copies sent to other receivers)

Subject: (specific heading related to e-mail content)

Read Case Study 6; then complete the e-mail. (Refer to model on p. 91)

Send an e-mail from Wendy Palez, Show Coordinator, to Ms. Kim Lang
(Klang@worldnet.com) inviting her to attend the Electronics and Media
Show to be held on June 10 and 11 at the San Diego Convention Center.

Inform Ms. Lang that the major electronics companies will be
displaying their latest equipment. It will give her an opportunity
to compare products before making any buying decisions. She
needs to make a reservation if she plans to attend. The Web site is
www. elecshow.com.

Case Study 7: E-Mail Memorandum Within a Company

Read Case Study 7; then complete the e-mail.

Send an e-mail memo to the human resources manager, Marta Santiago (martainteractive@opcit.com). Inform her that you would like to meet with her on June 10 at 9 a.m. to discuss management's plan for implementing a company policy for the personal use of the Internet and e-mail. Explain to her that the company is aware that this is a growing problem among the employees who see no wrongdoing, especially when the computer is used at the end of the workday. Indicate to Marta Santiago that you would like to hear suggestions and recommendations that relate to this issue and that employees would accept as a new policy.

Suggestion: You may want to include reasons why management is concerned with the problem.

The subject of this e-mail is "Meeting to Discuss Internet and E-Mail Usage."

➤ Cultural Communication

Canada:

- Country is officially bilingual, English and French.

- It is a multicultural society which is reflected in their customs.

- In business dealings, maintain a formal attitude; refrain from aggressive statements.

- They expect punctuality; avoid wasting time at meetings.

See www.executiveplanet.com

Self-Assessment
English Power

Directions: In each of the following sentences, change each italicized verb to the tense indicated in parentheses.

_____ 1. Photos *store* on the computer can be accessed on the cellphone. (simple past)

_____ 2. Analysts *predict* that sale of mobile phones will increase this year. (present perfect)

_____ 3. The software engineers *write* the program for the video game. (simple past)

_____ 4. The company *offer* a $25 rebate on its digital camera. (past perfect)

_____ 5. The president of the firm *issue* a statement on the progress of the lawsuit. (simple future)

_____ 6. Metrofone, a large cellphone provider, *merge* with an Asian firm. (present perfect)

_____ 7. At the last meeting, the negotiators *agree* on the terms of the settlement. (past perfect)

_____ 8. The settlement *announce* by the representatives of both firms. (present perfect, passive voice)

_____ 9. Before the next general meeting, the executive board *choose* the new director of the electronics division of the firm. (future perfect)

_____10. Companies *spend* millions on digital research. (present perfect)

Editing Power

Directions: Edit, format, and proofread the following letter for errors in verb tense, subject-verb agreement, sentence structure, and word usage. Then key it correctly. Address this letter to Mr. John Rodriguez, Customer Relations Manager, Telnex Company, 15 Midland Avenue, White Plains, NY 10533-2400.

```
In the passed, Telnex products has always been

competitively priced and has given excellent service. As

a satisfied customer, I decide to purchase your new X3

laptop model at the Best Services store. this particular

item carried a rebate offered by your company.
```

It is now three months since the purchase, and I have not receive the $200 rebate. At the time of the sale, I was direct by one of the sales assistance to fill out the rebate form and mail it with the receipt to your address. I did so promptly.

The retailer claims that the manufacturer has been responsible to send the refund. I can only assume that this is an oversight by your company please look into this matter and notify me when I receive this rebate.

Sincerely yours, Sarah Mitchell

Writing Power

Directions: After reading the case that follows, draft an e-mail memorandum to the sales staff from their manager, Thomas Saunders. Provide a subject topic.

Thomas Saunders wants to notify the sales staff that a meeting will be held next Monday (insert correct date) at 9 A.M. in the conference room. The agenda of the meeting will be the price increase for the entire line of computers. The reason for the increase is the escalating manufacturing costs. This price increase will take effect at the beginning of next month. The staff should be prepared to offer suggestions on ways to maintain clients' goodwill when they are informed about the price increase.

"Alone we can do so little; together we can do so much."

—Helen Keller

CHAPTER 5

Lots of Commas in Real Estate

*C*ORPORATE SNAPSHOT

Malls: An American Phenomenon

The automobile has had a profound impact on the American lifestyle. In the 1920s, shopping centers with plazas surrounded by stores with parking spaces began to appear.

When Americans began to leave the cities to settle in suburban areas, retail stores also began moving from downtown areas. The regional mall was introduced in the 1950s. Shoppers began to travel distances to malls that were anchored by department stores, specialty shops, and a central pedestrian walk conducive to browsing. The shift of retail businesses from city centers to suburban areas had taken place.

Gradually developers expanded regional malls into the popular mega malls. The most recent real estate concept is the upscale mall with a cityscape environment that includes walkways, flowers, fountains, as well as restaurants, office space, and apartments.

Are malls headed for extinction? Probably not as long as architects and real estate developers can create space that contributes to a good quality of life.

WHAT YOU WILL LEARN IN THIS CHAPTER

- To identify compound sentences
- To punctuate compound sentences with a comma
- To identify adjectives and adverbs
- To develop a business vocabulary in **REAL ESTATE**
- To proofread and edit correspondence and reports
- To compose collection letters at various stages
- To compose a request letter
- To compose an invitation letter with subject line
- To write an e-mail correspondence

Job Snapshot

REAL ESTATE AGENT: Represents the buyer or seller of a property, locates and examines available properties on the market, assists in executing the sale.

Skills: state license required, on-the-job training, client recommendation, personal integrity and reputation, interpersonal skills.

APPRAISER: Estimates value of property to determine the sales price or amount of mortgage that can be obtained, works on client-to-client basis, can be specialized in dealing with residential homes or commercial properties.

Skills: state license required, on-the-job training, appraisal courses given at community college.

PROPERTY MANAGER: Manages an individual or multiple properties, responsible for the day-to-day operations of a building site, reviews work contracts, oversees building projects, interviews potential contractors, acts as liaison among various groups of individuals, such as maintenance personnel, contractors, tenants, board of directors, lawyers.

Skills: college degree majoring in management or real estate, knowledge of building structure and construction, experience in related fields, interpersonal skills, communication.

Activity A   Language Arts Recall

Sentence Structure: Compound Sentence

A **compound** sentence has two or more independent clauses that are connected by a coordinating **conjunction** (and, or, but, nor).

As you learned in Chapter 1, an independent clause consists of a subject and a verb with its modifiers. The independent clause must make sense grammatically.

Comma—Conjunction

Rule 5.1: Use a comma before a conjunction that joins two independent clauses.

Example: The application must be completed by the borrower, and it will be processed as soon as it is received.

Rule 5.2: When a subject does not follow the conjunction, no comma is needed.

Example: The application blank must be completed by the borrower **and returned** within ten days. (The subject is missing after the conjunction "and.")

> **Rule 5.3:** When the conjunction "and" is followed by the word *that*, do not place a comma before the conjunction unless the word *that* is the subject of the clause.

Example: The real estate broker believed the property was priced at market value ***and that*** a sale would occur shortly.
The mortgage was approved by the bank, ***and that*** expedited the closing date for the house. (The word *that* is the subject.)

Check for Understanding

Directions: Compare the sets of sentences and answer the questions that follow.

1. a. We will be happy to meet with you and discuss possible sites.

   b. We will be happy to meet with you, and our salesperson will discuss possible sites.

2. a. Our representatives have expertise in the field of real estate and charge reasonable fees.

   b. Our representatives have expertise in the field of real estate, and they charge reasonable fees.

3. a. Our real estate office has relocated to a site that is much larger and more convenient for our customers.

   b. Our real estate office has relocated to the Downtown Mall, and that is a site our customers find more convenient.

QUESTIONS

  1. What do sentences 1b, 2b, and 3b have in common?

    _____

  2. What is the difference between sentences 1a and 1b?

    _____

  3. Which other two sentences have this same difference?

    _____

  4. Why isn't there a comma before the word that in sentence 3a?

    _____

(Answers are given below.)

Conclusion: Complete the following sentence.
When a _____ sentence contains two or more _____ clauses, there is a _____ before the conjunction.

Building English Power: Comma-Conjunction

Directions: Insert commas where required. If no comma is needed, write "C" (correct) in the space provided.

_____ 1. The home improvement business has become a major industry and future trends indicate a growing market. (5.1)

_____ 2. The custom-built homes are designed by a well-known architect but the prices are moderate. (5.1)

_____ 3. The residential community is located near the highway and is convenient to major shopping malls. (5.2)

_____ 4. The five acres of land will be sold to individual buyers or to a real estate developer. (5.2)

_____ 5. Mortgage rates have been low during the last year and that will affect future sales. (5.3)

_____ 6. Office space rents by the square foot and is quite costly in desirable business districts. (5.2)

_____ 7. Waterfront property has become increasingly expensive but buyers are always interested in purchasing such real estate. (5.1)

_____ 8. The tenant owes three months' rent and that is the reason the landlord will take legal action. (5.3)

_____ 9. Congratulations on your election to the governance committee of the building and the board thanks you for your contributions to good management. (5.1)

_____ 10. The architect's design for the neighborhood park has been completed and construction should begin in two months. (5.1)

_____ 11. The land will be sold by the acre and parceled out in smaller lots. (5.2)

_____ 12. The property has easy access to the downtown area and that site is located right off Exit 23 on the interstate highway. (5.1)

_____ 13. The court ruling prohibits the use of wetlands for commercial development but the firm will appeal the case. (5.1)

_____ 14. A day-care center will be built in the new corporate park and it will be available to employees and the community. (5.1)

_____ 15. The Association of Realtors will hold its annual conference in June and we urge individuals who are interested in the field of real estate to attend the meeting. (5.1)

Still Puzzled? See *One Writer's Key* Home Page: Commas. Click on: When do I use commas? (p. 1) How do I use a comma before a coordinating conjunction? (p. 3)

Note: no specific exercise for this rule available

_____ 16. Tara accepted the position at the real estate firm and will begin next week. (5.2)

_____ 17. Either the construction company will build on the old railroad site or it will move to the new industrial park. (5.1)

_____ 18. Mortgage rates have been low and that is good news for home owners. (5.3)

_____ 19. Our company has grown rapidly but it is not planning to expand in Europe. (5.1)

_____ 20. The community voted for a town park and that the residents would be able to use the new facilities free of charge. (5.3)

Activity B   Building Word Power

A cluttered, messy desk makes a poor impression. Keep personal pictures and mementos to a minimum.

The words that follow are commonly used in the real estate industry. From this list, select the word or phrase that correctly completes each statement. Refer to the personal dictionary if you are uncertain of the meaning of a word.

condominium
cooperative
corporate park
debris
delinquent
index
lease
mortgage

periodically
principal
prorating
realtors
references
security deposit
town code

_____ 1. Before approving a loan, a bank secures _____ on the borrower's credit rating and character.

_____ 2. Home builders must follow government regulations, which are written in the _____.

_____ 3. _____ that accumulates during construction must be discarded according to environmental regulations.

_____ 4. Fire inspectors _____ inspect buildings for fire-code violations.

_____ 5. Interest rates on adjustable-rate loans are based on a(n) _____, which is a mathematical calculation that determines the amount a borrower pays each month.

_____ 6. The _____ on a mortgage is the total amount borrowed to purchase property.

_____ 7. A tenant is usually required to sign a legal agreement with the landlord, known as a(n) _____, which states the terms and conditions of rental.

_____ 8. A(n) _____ is a stipulated amount of money given to the landlord by the tenant to cover potential damages or nonpayment of rent.

_____ 9. The architect plans to design a(n) _____, which will be a cluster of office buildings in a park-like setting.

_____ 10. Individuals known as _____ are experts in the field of buying and selling real estate.

_____ 11. Most individuals will need to obtain a(n) _____ from a bank or other lending institution to finance the cost of purchasing a house.

_____ 12. A(n) _____ offers an individual the opportunity to own a unit within a multi-dwelling complex. A monthly maintenance fee covers the cost of common facilities.

_____ 13. A form of property ownership in some cities is the purchase of shares in a corporation that owns the building and the land. The shareholder owns the apartment. This type of real estate is known as a(n) _____.

_____ 14. The method used to divide utility and heating bills equally over a 12-month period is known as _____.

_____ 15. Customers who are _____ in paying bills are sent monthly reminders to settle their charges.

On the Alert

- *of (preposition)*—used to indicate relationship

    Example: He is president **of** the Real Estate Board.

- *off (adverb)*—not on

    Example: Shingles were blown **off** the roof.

- *perspective (noun)*—a point of view

    Example: The guide gave an account of the lifestyles of the early 1900s from an historical **perspective**.

- *prospective (adjective)*—pertaining to the future

    Example: The **prospective** buyer filed an application for a mortgage.

- *principal (noun)*—

    1. the head of a school
    2. a sum of money owed, not including interest

    Example: The school **principal** repaid the **principal** on her loan in 24 months.

- *principle (noun)*—a basic truth

    Example: The landlord's renting practices were based on unfair **principles**.

Activity C   Industry Perspectives: Home Mortgages

Directions: Using appropriate revision marks, proofread and key the following report.

Purchasing a home is one of the most important financail decisions you will make. Shopping for a home mortgage

Rule Reference

5.3

can be confusing and that often frustrates a perspective buyer. The real cost of a house is the purchase price plus the financing charges. These charges often amounts

2.1, 5.1

to twice the cost of the house and the buyer should shop around for the best morgage deal.

There are key words that a borrower should understand when applying for a mortgage. The two most common key words is fixed rate and adjustable rate. With a fixed-rate mortgage, the monthly payments of principle and

interest never changes; and the debt is paid of at the end of the term.

The interest rate on an adjustable mortgage can

change periodically, and is based on an index or formula. A borrower must be aware that the interest rate can increase or decrease during the life of this type of mortgage.

Frequently, a buyer is charged points on the mortgage. This means that the borrower pays the lender a set fee that is based on the amount of the mortgage.

Buyers should compare different mortgage plans that meet there financial needs.

Did you find these errors?

3 punctuation
3 subject–verb agreement
4 word usage
3 typographical/spelling

Paragraphs

A **paragraph** is a group of sentences pertaining to the same idea or topic. Paragraphs are interrelated to form a cohesive letter or report. Skip a line to separate each paragraph.

In this and subsequent chapters, you will be expected to insert paragraphs. As a reminder, in a letter there is an opening sentence or sentences forming the introductory paragraph. The body of the letter, which discusses in detail the main topic, may have more than one paragraph. The body of the letter is followed by a closing paragraph.

Activity D   Editing Power

Task A: Edit, format, and proofread the following form letter. Be aware that commas have been inserted incorrectly in several places.

Use proofreaders' symbols to mark the errors, insert paragraphs, and then key the letter correctly. Use "Dear Neighbor:" as the salutation for this letter.

Errors
- commas
- subject-verb agreement
- word usage
- typographical

Our company, Capital Realtors, have been engaged in the Westchester real estate industry for over 25 years and our firm have earned a fine reputation in the community. We take pride in analyzing a perspective client's needs, and matching the proper house to the client. Our experienced brokers carefully research each property but the cost is never past on to the buyer. We believe that the market in this area is recovering, and that there are many good opportunities to buy real estate. If you are interested in either a new home or a parcel of land for development, visit our office and speak to one of our experienced representatives. Satisfied clients are the best source of references and a list of repeat clients are available to you.

We look forward to serving you. Don't hesitate to call Capitol Realtors at 914-623-1000.

Sincerely yours,

John Costello

Vice President

ri

Challenge Task B: Edit, format, and proofread the following unarranged letter for all errors. Supply missing parts and insert paragraphs, then key the listing correctly. (See appendix B for a model of a listing.)

This letter is being sent from James Hoffer, Managing Agent, to Mr. and Mrs. David Ewing, One Circle Drive, Boston, MA 02106–3540.

We have examine your plans for the renovation of your kitchen and they have been approved by us. The following procedures must be observe: 1. Contractors must submit

certificates of insurance before work begins. 2. All
electrical and plumbing work must be performed by
licensed persons and must comply with town codes. 3. You
are liable for any damages to electrical and telephone
wiring that may occur during construction and all costs
will be billed to you. 4. Removal of old appliances and
debris are you responsibility but we can arrange for
pickup. If you have any questions, please call me at
my office.

Activity E   Writing Practicum

The following chart reviews the use of **adjectives** and **adverbs**. Study
these rules before you complete the exercises.

Introduction: Adjectives and Adverbs

> **Rule 5.4:** **Adjectives** *modify* or *describe* nouns or pronouns.
> Adjectives may add clarity or additional information to a
> sentence.

Example: The **large** house is built in a **wooded** area of
the **suburban** town. (descriptive)

Adjectives are used to *compare* items. To most
adjectives, add **er** when **comparing two** items; add **est**
to **compare three or more** items.

Examples:	*Adjective*	*Comparative*	*Superlative*
	large	larger	largest
	warm	warmer	warmest
	happy	happier	happiest

To compare adjectives of **three or more** syllables or
words **ending** in **able/ible** use **more/most**, **less/least**.

Examples:	*Comparative*	*Superlative*
	more competent	most competent
	less effective	least effective
	more desirable	most desirable
	less accessible	least accessible

Larry is considered to be the **most competent** architect
in the town. (superlative)

I prefer the **less traveled** country road rather than the
highway. (comparative)

Rule 5.5: Adjectives **a, an** or **the** are also referred to as **articles**. **A** and **an** are general; **the** is specific.

Use **a** when the word that follows **begins** with a **consonant** or the sound of a **long u**.

Use **an** when the word that follows begins with a **vowel** or **silent h**.

Examples:	a skyscraper (consonant)	an attorney (vowel)
	a house (consonant)	an hour (silent h)
	a university (long u)	an uncle (vowel)

Rule 5.6: When **regular form verbs** are used as **adjectives**, add **d** or **ed**.

Examples:	*Verb Form*	*Adjective*
	reduce	reduced rate
	revise	revised draft
	correct	corrected copy

Rule 5.7: **Adverbs** modify verbs, adjectives, or other adverbs. They tell when, where, how, and how much.

Examples: The contractor **reluctantly** submitted the building blueprints. (adverb *reluctantly* modifies verb)

The **closely** guarded plans for the monument will be presented at the town board meeting. (adverb *closely* modifies adjective)

The design team worked **really** well with the architect on the plans for a cultural center. (adverb *really* modifies adverb)

Most adverbs are formed by adding **ly** to an adjective.

Examples:	beautiful	beautiful**ly** decorated house
	effective	presented effective**ly**

Note: Like adjectives, adverbs use the same comparative form.

Examples: more desirable location (comparative, *more* is an adverb modifying adjective *desirable*)

most influential speaker (superlative, *most* is an adverb modifying adjective *influential*)

Rule 5.8: **Troublesome Adjectives/Adverbs** There are some adjectives and adverbs that can be troublesome.

Adjectives: **good** and **bad**

Examples: The building department submitted a **good** survey report. (adjective modifying noun)
The rejection of the proposed stadium was **bad** news for the local team. (adjective modifying noun)

Adverbs: **well** and **badly**

Examples: The project is not going **well.** (adverb describes verb)
The proposal was written **badly.** (adverb modifies an action verb)

Almost—meaning **nearly**

> **Examples:** almost half (nearly half)
> almost all (nearly all)

Most—superlative form of the adjective

> **Examples:** most desirable (superlative comparison)
> most experienced (superlative comparison)

EXERCISE 1   USE OF ADJECTIVES AND ADVERBS

Directions: Complete each sentence with the correct form of the word in parentheses. Write the *adjective* or *adverb* form in the space provided.

_____ 1. The _____ date for a site inspection has been postponed. (schedule)

_____ 2. The _____ report on real estate investments is available in my office. (revise)

_____ 3. The _____ parties met to reach an agreement. (interest)

_____ 4. The community envisions a small park in the _____ populated area. (dense)

_____ 5. You performed _____ on the real estate licensing examination. (satisfactory)

_____ 6. The _____ signatures were missing from the _____ contract. (require, revise)

_____ 7. The _____ land could be used only for commercial purposes. (lease)

_____ 8. The _____ _____ building will be open this weekend for prospective tenants. (new, renovate)

_____ 9. The developer anticipated major renovations to the _____ _____ properties. (recent, acquire)

_____ 10. The _____ broker will get you a _____ good purchase price on the vacant building. (experience, fair)

EXERCISE 2   COMPARATIVE AND SUPERLATIVE FORMS

Directions: Choose the comparative or superlative form (as indicated in parentheses at the end of each sentence) for the word in parentheses.

_____ 1. The (large) one-bedroom apartment will become vacant next month. (superlative)

_____ 2. A (more, most) favorable city in which to relocate our offices is Seattle. (comparative)

_____ 3. Our city has a (high) tax rate than other areas of the state. (comparative)

_____ 4. You will find the (fine) selection of home furnishings at the Design Showroom. (superlative)

_____ 5. One of the (more, most) popular tourist attractions is Disneyland. (superlative)

_____ 6. The property manager gave a (more, most) informative presentation than the other speakers. (comparative)

_____ 7. The (less) elegant furnishings in the estate will be auctioned. (superlative)

_____ 8. Online realtors often charge (low) commission rates than full-service real estate agents. (comparative)

_____ 9. I will try to submit the proposal (early) than the deadline date. (comparative)

_____ 10. The (great) amount of pollution occurs in major industrial cities. (superlative)

EXERCISE 3 **CORRECT WORD CHOICE**

Directions: Choose the correct word in parentheses and write the answer in the space provided. If necessary, refer to rules 5.5 and 5.8

_____ 1. (Almost, Most) of the reports show an increase in the sale of higher priced homes.

_____ 2. (Almost, most) half of the respondents favor reclaiming the wetlands.

_____ 3. We received (bad, badly) news about the proposed variance to build a garage.

_____ 4. He spoke (bad, badly) about the environmental report.

_____ 5. The students performed (good, well) at the state competition.

_____ 6. (A, An) added bonus will be one month's free rent.

_____ 7. (A, An) unique feature of the house is the shape of the swimming pool.

_____ 8. The judge gave (a, an) unfavorable ruling on the housing project.

_____ 9. The gardener is paid at (a, an) hourly rate.

_____ 10. The expansion proposal by the university is (a, an) highly featured newspaper story.

INTRODUCTION: ACTIVE/PASSIVE VOICE

■ Use the **active voice** of the verb to strengthen a message. In an active sentence, the doer of an action, the subject, precedes the verb. The *subject* of the sentence *performs* the action.

Example: The bank approved the home mortgage for the young couple.

■ The **passive voice** indicates who or what is receiving the action. A sentence in the passive voice is generally considered weak because the *subject receives* the action rather than performing the action. It is occasionally used for emphasis, tact, and sensitivity.

Example: The young couple's home mortgage was approved by the bank.

Note: The use of active/passive voice pertaining to perfect tense was discussed in chapter 4.

EXERCISE 4   CONVERTING FROM PASSIVE TO ACTIVE VOICE

Strengthen the following sentences by changing them from passive voice to active voice. You will need to alter the sequence of the words within the sentence.

Example: Your rent for the month of September **was paid** by John. (passive voice)

John **paid** your rent for the month of September. (active voice; subject is doer of action)

1. Fifty single-family homes will be built by the local construction firm.

   _____

   _____

2. An increase in real estate taxes has been proposed by the city council.

   _____

   _____

3. A reduction in the price of the new homes was announced by the builder.

   _____

   _____

4. The plan for urban development was submitted to the town board by the engineer.

   _____

   _____

5. Mortgage financing is offered to first-time home buyers by Union Bank.

   _____

   _____

6. A plan to convert the building to cooperative ownership has been submitted by the landlord.

   _____

   _____

7. Renovations were vetoed by the Board of Directors.

_____

_____

8. The mortgage application that was submitted by the young couple was rejected by the bank.

_____

_____

9. The difficulty in changing the existing building code was mentioned by the speaker.

_____

_____

10. The annual meeting of the condominium was attended by the majority of the shareholders.

_____

_____

Collection Letters

To collect overdue accounts, businesses use **collection letters.** They are written in several stages from sensitive reminders to a stern tone that indicates readiness to take action. The first stage is a simple reminder to pay the bill. The letter is written in a tone that maintains goodwill and at the same time obtains a positive response.

At the second stage, the customer still neglected to pay the bill. The letter is written in stronger language persuading the customer to make payment. At this stage, the letter may indicate a willingness to help the customer meet the financial obligation.

The final stage is where action needs to be taken. The letter is firm and explains the consequences if the bill remains unpaid.

Writing Pointers—Collection Letters

FIRST STAGE—REMINDER

1. Remind customer of overdue payment in a cordial tone.

2. Appeal to customer's responsibility for payment.

3. Assume person intends to make payment but has forgotten.

SECOND STAGE—REQUEST

1. Remind customer of failure to respond to first reminder.

2. Ask if a problem exists in paying the bill.

3. Suggest a willingness to cooperate in a plan for making payment.

4. Communicate your desire to receive payment promptly or to hear from the customer.

5. Refer to the consequences of nonpayment (late charge, poor credit rating).

FINAL STAGE—ACTION

1. Convey stern tone in demanding payment.

2. Stress consequences of nonpayment, which can result in poor credit rating.

3. Threaten customer with turning the matter over to a collection agency or taking legal action.

4. Send letter certified, return receipt requested.

Writing Pointers—Letter of Invitation

- Mention purpose of invitation.

- Include specific information—time, place, location, and topic.

- Express benefit(s) to reader.

- Indicate where further information can be obtained.

- Request confirmation or response.

- Close on a positive note.

SUBJECT LINE

A **subject line** states what the letter is about. It appears between the salutation and the body of the letter. Leave a blank space before and after the subject line.

ATTENTION LINE

The **attention line** is used when a letter is directed to a company rather than to a particular individual. When this type of letter is received by an organization, it is assumed that it relates to company business that can be handled by an employee of a particular department or the business.

The attention line usually appears on the first line of the inside address or envelope. Use "Ladies and Gentlemen" for the salutation in correspondence. (See model in appendix.)

Examples:

Attention: Planning Board	ATTENTION PLANNING BOARD
Town of Greenburgh	TOWN OF GREENBURGH
142 Central Avenue	142 CENTRAL AVENUE
Tarrytown, NY 10532-2315	TARRYTOWN NY 10532-2315
Ladies and Gentlemen:	Ladies and Gentlemen:

If you are using *window envelopes,* place the attention line as the first line of the address with or without the word *Attention.* The omission of the word *Attention* is also acceptable in the inside address.

Date

Mr Sam Burns
11 Boulevard Avenue
Boston, MA 02175-3342

Cordial tone   Dear Mr. Burns:

Gentle   This letter is a reminder that your rent for the month of August is past due.
reminder   We are sure that this is an oversight. Your prompt payment of $725 would
                      be appreciated.

Goodwill   Keep up your good credit rating.

                      Sincerely yours,

                      Rose O'Malley
                      Building Manager

                      ri

Date

Mr. Sam Burns
11 Boulevard Avenue
Boston, MA 02175-3342

Dear Mr. Burns:

Subject: Reminder Rent Overdue

Follow-up   Perhaps you have overlooked our first reminder that the rent for your
reminder   apartment is still unpaid. As of this date, you are two months behind in rent,
                      totaling $1,450. As a valued tenant, you must have a reason for this
Appeal to self-   nonpayment.
respect
                      To avoid an unfavorable credit rating, please call our office at 617-567-9832
Refer to   within the next few days to discuss the matter. If you are unable to make full
consequences   payment, we shall try to work out a satisfactory solution.
of nonpayment
                      Your cooperation will be appreciated.
Communicate
willingness to
cooperate   Sincerely yours,

Offer solution

                      Rose O'Malley

                      ri

Date

Certified Mail

Mr. Sam Burns
11 Boulevard Avenue
Boston, MA 02175-3342

Dear Mr. Burns:

Severe tone

Stress consequences

Your rent is now five months overdue. We sent you several reminders but no response has been received. The delinquent stage of your account leaves us no alternative but to begin eviction proceedings.

Give time limits

We must hear from you or receive a check for $3,625 within the next ten days; otherwise, your account will be forwarded to our attorney for legal action.

Maintain goodwill

No negative language

We are confident that you will resolve this matter.

Sincerely yours,

Rose O'Malley
Building Manager

ri

(Current Date)

Mr. Pat Jackson
230 Alta Vista Road
Annapolis, MD 21405-3321

Dear Mr. Jackson:

Subject: Seminar on "Smart Strategies in Real Estate"

Purpose of invitation

Specific information

Many individuals are exploring alternate ways of investing money. You are invited to attend a special seminar on "Smart Strategies in Real Estate." This exciting event will be held on Saturday, June 10, 20xx, at the Brunswick Hotel.

Gives further details

Expresses benefits to reader

This seminar will present workshops on various aspects of the real estate market. Representatives from new real estate developments throughout the country will be on hand to discuss specific areas. Of great interest to you will be our featured speaker, Melissa Hodge. She is a successful realtor and developer of middle income housing and luxury resorts. Her lectures are both interesting and informative.

As our invited guest, you will be able to attend all the sessions free of charge. Simply return the enclosed reply card to confirm your participation. You are welcomed to visit us online at www.realestate.com. We are confident that you will obtain valuable suggestions on how to make money owning property.

Sincerely yours,

Greg Werner
Coordinator

ri

Activity F   Writing Power

Case Study 1: Rewrite of Poorly Written Collection Letter, Second Stage

Rewrite the following poorly written collection letter. It is a second stage reminder letter to Ms. Lauren Foley, One Wood Avenue, New City, NY 10956–1008 about her past-due mortgage payment.

To help you complete this task, (a) answer the questions that follow, (b) rephrase sentences, if needed, and (c) rekey the letter for mailing.

Case

Dear Ms. Foley:

Mortgage payment for the months of September and October are late. We sent you a previous letter reminding you of the situation. There is a penalty of $50 for this delayed payment. Please be so kind to send us a check for $1,150 to cover the two months. If we do not hear from you, we will be forced to take legal action.

QUESTIONS

1. What is the overall tone of this letter?

_____

2. What should the writer's main goal be for a second reminder letter?

_____

3. What is wrong with the last sentence?

_____

_____

4. What is a closing sentence that would get results?

_____

_____

Case Study 2: Collection Letter, Final Stage

After reading this case, respond to the questions that follow, which will help you organize your ideas. Then draft a letter.

Case: You are the managing agent of a building at 150 Poe Lane, St. Louis, MO 63100–4509, in which Mr. and Mrs. Richard Greene reside. After a reminder sent to the Greenes that their rent is three months past due, the rent remains unpaid. In your letter, request that they pay their total bill of $2700. Payment must be received immediately or management will be forced to take legal action.

ORGANIZE YOUR IDEAS

1. At what stage of the collection process should you write this letter?

_____

2. What is the most important point that you want to make to Mr. and Mrs. Greene?

_____

_____

3. What would you include in the opening sentence?

_____

_____

4. What specific details should you include in the body of the letter?

_____

_____

_____

5. What would you include in the closing statement to get a positive reaction from the tenant?

_____

_____

_____

Case Study 3: Collection Letter

Read Case Study 3; organize your ideas before composing the letter.

Case: Ms. Eileen Robb, a shareowner at Rockledge Cooperative Apartments at 11 Rockledge Road, Hartford, CT 06180–1254, refuses to pay a $25 late penalty fee for nonpayment of her monthly maintenance charge. According to the rules of the cooperative, any shareowner who does not pay the monthly charges on the first of each month will be charged a penalty.

Ms. Carole Ponte, managing agent, has been asked to send a letter to Ms. Robb requesting that this fee be paid immediately; otherwise, the amount will be doubled after ten days.

Case Study 4: Letter of Request

Read Case Study 4; then compose a letter.

Case: Mr. and Mrs. John Tisch, who reside at 2 Maiden Lane, Tarrytown, NY 10532–0050, are planning to expand their kitchen 12 feet by 14 feet in their single-family home. The town requires that owners receive permission from the Planning Board to expand existing structures. Write a letter to the attention of the Planning Board, Town of Greenburgh, 142 Central Avenue, Tarrytown, NY 10532–2315 on behalf of the Tisches' request that a variance be granted for the construction to take place. Architectural plans will be enclosed with the letter.

Challenge Level Case

Case Study 5: Invitation Letter

Read Case Study 5; then compose the letter.

Case: Send a letter from Susan Jackson, Expo Coordinator, to Mr. Joel Friedman, property manager of AMS Management Company, 14 Maiden Lane, Irvington, NY 10500. Subject: Tenth Annual Co-Op and Condo Expo

The Tenth Annual Co-op and Condo Expo is scheduled for Thursday, October 15, at the New Yorker Hotel. This conference is a free one-day event for property managers and members of the real estate industry.

When you write to Mr. Friedman, mention to him that he will be interested in the following seminars: Enforcing House Rules, Safeguarding an Apartment's Value, and Money-Saving Ideas for a Building. All individuals attending the Expo will find booths that exhibit products and services for building maintenance.

In addition, property managers and real estate agents will receive free advice on building operations and legal matters when dealing with clients. To attend the Expo, individuals must preregister on the Web site http://www.expo.com or call 800-543-1000.

Note: When composing the letter, list the three seminars in outline form.

Case Study 6: E-Mail Correspondence

Read Case Study 6; then complete the e-mail memo.

Case: Your manager, Luis Ortega, asks you to send an e-mail to John Ling (ling @gazette.com), a real estate agent, to inform him of an article that appeared in the *Gazette Weekly*. This article featured the suburban town of Greenburg, the area where John Ling sells real estate. Mr. Ortega believes that John Ling will find the article informative since it describes in detail the positive aspects of the Greenburg community, its zoning restrictions, prices of area homes, and future development.

The subject of this e-mail is "Gazette Weekly Article on Greenburg Community."

Self-Assessment
English Power

COMMAS

Directions: Insert commas where required. If no comma is needed, write **C** (correct) in the space provided.

_____ 1. The staff has revised the monthly billing statements and they will be mailed shortly.

_____ 2. We have mailed you a second notice for the monthly maintenance fee but you have not responded to our request.

_____ 3. The city council has raised taxes for next year and that has caused a protest by the homeowners.

_____ 4. The monthly publication suggests ways to renovate houses and lists licensed contractors.

_____ 5. The town board meeting did not begin until 8 p.m. but a large group of people congregated early.

_____ 6. My friend plans to build a home in the suburbs or she will move out of state.

_____ 7. The realtor believed the condominium was a good value and that a sale would occur quickly.

_____ 8. The recent zoning changes will not allow builders to replace the older homes or build multi-family dwellings.

_____ 9. Mortgage rates are on the increase but home sales are still strong.

_____ 10. The planning board approved plans for a housing development to be built on the site of the former airport and construction will start in the spring.

ADJECTIVES/ADVERBS

Directions: Complete each sentences with the correct form of the adjective or adverb in the space provided.

_____ 11. The construction of the building is not going (good, well).

_____ 12. I feel (bad, badly) that we lost the bid to host the convention.

_____ 13. (Most, almost) all of the applicants had their real estate licenses.

_____ 14. The (increase, increased) cost of the building materials will affect the price of the house.

_____ 15. There is (a, an) additional fee to notarize the contract.

_____ 16. The inner city is the most (dense, densely) populated area.

_____ **17.** The storm (heavy, heavily) damaged the downtown buildings.

_____ **18.** You should always read (careful, carefully) all contracts.

_____ **19.** The (revise, revised) figures show a decrease in purchases of homes.

_____ **20.** The building of the stadium was (good, well) news to the community.

Editing Power

Directions: Edit, format, and proofread the following unarranged letter. Supply paragraphs, punctuation, correct verb tense, adjective and word usage.

```
Mr. and Mrs. John Reilly, 177 Hartsdale Road,

Eastchester, NY 10547-1220

    One of the most important decisions of your life are

the purchasing of a home. Brothers Realtors can help you

make the decision careful. We have the more

comprehensive sales and service organization in the area

and our agents are full licensed. We will help you

identify your needs and introduce you to the right home.

Our agency was in this county for the passed 25 years

and can offer valuable advise on the neighborhoods and

schools. Our real estate agents work with the local

banks and they will help you get the lowest mortgage

rate. As a added service, we will coordinate your title

search and closing procedures. Without a doubt, Brothers

Realtors will serve you good. It is a pleasure to

provide you with a complimentary copy of Home town Guide

which contains important community information. Visit

our Web site at www.brothersrealtors.com. Louis Reyes,

Manager
```

Writing Power

Directions: Draft a second stage collection letter to Mr. William Wade, 250 West Drive, Chicago, IL 60605-2220, from Sonja Edwards, Managing Agent. Mr. Wade has not paid his rent for the past two months. Inform Mr. Wade that he owes $1600 plus $100 late fees. The total amount of $1700 is due immediately. If this amount is not paid within ten business days, legal proceedings will start. Suggest to Mr. Wade that he call the office if he has any questions or to seek assistance in solving the problem.

➤ Cultural Communication

China:

- To save face is important in the Chinese culture.

- Don't confront someone; show proper respect.

- Use a single nod when greeting an individual.

- Address an individual by the last name with the title.

- Believe in a network of contacts; exchange favors.

- Loyal to their inner social circle—family, friends, colleagues.

- Exchange business card written in both English and Chinese.

See www.executiveplanet.com

"Diversity: the art of thinking independently together."

—*Malcom S. Forbes*

CHAPTER 6

Maintaining Healthy Complex Sentences

CORPORATE SNAPSHOT

PFIZER, INC., one of the world's leading health-care companies, discovers, develops, and markets medicines for humans and animals. Fundamentally, Pfizer's business is about saving, improving, and enhancing lives. It values the highest ethical standards to manufacture quality products both in prescription and over-the-counter drugs.

Pfizer is committed to being an exemplary corporate citizen. This is reflected in the company's extensive efforts to actively improve access to health care both in the United States and around the world, to care for the environment, and to encourage employee volunteerism in the community. Pfizer employees can be found offering their services in health organizations, hospitals, schools, and libraries. This firm is an example of a corporation that utilizes its size and resources to better the global community.

Source: Pfizer, Corporate Communications

WHAT YOU WILL LEARN IN THIS CHAPTER

- To identify complex sentences
- To punctuate complex sentences
- To punctuate parenthetical expressions
- To develop a business vocabulary in **HEALTH CARE**
- To proofread and edit correspondence and reports
- To compose letters of refusal
- To compose a collection letter
- To compose a sales letter
- To write an e-mail memo
- To compose an informational memo report

MEDICAL OFFICE MANAGER: Provide administrative support for departments in hospitals, schedule meetings, prepare materials, assist with budget reports, order supplies.

Skills: computer, communication, managerial, interpersonal.

MEDICAL ASSISTANT: Maintain billing and medical records, perform clerical duties, prepare patients for examination.

Skills: computer, communication, clerical skills, on-the job training.

MEDICAL RECORDS TECHNICIAN: Compile, process, and maintain accurate and updated medical records.

Skills: computers, customer relations, communication, knowledge of specific procedures of an organization, team worker.

Activity A *Language Arts Recall*

Sentence Structure: Complex Sentence

A **complex** sentence consists of an **independent** clause and one or more **dependent** clauses that appear anywhere within the sentence. (A clause is a unit that includes a subject and a verb.)

An **independent** clause, as you reviewed in chapter 5, can stand alone as a sentence because it has a subject and a predicate (verb and its modifiers) and expresses a complete thought.

Example: Good *nutrition and exercise are* two basic factors in maintaining a healthy body.

A **dependent** clause does not express a complete thought; therefore, it cannot stand alone.

Example: *If individuals exercise and follow nutritious diets,* they will maintain healthy bodies. (The dependent clause cannot stand alone because it does not express a complete thought.)

Comma Usage in Complex Sentences: Introductory Clauses

Rule 6.1: When there is an introductory clause at the beginning of a sentence before the independent clause, place a comma after it. Some common introductory words are: although, after, because, before, if, when, since.

Example: *As we discussed yesterday,* a registration form will be mailed to you. (introductory clause)

continued

Rule 6.2: A dependent clause at the end of a sentence in its usual grammatical position is usually not set off by a comma.

(When the clause is at the beginning of a sentence, it is an introductory clause.) Example: You may be interested in the health options *although you are enrolled in the community insurance program.*

Although you are enrolled in the community insurance program, you may be interested in the health options.

Comma Usage: Introductory Phrases

A **phrase** consists of two or more words that do not contain a subject and a verb. It expands the meaning of the sentence.

Example: *If available,* our spring catalog will be sent to you.

Rule 6.3: When a phrase occurs at the beginning of a sentence before the independent clause, place a comma after it.

Example: *At the beginning of the month,* a seminar on medical insurance plans will be held. (introductory phrase)

Rule 6.4: When an introductory clause or phrase is the subject of a verb, do *not* place a comma after it.

Example: *To secure adequate health insurance coverage* is a necessity for individuals and families.

Comma Usage: Parenthetical Expressions

Parenthetical expressions are unnecessary words that do not add meaning to the sentence.

Rule 6.5: Use commas around parenthetical expressions (unnecessary words) that occur within a sentence or at the beginning of a sentence.

Example:

In our opinion, a greater number of people maintain a healthy diet and follow an exercise program.

Nutritionists, *without a doubt,* recommend a healthy diet and moderate exercise.

Rule 6.6: If a phrase at the end of a sentence gives additional but nonessential information, place a comma before the phrase.

Example: Individuals are interested in weight loss diets, *such as low carb diets.*

Check for Understanding

Directions: Compare the sentences and answer the questions that follow.

PHRASES AND CLAUSES

1. If you belong to an HMO plan, you have a limited choice of doctors.

2. You have a limited choice of doctors if you belong to an HMO plan.

3. To control costs, we are increasing the deductible on medical insurance.

4. We are increasing the deductible on medical insurance to control costs.

5. To offer a national health plan is the senator's proposal.

QUESTIONS

a. What do sentences 1 and 3 have in common?

_____

b. What do sentences 2 and 4 have in common?

_____

c. How is the structure in sentences 1 and 3 different?

_____

d. Why isn't there a comma after the phrase in sentence 5?

_____

(Answers are given on page 125)

Conclusion: Complete the following sentence.
Place a(n) _____ after a(n) _____ phrase or clause at the beginning of a sentence.

PARENTHETICAL EXPRESSIONS

6. Many corporations, for example, have set up optional health insurance plans.

7. Undoubtedly, the cost of medical insurance is rising.

8. You will realize, without a doubt, that our health benefits are superior.

9. Finally, the committee completed its findings.

e. What is similar about the phrases in sentences 6 and 8?

_____

f. How is a parenthetical phrase within a sentence punctuated?

_____

g. What is similar about the first word in sentences 7 and 9?

_____

h. How is a parenthetical word at the beginning of a sentence punctuated?

_____

(Answers are below.)

Conclusion: Complete the following sentence.
When there is a(n) _____ word or phrase within a sentence, it must be set off by _____.

Answers to "Check for Understanding"

a. There is a comma after the introductory clause and phrase.

b. The phrase and clause appear in their usual grammatical order; therefore, no comma is required.

c. Sentence 1 has an introductory clause, and sentence 3 has an introductory phrase.

d. The introductory phrase is the subject of the sentence.

e. There is a parenthetical expression within each sentence.

f. There is a comma before and after the parenthetical phrase.

g. Each word is a parenthetical.

h. There is a comma after the parenthetical expression.

Conclusion: comma, introductory

Conclusion: parenthetical, comma

Building English Power: Introductory Clauses, Phrases, and Parenthetical Expressions

Directions: Insert commas where required. If no comma is needed, write "C" (Correct) in the space provided.

_____ **1.** For many workers health care is a major expense. (6.3)

_____ **2.** If you wish to continue to participate in the insurance plan please return the signed form. (6.1)

Still Puzzled? See Writer's OneKey Home Page: Commas. Click on: How do I use a comma to set off introductory words? (p. 2)

_____ 3. To include vegetables and fruits in your daily diet is recommended for good health. (6.4)

_____ 4. Since your last bill premium rates have increased slightly. (6.3)

_____ 5. You will receive supplemental insurance benefits if you are hospitalized. (6.2)

_____ 6. More than ever you need adequate medical insurance. (6.5)

_____ 7. We cannot process your claim however without a detailed statement. (6.5)

_____ 8. In an effort to control costs we increased the deductible on the dental plan. (6.3)

_____ 9. We have served one million members since we offered our plan. (6.2)

_____ 10. To exercise regularly is important for physical fitness. (6.4)

_____ 11. As you know a smoke-free workplace is endorsed by most Americans. (6.1)

_____ 12. DWI laws without a doubt have become stricter in the past decade. (6.5)

_____ 13. After the public debate Congress will address the issue of health insurance. (6.3)

_____ 14. Within the last few years HMOs have become an alternative approach to medical treatment for patients. (6.3)

_____ 15. Arthritis problems according to some doctors can be treated with a proper nutritional diet. (6.5)

_____ 16. You need to make reservations before next week if you plan to attend the health fair. (6.2)

_____ 17. There are a number of medical Web sites such as WebMD. (6.6)

_____ 18. If individuals exercise they will lower their stress levels. (6.1)

_____ 19. To surf the Web for information can be time-consuming. (6.4)

_____ 20. As you know you are entitled to health and dental insurance. (6.1)

Activity B   Building Word Power

Manage your time wisely—prioritize things to be done, prepare advance agendas, and designate a work period with no interruptions.

The words that follow are commonly used in the health-care industry. Study the meaning of each word. From the list that follows, select the word or phrase that correctly completes each statement. Refer to the personal dictionary in the appendix for the meaning of each word.

biomedical	network
cholesterol	nutrition
comprehensive	nutritionist
DWI	ophthalmologist
HMO	orthopedic
mammogram	outpatient
metabolism	transition

_____ **1.** The eye infection was treated by a(n) _____.

_____ **2.** Some people have high levels of blood _____, which may indicate an excessive amount of fat in the diet.

_____ **3.** A balanced, healthy diet is affected by sensible _____.

_____ **4.** Advanced technology has brought about _____ systems, which interconnect communications throughout the world.

_____ **5.** _____ groups, or health maintenance organizations, offer medical services and doctors to their subscribers.

_____ **6.** The football player consulted a(n) _____ doctor who specializes in bone injuries.

_____ **7.** The _____ from one stage of life to another can be stressful.

_____ **8.** _____ is the process by which the body converts food, oxygen, and other substances into tissues and energy.

_____ **9.** The _____ met with the patient to plan a low-cholesterol diet.

_____ **10.** The research team completed a(n) _____ study that describes in detail the relationship between smoking and heart disease.

_____ **11.** _____ is a term that refers to high-tech medical equipment used in the replacement of parts of the human body.

_____ **12.** A(n) _____ department treats individuals who go to a hospital on a regular basis for treatment.

_____ **13.** Women are advised to have a(n) _____ every year to examine for breast cancer.

_____ **14.** _____ laws refer to those that penalize individuals who drive while intoxicated.

On the Alert

- *patient (adjective)*—1. able to wait, showing self-control

    Example: The passenger was **patient** after the delayed flight.

    2. *patience (noun)*—the ability to remain calm

    Example: Nurses need a great deal of **patience** when dealing with a troubled patient.

    3. *patients (plural noun)*—individuals receiving medical treatment

    Example: The **patients** waited a long time at the clinic.

- *to (preposition)*—express direction

    Example: The free tickets **to** the seminar on nutrition were sent **to** your house in the mail.

    too (adverb)—1. more than enough

    Example: The patient is **too** sick to leave the hospital.—

    2. also

    Example: Mary's brother is attending the health fair, **too.** ("Too" is used as a parenthetical expression.)

- Use a hyphen between compound words that begin with "self."

    Example: self-esteem

- Hyphenate compound adjectives (one-thought modifiers) that precede nouns.

    Example: one-year study

- Omit the word *dollars* after the number when the dollar symbol ($) is used.

    Example: $200

Activity C   Industry Perspectives: Physical Fitness

Directions: Using appropriate revisions, proofread and key the report that follows. There are some built-in punctuation errors.

Rule Reference	
	In america today individuals care about physical fitness
6.3	and good nutrition. The trend is toward a lifestyle that
6.1	balances moderate exercise with a sensible diet. As we
	know individuals who are physically fit are better able
	to cope with daily stress.

Doctors recommend a regular routine of physical activity for thirty minutes that is preformed three days a week. Doctors warn against strenuous exercise, which can be harmful. Sensible exercise, such as running and walking can help raise your metabalism and control weight to.

A good diet plan and regular exersise will help to lower cholesterol levels, and reduce heart problems. As recommended by nutritionists fruits, vegetables, and whole grains should be the basis for every diet. Diet fads on the other hand are not the answer to good health. Individuals who follow these diets often regain lost weight. This failure to control weight can effect a person's self esteem. To develop a long-term fitness plan, is the best way to maintain lifelong health.

To be physically and mentally fit is a goal of every person. This goal however can only be achieved by a long-term commitment to exercise and nutritious eating.

Did you find these errors?

11 punctuation
1 hyphen
1 capitalization
3 typographical/spelling
2 word usage

Activity D Editing Power

Task A: Edit, format, and proofread the following form letter for introductory phrases and clauses as well as for parenthetical expressions and other errors. Use proofreaders' symbols to mark the errors, then key the letter correctly. Use "Dear Participant:" for the salutation.

As a result of a comprehensive one year study on medical insurance costs sections of our medical plan has been restructured.

In an effort to control future costs the following changes will become affective immediately:

1. Your deductable will increase to $200 for an individual and $350 dollars for a family.

2. There will be a five percent increase in the premuim rate.

3. You will need a second opinion for major surgery. If this procedure is not followed payment will be denied.

You may wish however to consider our monthly payment plan, if you find that an increase in premiums may be difficult to absorb. Please feel free to call our Customer service Department at 800-336-1000, if you need assistants.

Sincerely yours,

Cynthia Washington
Director

Challenge Task B: Edit, format, and proofread the following unarranged memorandum for all errors. Supply missing parts and insert paragraphs; key the memorandum correctly.

This memorandum should be sent to the staff of the Department of Orthopedics from Dr. Luis Alvarez, Chief of Orthopedics. The subject is "Moving Procedures."

Errors
- commas
- subject-verb agreement
- capitalization
- hyphen
- spelling
- typographical
- word usage
- number usage

You will be happy to know that the new surgical wing of the hospital will be in full operation on September 1, 20_. This wing has the most advanced biomedical equipment and patience services. The move will take place on August 31 and the department will occupy the fifth floor of the building. The staff is asked to label all equiptment and supplies which needs to be transferred. Special boxes therefore will be provided to pack all your supplies and records. As of 5 p.m. on August 30 all computers will be shut down. Therefore be sure to have backup copies of all data stored in the computer. In your new quarters you will have a state-of-the-art telephone network system. These new telephone numbers however are not available now. Please be patient during this transition period and your corperation will be appreciated.

ri

Reference Tools: Dictionary and Thesaurus

Proper word choice will help make a message attractive to the reader. In turn, you will get the response you want. Two valuable tools in aiding you to choose the most appropriate words are the **dictionary** and a **thesaurus**.

A **dictionary** is primarily a word reference text; it defines words, gives correct spelling, identifies word usage, and provides correct word pronunciation. It also covers biographical and geographical information, explains abbreviations, and includes a writing style guide.

A **thesaurus** is a book of words and their synonyms and antonyms. A writer can check to find alternative words to express ideas rather than overusing certain words. This will make for more interesting reading.

When composing documents, you should have these two reference sources on hand. These books will be most helpful in providing words and phrases needed to express your ideas more clearly and effectively. Most word processing programs include thesaurus and spell-and-language check features. After proofreading your work, use these software programs to recheck for any possible errors.

You are reminded that the software has limitations and does not always catch a language error. For example, it does not recognize words spelled correctly but used incorrectly in context, such as, *their there*. It is up to you to decide which word is correct for the sentence.

The computerized **thesaurus** lists words as nouns, verbs, adjectives, or adverbs. In order to substitute words effectively, you will need to identify the part of speech needed in the particular statement.

Activity E   Writing Practicum

EXERCISE 1   USING A THESAURUS

Directions: Use a thesaurus to find another word with a similar meaning and then replace the italicized word in each sentence. (You can use a text copy or a word processing version. If you use the computerized form, go to Menu Bar and click on Tools, click Language, and go into Thesaurus).

_____ 1. The insurance company will offer a **cheap** prescription drug plan to its members.

_____ 2. A test program will give patients online **contact** with the local hospital.

_____ 3. A new Web site, known as Tel Doc, was **launched** last month.

_____ 4. Now you can **pick** the HMO that you believe will give you the best services.

_____ 5. The health fair offered a **vast** amount of information on fitness and stress management.

_____ 6. The patient used natural herbs to **alleviate** the pain.

_____ 7. Saturated fat can **raise** your cholesterol level.

_____ 8. There are many **remedies** on the market to slow the aging process.

EXERCISE 2   REPLACING DESCRIPTIVE WORDS

Descriptive words can express messages distinctly and vividly. They can make a dull sentence come alive.
Directions: Rewrite each sentence. Replace the general descriptive word (italicized) with a different, specific term.

Example: The lecture on controlling health costs was **interesting**.
Rewrite: The lecture on controlling health costs was **informative**.

1. The National Heart Association states that foods filled with saturated fats are *bad* for your health.

   Rewrite: _____

   _____

2. Selecting a *good* medical plan can be one of the most important choices a family can make.

Rewrite: _____

_____

3. Reading numerous health coverage brochures can be *boring*.

Rewrite: _____

_____

4. The nurse who administered my blood test was *nice*.

Rewrite: _____

_____

5. In addition to improving your health, a well-structured exercise plan can be *fun*.

Rewrite: _____

_____

6. Filling out medical forms is a *dull* activity.

Rewrite: _____

_____

7. Everyone hopes that medical reimbursement checks are issued *fast*.

Rewrite: _____

_____

8. The choice of a physician is an *important* factor when selecting a health plan.

Rewrite: _____

_____

9. My yearly physical revealed that I was in *fine* health.

Rewrite: _____

_____

10. Recuperating after a surgical procedure can be a *slow* process.

Rewrite: _____

_____

EXERCISE 3   CHOOSING POSITIVE OPENING SENTENCES IN LETTERS OF ADJUSTMENT AND REFUSAL

Select the statement that best expresses opening sentences with a positive tone and give the reason for your choice. Choose Option 1 or 2 in each group. Check the "Writing Pointers" before completing this exercise.

Reminder: Avoid negative language. Reflect a friendly tone by avoiding "cannot do" statements. Message should appear encouraging to the reader.

A. TOPIC: REFUSING AN INVITATION

1. Your organization, Society for Protecting the Environment, has honored me with an invitation to address its annual meeting. I look forward to your professional and exciting meetings; however, I am unable to accept this invitation.

2. I received your invitation to address the annual meeting of the Society for Protecting the Environment. I am sorry that I cannot accept this invitation.

   Option 1. _____ 2. _____

   Reason: _____

B. TOPIC: REFUSING AN INVITATION

1. Thank you for the invitation to be a moderator for the one-day workshop. I am sorry to say that I cannot accept this invitation.

2. I was pleased to receive your request to give a one-day workshop to your employees on critical decision making. I always enjoy leading a workshop on this important topic; however, I have a previous commitment.

   Option 1. _____ 2. _____

   Reason: _____

C. TOPIC: REFUSING A CLAIM

1. We are sorry that we cannot process your prescription claim as submitted. We need additional information.

2. We have received your prescription claim for reimbursement. However, we are unable to process this claim without further explanation of the charges.

   Option 1. _____ 2. _____

   Reason: _____

D. TOPIC: REFUSING A CLAIM

1. We are sorry that we cannot process your claim for the routine eye examination performed by your ophthalmologist. Unfortunately, this procedure is not covered in your present medical policy.

2. You have submitted a claim for a routine eye examination performed by your ophthalmologist. This procedure is not covered in your policy.

   Option 1. _____ 2. _____

   Reason: _____

E. TOPIC: REFUSING AN APPLICANT

1. We appreciate your interest in enrolling in our comprehensive health insurance plan. However, your preexisting heart problem, unfortunately, makes you ineligible for our plan.

2. I am sorry we cannot offer you our comprehensive health insurance plan since you have a preexisting heart problem.

Option 1. _____ 2. _____

Reason: _____

F. TOPIC: REFUSING AN APPLICANT

1. You missed the deadline for our special rate for catastrophic health insurance. We can offer you the plan at the enclosed rates.

2. Thank you for expressing an interest in our catastrophic health insurance plan. We are sorry that the deadline for the special rates has elapsed. We have enclosed our present rates for coverage that is available.

Option 1. _____ 2. _____

Reason: _____

G. TOPIC: REQUESTING AN ADJUSTMENT

1. I have received a reimbursement check for $75 for my recent foot examination charges. I believe that this amount is insufficient payment for the $200 fee that I submitted to you.

2. I received your reimbursement check of $75 for a recent bill submitted to you for foot examination charges. My records indicate that I may be entitled to a larger refund.

Option 1. _____ 2. _____

Reason: _____

H. TOPIC: REQUESTING AN ADJUSTMENT

1. I cannot understand why I continue to be billed for an electrocardiogram test I took six months ago. This bill was paid by check at your office immediately after the test.

2. Your office has repeatedly billed me for an electrocardiogram test taken six months ago. Your records will show that this bill was paid immediately after the test in your office.

Option 1. _____ 2. _____

Reason: _____

Letters of Refusal

Letters of refusal must be written with tact so that the firm's goodwill will not be adversely affected. Never start the letter with bad news. With a friendly, pleasant opening, the reader is in a better frame of mind to accept a decision to refuse a request. Offer a reasonable explanation to support your answer. The "No" can be implied. The closing should be a positive statement indicating that the business relationship will continue.

Writing Pointers

LETTER OF REFUSAL

- Use an opening sentence as a buffer statement introducing the situational problem.
- Use a positive, upbeat approach; start a letter with a statement of thanks.
- Be direct but polite.
- Offer reasonable explanation.
- Offer alternative course of action and assistance.
- Apologize for inconvenience.
- Close with a goodwill statement.

Model Letter of Refusal

Date

Ms. Lucy Brito
1042 Maple Drive
Sacramento, CA 95680–7391

Dear Ms. Brito:

Positive buffer statement
Thank you for your interest in enrolling in our Basic Health Plan. We would like to have you as one of our participants.

Reasonable explanation for refusal
After serious review of your medical background, we regret that we cannot accept you as one of our subscribers. A prerequisite for membership is that an applicant has not had a heart problem for the past five years. Your records indicate that you had a triple bypass last year.

Offer suggestions
There are other medical plans that focus on cases similar to yours. Unfortunately, we do not have such a plan. I suggest that you discuss this matter with your doctor or local medical facility.

Apology for non-acceptance
We are sorry that you cannot be a participant in our plan, but we hope that we can be of service to you in the future.

Goodwill statement
Sincerely yours,

Henry Sainville
Director

ri

Case Study 1: Rewrite of Poorly Written Letter of Refusal

After reading the poorly written letter sent to Alberto Genao, an individual who inquired about joining your medical group, respond to the questions that follow to help you organize your ideas before rewriting this letter. Then draft the letter. Send the letter to Mr. Genao, 21 Thornwood Drive, San Diego, CA 92100–2324.

Case

Dear Mr. Genao:

  We would like to thank you for the interest in wanting to join our medical group.

  Unfortunately, you are ineligible to join our group plan. Your company does not belong to our group. We allow only employees of companies that are members to participate.

  Ask your human resources representative to suggest a medical group.

QUESTIONS

1. How would you rewrite the opening sentence to set a tone of appreciation and courtesy?

   _____

   _____

2. Following the opening statement, how would you convey the message of refusal?

   _____

   _____

3. What other statements should you include in this letter of refusal?

_____

_____

Case Study 2: Letter of Refusal of a Claim

After reading this case, respond to the questions that follow, which will help you organize your ideas. Then draft the letter to Ms. Lori Young, 30 East Lane, Denver, Co 80215–3460.

Case: Ms. Lori Young submitted a claim to her insurance company for her $200 dental expenses. The company reviewed it and did not accept the claim. The claims supervisor, Suzanne Martel, must notify Ms. Young of the claims refusal. Ms. Martel must inform Ms. Young that she should resubmit the claim with a detailed explanation of the dental procedure for a reevaluation of the claim. If Ms. Young has any questions, she can call the Claims Department office at 202-667-3000.

ORGANIZE YOUR IDEAS

1. What is the most important point that Ms. Martel needs to make to Ms. Young?

_____

_____

_____

2. What would you include in the opening sentence?

_____

_____

_____

3. What specific details would you include in the body of the letter?

_____

_____

_____

4. What should Ms. Martel say in her closing statement to maintain goodwill?

_____

_____

_____

Case Study 3: Collection Letter

Read Case Study 3, and then develop an outline before composing the letter.

Case: A patient, Mr. Gerard Coleman, received six eye treatments from Dr. Larry Cutler. Mr. Coleman was informed before he started the treatments that his insurance would not pay for the procedure. The patient was willing to pay for the total cost of $1200. The account is four months past due, and no payments have been made.

Write a letter on behalf of Dr. Cutler requesting payment.

Case Study 4: Refusal of an Invitation

Read Case Study 4; Organize your ideas before composing the letter.

Case: Your employer, Dr. Carolyn O'Connell, has been invited to speak at a regional medical conference in Kansas City on May 15, 20xx. The topic is "Stress in the Workplace." Dr. O'Connell is unable to accept the invitation because she will not be returning to the United States before the date of the conference. She is presently on a special assignment in South America. As administrative assistant to Dr. O'Connell, draft a letter to send her regrets and inform the group that she will be available at another time. Address the letter to Dr. Ivan Ruiz at County Medical Center, 344 Eastern Parkway, Kansas City, KS 64100–4301.

Challenge Level Case

Case Study 5: Information Letter

Read Case Study 5; then compose the letter.

Case: The Americana Health Insurance Company is introducing a new prescription drug discount plan for its members. It is good news because the rates will be 15 percent lower than drug prices at the pharmacy.

It is easy to order the prescription drugs. Initially, the member sends in the doctor's prescription, and afterward the individual simply calls in for refills. The order is mailed within a week. There are no shipping charges. There is overnight delivery for emergencies. With a generic drug, the savings are greater. The charge is billed directly to the credit card account.

There is also a health product catalog that lists many over-the-counter medications and beauty products at savings of 25 percent off listed prices.

Members can receive an information kit by returning the attached card. There is no obligation.

Send a form letter; salutation should read "Dear Member:" The letter is from Alicia White, Director of Sales.

ADDRESS BOOK

When the same e-mail message is to be forwarded to a group of individuals, a mailing group of names is created in the address book. When you send the e-mail message, you place the name of the mailing group in the **To** block. The message will be automatically delivered to all the names listed in the mailing group.

Case Study 6: E-Mail Memorandum

Read Case Study 6; then complete the e-mail memo.

Case: Henry Kinnel, chief executive officer of Beard Pharmaceutical, is writing an e-mail to the staff announcing the approval of the drug Arpsin by the U.S. Food and Drug Administration. He congratulates the Research and Development Department for its work on developing the drug. Arpsin was tested for two years. The drug greatly improved the survival rate of heart attack victims. Mention that doctors will welcome this breakthrough. Arpsin will be available within a few months. Mr. Kinnel thanks everyone for their support in making the company a leader in its field.

Write the e-mail memo to be sent to all the staff members of the company. (In an office, this e-mail would be sent through the mailing group list in the address book.)

Include Mr. Kinnel's name and title in the closing.

The subject of this e-mail is "Approval of New Drug Arpsin."

Activity G   Report Writing Power: Memo Reports

The ability to write reports is an important skill to master to communicate effectively in business. The two types of report writing are formal and informal.

The formal report, which is sent outside the company, is usually a lengthy, well-structured, and documented report. The informal report, both letter and memo format, is used widely to disseminate information. Within the organization, the memo report is the accepted format for communicating with employees. To summarize a problem, to present a rationale for a project, or to recommend specific practices, the one-page memo is accepted as the most expedient type of report.

In the next six chapters, section G will focus on sharpening the skills of business report writing.

INFORMATION ON MEMO REPORTS

Functions

- To present relevant facts and information to help staff make decisions

- To provide analytical data

- To make recommendations based on factual information

- To report on the progress of a project

Types

- Status or progress reports to keep staff informed on the status of special projects

- Periodic reports prepared at set intervals to keep staff informed about company business (example: sales and financial reports)

- Informational reports to give facts, trends, and statistics to staff for decision making

Writing Pointers—Memo Reports

- Identify the purpose of the report.

- Write a clear, accurate introductory statement explaining the purpose of the report.

- Know your audience who will read the report.

- Write a draft and then edit and revise for correct English, grammar, and organization.

- Write in an informal manner; use of first person (I, we) is acceptable.

- Use memorandum format.

- Provide sideheadings for focus.

- State the purpose of the memo report in the subject line.

TO: Staff Supervisors

FROM: Jane DeSanctis, Vice President
            Human Resources

DATE: January 10, 2005

*Purpose
identified*

SUBJECT: CHANGES IN EMPLOYEE PRACTICES AND PROCEDURES

As newly appointed vice president of human resources, one of my priorities has been to review company policies and practices in dealing with our home health care personnel. We are very much aware that the employee turnover rate in the industry is high. However, at Wellcare Agency, the rate is above the norm. A firm's workforce is its greatest asset. High employee turnover and poor performance affect our business through increased costs and loss of clients.

*Explains
need for
change*

I have met with each of you personally to discuss ways to improve employee relations and have sent a questionnaire to all home health care personnel. The responses revealed some disturbing facts; however, they also offered constructive suggestions to improve the working climate within the organization.

*Use of
personal
pronoun*

*Side heading for
focus*

FINDINGS

*Presents
facts*

During the past year, our turnover rate was 40 percent, and a poor working climate was the main reason for individuals leaving the agency. Responses from our present employees highlighted the following reasons for job dissatisfaction: inadequate on-the-job training, poor internal communications, lack of self-worth, and little recognition by management for outstanding work.

*Provides
recommendations
based on
findings*

RECOMMENDATIONS

Based on the findings, the following changes in practices and procedures will be implemented immediately:

*Clarity of
reading*

- Formation of a task force to review and improve on-the-job training
- Monthly meetings of supervisors with their employee teams to interact and communicate
- Involvement of personnel in decision making (example: updating home health care practices)
- Willingness of management to listen to the rank-and-file who are on site every day
- Periodic visits by supervisors to assess the care given to patients in their homes
- Implementation of a program to reward outstanding employees

It is through a cooperative effort that we shall be able to energize our employees to make Wellcare Agency a great place to work and to do business.

Case Study 1: Memo Report

After reading the following case, respond to the questions in the section that follows in "Organize Your Ideas," then compose the memo report.

Case: You are working in the Community Relations Department of your local hospital. The neighborhood surrounding the hospital has a multicultural population, and many of the residents are recent immigrants who are not familiar with our health services.

As a member of the Community Task Force, you have been involved in a recent study that shows a need to offer programs in English and other languages for expectant parents. These programs would include courses on infant care and parenting skills. The need is supported by data that shows that 50 percent of the respondents spoke English as a second language. Of the 500 families who responded, 30 percent of them have been living in the community less than three years and are unaware of the services provided by the hospital.

In a memo report to Dr. Louis Farnsworth, director of the hospital, discuss the findings of the study, the educational programs recommended by the Task Force, and the implementation of courses. The recommendations include offering monthly classes to discuss topics of interest for expectant parents; conducting tours of the state-of-the-art maternity, nursery, and delivery units; forming a support group of knowledgeable parents to teach parenting skills; and holding weekly classes on infant care. These programs should be bilingual to accommodate the community. At present, a bilingual evening course on parenting skills and a weekend class on infant care have been started.

Remind the hospital administration that it is important for the hospital to reach out using a preventive approach to avoid health problems later. Also, invite Dr. Farnsworth to meet with the task force.

ORGANIZE YOUR IDEAS

To help you write an effective report, respond to the following questions before composing it. The questions are organized in a logical sequence; therefore, as you write the report, use your responses to the questions as a reference. When completed, your response list, in effect, will be the outline you should follow step by step during the writing process. This section reviews important points that need to be considered when writing this report.

1. What is the purpose of this memo report?

   _____

2. Which of the following is the most appropriate subject line?
   a. Proposed Health Education Program
   b. Community Task Force Study
   c. Implementation of the Community Task Force's Recommendation

3. What will be the side-heading for your opening?

_____

4. What information do you plan to give the reader in the introductory paragraph?

_____

5. Which of the following is the most appropriate opening sentence of the memo report?

   a. I am reporting on behalf of the Community Task Force that the study on the health needs of our residents is completed.

   b. The study of the Task Force has completed its study of the health needs of the residents of our community.

   c. The Community Task Force has completed its study of the health needs of the residents of our community.

6. What other information would you include in your opening paragraph?

_____

7. What is the side-heading for the next section of your report?

_____

8. What is the best way to present the recommendations that are being implemented?

_____

9. What key words will your recommendation include? (Put the key words in order to form an outline.)

_____

10. What would you say in the closing section of the report?

_____

Case Study 2: Memo Report

Community General Hospital serves a 20-square-mile area with a population of 25,000 residents. Ninety percent of the families are middle in-come, and the remaining 10 percent are low income.

The Community General Hospital's emergency room is always crowded and often there is a two-hour waiting period. To alleviate this overcrowding condition, a pilot project was started by opening a neighborhood clinic on the opposite side of town. The clinic has been in operation for one year. It is open seven days a week from 8 a.m. until 11 p.m. and is staffed by physicians from the hospital, part-time specialists in child care and senior care, nurses, and technicians.

Over the past year, treatment at the clinic has included emergency and routine situations such as sprains, colds, fevers, chest pains, and x-rays. The clinic has been well received by the community and treats about 250 patients a week. There is also a decrease in attendance at the emergency room of Community General Hospital.

Write a report to the hospital's Board of Directors informing them of the success of the pilot program. Suggest expansion of the clinic to serve that section of the city. Important services that could be added include pediatrics and family care.

ORGANIZE YOUR IDEAS

Answer the following questions before writing your memo report:

1. What is the purpose of this memo report?

   _____

2. What is an appropriate subject line heading?

   _____

3. What will be the side heading for the opening paragraph?

   _____

4. What information would you include in the beginning paragraphs?

   _____

5. What recommendations would you offer?

   _____

➤ Cultural Communication

England:

- Senior executives make the final business decisions; follow a hierarchy pattern.

- Business people approach their work objectively; personal feelings are immaterial.

- Aggressive approach is not well received.

- Conservative dress is the norm; use formality in writing.

See www.executiveplanet.com

Self-Assessment
English Power

Directions: In the following sentences, insert correct punctuation. If no comma is needed, write C (correct) in the space provided.

_____ 1. As you realize the trend in medical care is to subscribe to an HMO.

_____ 2. Many people use the Internet to obtain medical information such as common health problems.

_____ 3. If possible the new clinic will open evenings.

_____ 4. Obesity without a doubt contributes to other illnesses.

_____ 5. To prevent work-related ailments firms are improving their office environment.

_____ 6. Many states as we know are enacting smoke-free laws.

_____ 7. The patient needless to say will seek a second opinion.

_____ 8. To choose a doctor ask the referral service at your local hospital.

_____ 9. I plan to attend the hospital fundraiser if it is held within the area.

_____ 10. Before the pharmaceutical company released the new drug it was approved by the FDA.

English Power

Directions: Edit, format, and proofread the following unarranged letter for errors; key the letter correctly. This form letter will be addressed to the residents of the county.

Dear Resident:

Get fit today by joining the Westchester Mall Walking Club. As we know walking is an non-stressful exercise for people of all ages. It provide many benefits such as reducing the risk of heart disease, helping to lose weight, and improving circulation.

The Westchester Mall is a ideal location for walkers. It offers more than one mile of climate-controlled walkways in a secure environment. The program is led by a fitness professional. Since the program began young

adults, parents with strollers, and seniors start the

day with a energetic walk. At the same time they enjoy

each other's company, and do a little window shopping.

At the beginning of each month special guests give talk

on health and fitness.

For more information log on to www.mallwalk.com. We

look forward to seeing you every Tuesday and Friday,

from 8 a.m. to 10 a.m.

Sincerely, Andrew Berger, Mall Manager

Writing Power

Directions: Read the following case; then draft a memorandum. Keep the message positive.

Address the following memorandum to the sales representatives from your boss, Henry Posner, Regional Sales Manager, at Argo Pharmaceutical. Notify them that the annual sales meeting is scheduled for June 1, 20xx, to be held at the company headquarters. The topics to be presented include the introduction of Anatol, over-the-counter drug for allergies, and the prescription drug Dextron for arthritis. Both drugs have tested well in trial tests.

Management is concerned with the lack of personal contact of the sales representatives with the primary-care physicians. Lori Balfour, Vice President of Sales, will review ways that will increase contact between sales representatives and doctors.

Ask the reps to contact you, Mr. Posner's assistant, to confirm attendance at the meeting and to make hotel reservations.

"Talent wins games, but teamwork and intelligence win(s)

championships."

—Michael Jordan

Retailing
Commas in
Words, Phrases,
and Clauses

WHAT YOU WILL LEARN IN THIS CHAPTER

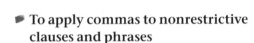

- To apply commas to nonrestrictive clauses and phrases

- To punctuate a series of items

- To apply commas to words and phrases in apposition

- To punctuate consecutive adjectives

- To punctuate items in dates

- To develop a business vocabulary in **RETAIL SALES**

- To proofread and edit correspondence and reports

- To compose a reply to a customer's letter of complaint

- To compose a reply to a letter of inquiry

- To compose a promotional letter

- To compose a periodic memo report

- To compose an informational letter

- To write an e-mail memo

- To search the Internet

SALES REPRESENTATIVE: Employed in a field encompassing a wide range of firms which sell consumer products, pharmaceuticals, electronics, and services; appeals to buyers and purchasing agents at the retail level in a particular company's products, takes orders, resolves any problems with the merchandise, maintains contact with clients.

Skills: college courses in marketing, knowledgeable in specific field or product, on-the-job training, goal-oriented, persuasive, communication skills.

SALES ASSOCIATE: Works in a retail specialty shop, department store, or consumer products establishment; assists customers in choosing merchandise, executes a sale, restocks merchandise on shelves/racks, monitors inventory of in-store sales.

Skills: Shows interest in retailing, on-the-job training, pleasing personality, interpersonal skills, well-groomed.

BUYER: Works for an organization purchasing a line of merchandise from a wholesaler or manufacturer to be sold at the retail level; reviews buying and fashion trends, attends trade shows, assesses in-store sales and consumer buying patterns.

Skills: college degree in retailing, marketing, on-the-job training, internships, fashion savvy, knowledgeable with the line of merchandise, interpersonal skills.

Activity A Language Arts Recall

COMMA USAGE

Commas that are used within a sentence show relationships between words, phrases, or clauses.

SERIES OF WORDS, PHRASES, AND CLAUSES

> **Rule 7.1:** Use a comma after each item in a series of words, phrases, or clauses, including the item before the conjunction **"and, or, nor. "**

Example: We stock **accessories, luggage, and stationery.**

NONRESTRICTIVE AND RESTRICTIVE CLAUSES

> **Rule 7.2:** Use commas around nonrestrictive clauses and phrases (clauses that are not essential to the meaning of the sentence).

Example: Your catalog order, **which was received today,** will be shipped immediately.

Rule 7.3: Do not use commas around restrictive clauses (clauses that are essential to the meaning of the sentence).

Example: The customer **who returned the damaged item** was given a refund.

Rule 7.4: Do not use a comma before the word *that* when it introduces a clause that is essential to the meaning.

Example: The one-day sale **that was scheduled for January 4** is canceled until further notice.

APPOSITION

Rule 7.5: Use commas to separate words or phrases in apposition (when words within commas explain the preceding noun or pronoun).

Example: Her first book, *Steps to Successful Selling,* was just published.

Rule 7.6: Do not use a comma when a word or phrase in apposition is essential to identify the preceding noun.

Example: The new book *How to Shop* is offered at a discount to customers.

CONSECUTIVE ADJECTIVES

Rule 7.7: Use a comma to separate two or more consecutive adjectives that modify a noun. To test for a comma, mentally insert the word *and* between the two adjectives or reverse the order of the adjectives.

Example: Soft, silky fabric was used in our collection of scarves. (Test: Soft and silky fabric. . . .)

DATES

Rule 7.8: Use commas to set off items in dates. When a year is used with other items in a date, place a comma after the year.

Example: **March 1, 2008,** is the date we scheduled for the flea market sale.

Omit commas when only month and year are given.

Example: The May 2008 issue is an anniversary edition.

Dates in foreign correspondence are expressed in day, month, year sequence.

Example: 3 April 2007.

CITIES AND STATES

Rule 7.9: Use a comma between the name of a city and the name of a state. Also, place a comma after the name of the state when it is preceded by the name of a city and is not followed by final punctuation.

Example: We will be visiting **Charleston, West Virginia,** and **Asheville, North Carolina.**

Check for Understanding

Directions: Compare the sentences that follow and answer the questions.

NONRESTRICTIVE AND RESTRICTIVE CLAUSES

1. The customer who was dissatisfied with the merchandise complained to the manager.

2. The customer, who had purchased the item on sale, returned it for a refund.

3. Our upscale line of clothing that has shown a net loss will be discontinued immediately.

4. Our upscale line of clothing, which is popular with our customers, will be expanded.

QUESTIONS

a. What do sentences 1 and 3 have in common?

_____

b. What do sentences 2 and 4 have in common?

_____

c. Why do sentences 1 and 3 have no internal punctuation?

_____

d. Why do sentences 2 and 4 have internal punctuation?

_____

(Answers are given on page 152.)

Conclusion: Complete the following sentence.
Use no _____ around restrictive clauses; use _____ around nonrestrictive clauses.

APPOSITION

5. We have enclosed our shopping credit card, Royalcharge, for your convenience.

6. The new credit card Royalcharge will offer shoppers many added features.

QUESTIONS

e. What is the difference in punctuation between sentences 5 and 6?

_____

f. Why is the word *Royalcharge* set off by commas in sentence 5?

_____

g. Why are there no commas in sentence 6?

_____

(Answers are given below.)

Conclusion: Complete the following sentence.
When a word or phrase is necessary to identify the preceding noun, do _____ use a comma. If the word or phrase describes the preceding noun, it is in _____; therefore, _____ need to be inserted.

Conclusion: not, apposition, commas

Answers to "Check for Understanding"
a. There are no commas in the sentences.   b. There are commas in the sentences.   c. There is a restrictive dependent clause in each sentence.   d. There is a nonrestrictive dependent clause in each sentence.   e. Sentence 5 has commas; sentence 6 has no commas.   f. *Royalcharge* is in apposition and explains the preceding noun ("credit card").   g. The word *Royalcharge* is necessary to identify the preceding noun (it is the name of the new credit card).

Building English Power: Comma Use in Series, Consecutive Adjectives, Nonrestrictive / Restrictive Clauses, Apposition, Dates, Cities, and States

Still Puzzled? See Writer's One Key Home Page: Commas. Click on: How do I use a comma with a series? (p. 4)

How do I use commas between adjectives? (p. 5)

How do commas work with non-restrictive and restrictive elements? (p. 6)

How do I use commas in dates, places? (p. 9)

Review exercises:
First, do *Comma Exercise* (reviews comma rules) *Commas—Additional Exercises* are optional.

Directions: Insert commas where required. If no comma is needed, write "C" (Correct) in the space provided.

_____ 1. You a valued customer are eligible for our money- saving bonus plan. (7.5)

_____ 2. On May 1 20xx our popular well-known rug sale will take place. (7.8, 7.7)

_____ 3. Price Cutter a national chain will open a store in Huntington New York a thriving suburban community. (7.5, 7.9)

_____ 4. Designer clothing which appeals to today's shopper can be purchased at discount stores. (7.2)

_____ 5. Appliances carry a manufacturer's warranty that offers consumers protection against product defects. (7.4)

_____ 6. Shoppers who look for affordable quality are joining warehouse price clubs. (7.3)

_____ 7. Our electronics store which is located in the mall is offering a 10 percent discount on VCRs camcorders and CD players. (7.2, 7.1)

8. As a valued respected charge customer you are invited to our annual two-day sale which will be held this weekend. (7.7, 6.1, 7.3)

9. If you are interested in discount stores Chet Edwards' latest guide *The Popular Discount Malls* is now available at your bookstore. (6.1, 7.5)

10. The seminar speaker discussed today's competitive market consumer preferences and new marketing trends. (7.1)

11. The new upscale mall that attracted huge crowds on the weekend will extend its shopping hours. (7.7, 7.4)

12. The popular home-furnishing store offers free shipping a convenient layaway plan and low credit rates. (7.1)

13. The firm has scheduled Friday July 31 for its annual physical inventory. (7.8)

14. Our spring catalog which was recently mailed to you illustrates the latest women's fashions. (7.2)

15. The bestseller *Repackaging Your Sales Approach* sells for $19.95 plus shipping. (7.6)

16. The lengthy informative sales report was distributed to the staff. (7.7)

17. The semi-annual sale that was scheduled for Wednesday March 1 has been postponed. (7.4, 7.8)

18. The European designer who specializes in women's sportswear will show his line of clothing at the fashion show. (7.3)

19. The retail store that sells organic foods is moving to the new shopping mall. (7.4)

20. Individuals can download music movies and games on the Internet. (7.1)

Activity B   Building Word Power

Directions: The words that follow are commonly used in the retail sales industry. From this list, select the word or phrase that correctly completes each statement. Refer to the personal dictionary, if necessary.

Stay calm through stressful or confrontational situations; avoid loss of temper.

backlogged	physical inventory
boutiques	privileged
electronic malls	redeemed
franchises	upscale
innovative	upsurge
megamalls	warehouse clubs
outlet malls	warranty

_____ 1. Shoppers find that _____ are good places to purchase large quantities of popular products at low prices.

_____ 2. High-styled clothing is sold in small, specialized stores known as _____.

_____ 3. Through the Internet, shoppers will be using _____ to make their purchases.

_____ 4. _____ are huge shopping sites that have expanded the variety of retail stores to include restaurants, movies, and entertainment.

_____ 5. When economic conditions are poor, there is a(n) _____ of unemployment.

_____ 6. Airlines offer bonus points for traveling that can be _____ for free trips.

_____ 7. _____ people can often find different, creative ways to design projects and solve problems.

_____ 8. The popular children's video has sold out, and production has been _____ for a month; therefore, shipment of the video will be delayed.

_____ 9. Well-known personalities from the fields of sports and entertainment are _____ individuals who can gain access to social events.

_____ 10. Clothing manufacturers often have stores in _____ to sell their overstocked and discontinued line of merchandise at lower prices.

_____ 11. The shopper was interested in visiting the _____ mall that features boutique stores and higher-priced department stores.

_____ 12. Retail stores conduct a(n) _____ each year to manually count merchandise for control purposes. (In retailing, the word _inventory_ means "merchandise.")

_____ 13. Most appliances carry a manufacturer's _____ that guarantees against defective parts of a product.

_____ 14. Many retail firms offer _____ to buyers, which gives them the right to use the company name and product while they adhere to specific company policies and conditions.

On the Alert

■ _build (verb)_—to construct

Example: The Town Planning Board voted to **build** a new mall.
built (verb, past tense)—constructed

Example: This historic home was **built** in the 1900s.

- *on-site*—on location (e.g., **on-site** hotel; compound adjective modifying the noun)

    Example: The fire department carried out an **on-site** inspection of the building.

- *plural of numbers*—Add "s" without an apostrophe.

    Example: During the **1990s,** the Internet became an alternative way of personal shopping.

- *percent*—Express percentages in figures except at the beginning of a sentence; spell out the word *percent.*

    Example: 10 percent

- *punctuation and question marks*—Periods and commas are always inside the quotation mark.

    Example: I read that his latest article, "Selling Tips," is available.

- *books*—Titles of books are generally italicized. All caps may be used to highlight a title.

    Example: *Repackaging Your Sales Approach*

    REPACKAGING YOUR SALES APPROACH

- *Internet*—Capitalize I in this widely used technology term.

- *Decades and centuries*—write as words and do not capitalize.

Activity C   Industry Perspectives: Retailing Trends

Directions: Using appropriate revision marks, proofread and key the report that follows. Refer to the appendix for a model report.

CURRENT RETAILING TRENDS

Rule Reference

The retailing industry has changed dramatically during the passed decade. Consumer demands for quality merchandise at competitive prices effect the way retailers sell their products. To meet the needs of specific consumer markets megamalls warehouse clubs and

6.4, 7.1   specialty boutique shops have become popular.

3.1, 7.2   The megamall which is especially popular with

2.1   families offer the consumer a combination of retail and

7.1	department stores fast-food eateries and entertainment
1.4	establishments. The mall has become the "Main Street of
	america." Also, the discount stores of the 1980s have
	been replaced by discount malls where outlet stores of
2.1	famous brand names offers customers merchandise at 20 to
	50% off the regular prices.
7.2	Warehouse clubs which are membership-only discount
	stores also are targeted for family-oriented shopping.
2.1	These supercenters offers a variety of bulk merchandise
6.3	at low prices. At the other end of the marketing
	spectrum specialty boutiques are favored by shoppers who
	believe that brand names reflect status symbols.
2.2	TV and the Internet has become powerful forces in
1.7	changing the shopping habits of americans. Individuals,
7.3	who have limited time, use the TV shopping channel to
	make their purchases. The Internet with it's vast source
	of information has been attracting retailers to sell
	there merchandise through electronic malls.
6.3	In the 21st century retailing will not be "business
7.7	as usual" but an exciting innovative industry.

Did you find these errors?

12 punctuation
2 capitalization
3 word usage
3 subject–verb agreement
1 number usage
1 symbol usage

Activity D   *Editing Power*

Task A: Edit, format, and proofread the following unarranged form letter. Use proofreaders' symbols to mark the errors, then key the letter correctly. Remember to insert paragraphs.

Errors

■ commas
■ verb tense
■ word usage
■ typographical

Dear Customer: We value you as a customer, and want to show our sincere appreciation for your support and loyalty. A special weekend has been reserve for our preferred customers. This weekend, June 15 16 and 17 you are invited to take 10% off our entire line of merchandise which includes jewelry clothing and home furnishings. To get this extra 10 percent of the ticketed price present this letter and use your Albertson's charge card when making you purchase. We are introducing a new service for our busy customers. The Shopper's Cafe will serve salads sandwiches and gourmet coffees throughout the day. We look forward to serving you. Sincerely yours, Sam Ross, Vice President

Challenge Task B: Edit, format, and proofread the following rough-draft letter for all errors; key it correctly.

Address this letter to Ms. Sylvia Atkins, 11 Secor Drive, Memphis, TN 38111-0700. The letter is from Thomas Butler, sales representative.

I invite you to take advantage of our convenient home-buying service Value Shopping. As a busy individual you know your time is precious. With our plan you do not face crowded stores long lines and limited stock. Our catalog which is published twice a year advertizes our fine line of fashion clothing. Our order forms are simple to to complete and we have an easy payment plan. With every order you receive bonus shopping points which can be redeemed toward future purchases. Please read this enclosed mailing and become a priviledged customer. We look forward to providing you with efficient reliable service.

Activity E *Writing Practicum*

Introduction: Parallelism

Sentences should be easy to read and understand clearly. One way to ensure this is to express similar words in the same grammatical form to communicate corresponding thoughts.

Examples:

- pairing a noun with a noun
- pairing a verb with a verb
- pairing a phrase with a phrase
- pairing an infinitive with an infinitive ("to" + verb)
- pairing a clause with a clause

This construction is known as **parallelism**, which improves readability and enhances clarity.

EXAMPLES OF PARALLEL CONSTRUCTION

Incorrect:

- The management team was responsible for **company strategy, finance,** and **directing** the administrative team. (noun forms mixed with verb form)

Correct:

- The management team was responsible for **company strategy, finance,** and **administration.** (noun form)

Incorrect:

- This month's window display was **chic, creative,** and **appealed** to consumers. (adjectives mixed with verb form)

Correct:

- This month's window display was **chic, creative,** and **appealing.** (adjective form)

Incorrect:

- Advertising is an important tool that retailers use to **attract** the attention of the public, **influence** a potential shopper, and **for arousing** the consumer's curiosity. (mixed verb forms)

Correct:

- Advertising is an important tool that retailers use to **attract** the attention of the public, **influence** a potential shopper, and **arouse** the consumer's curiosity. (infinitive form)

Incorrect:

■ In the retailing seminar, I learned about fashion **merchandise,** customer **service,** and **motivating** employees. (noun forms mixed with verb form)

Correct:

■ In the retailing seminar, I learned about fashion **merchandise,** customer **service,** and employee **motivation.** (noun form)

EXERCISE: PARALLELISM

Directions: Revise the following sentences so that they are balanced and so that the parallel ideas are written in the same grammatical form. Occasionally, a word or phrase may have to be added or deleted in the sentence.

1. The goals of the manufacturer are to mass produce custom-made clothing and selling directly to the consumer. (infinitive form)

_____

_____

2. The antiquated marketing system has been updated by using computer technology and by employees being sent for training. (verb form)

_____

_____

3. In marketing, computers are used for product inventory control, to record daily sales, and to get customer feedback. (noun form)

_____

_____

4. Suburban malls have replaced downtown shopping areas because they are centralized, diversified, and parking is accessible. (adjective form)

_____

_____

5. Our entire line of merchandise, which includes jewelry, furniture, and introduces new fall fashions, is on sale. (noun form)

_____

_____

6. This month's sales of winter clothes will be a huge success because of two-day sales and 20 percent off retail price will be given. (noun form)

_____

_____

7. Come to the selling course prepared to take notes, listen to the guest speaker, and asking some questions. (infinitive form)

_____

_____

8. Your mail-order catalog was received yesterday and my order for furniture sent to the purchasing department today. (verb form)

_____

_____

9. Good salespersons should have knowledge and familiarity with their stock. (preposition form)

_____

_____

10. The department store, specializing in sporting goods, also features designer clothing, equipment to exercise, and has books for traveling. (noun form)

_____

_____

11. The mall has increased its budget for hiring security personnel and to prevent shoplifting. (verb form)

_____

_____

12. The company sent out direct mailers advertising the sale and to promote new merchandise. (infinitive form)

_____

_____

13. When the shopping mall was designed, the architect considered mall motif, laying out of the stores, and accessibility to roads. (noun form)

_____

_____

14. The shopper purchased groceries at the supermarket, at the drug store bought cosmetics, and bought a sweater at the boutique. (phrase form)

_____

_____

15. Service, being dependable, and having product value are the major goals of our firm. (noun form)

_____

_____

Writing Pointers

REPLY TO A CUSTOMER COMPLAINT

- Respond immediately to a complaint.
- Begin with a pleasant buffer statement.
- Offer a logical explanation for the action taken.
- Offer to correct the problem, if possible.
- Offer alternative solutions where applicable.
- Be sympathetic but firm.
- Respond positively to maintain goodwill.
- Use a friendly closing.

Date

Ms. Eva Johnson
5872 Jackson Plaza
Spokane, WA 99200-3274

Dear Ms. Johnson:

Buffer
statement

Logical
statement

Positive tone

Stress firm's
policy

Goodwill
gesture

End positively

Our firm is committed to offer its customers quality merchandise at competitive prices. Therefore, it is important that our inventory control be maintained. To achieve this, we have a policy to give cash refunds on merchandise that is returned within 30 days of purchase.

The garment you returned was purchased three months ago; therefore, our sales associate was only able to offer you a store credit and not a cash refund. To avoid any misunderstanding, the refund policy is posted at each register. We trust that you understand the company's position.

We invite you to continue shopping at our store and have enclosed a 10 percent discount coupon toward your next purchase.

Sincerely yours,

Chris Adamo
ri
Enclosure

Activity F   Writing Power: Composing Correspondence

Case Study 1:   Rewrite of Poorly Written Letter of Reply to Complaint

Richard Santana attempted to return merchandise that he purchased more than 30 days ago. The salesperson displayed a negative attitude and did not explain the store's policy on returned merchandise. A poorly written letter was sent to Mr. Santana by the manager. After reading it, respond to the questions, then rewrite the letter. Send the letter to Mr. Richard Santana, 15 Lotus Street, Nashville, TN 37200-8426.

Case:

Dear Mr. Santana:

I received your letter describing the poor attitude that was shown to you by our salespeople when you returned some merchandise. This was wrong behavior.

Our store's policy is to give store credit only if the merchandise was not returned before 30 days after date of purchase.

We know you will understand.

Sincerely yours,

Timothy Jenkins

Manager

ri

Enclosure

QUESTIONS

1. What type of letter appears on the previous page?

   _____

2. Is the first sentence a good buffer statement? Why?

   _____

3. Has an apology been offered in the letter?

   _____

4. Does the letter have a sympathetic tone?

   _____

5. Is there a statement of goodwill to offset the customer's poor experience?

   _____

6. What type of closing statement would get results?

_____

_____

_____

Case Study 2: Reply to Customer Complaint

Read the case that follows; then answer the questions that follow. Using your answers, respond to Mrs. Jessica Silvers, One Poplar Drive, Springfield, IL 62705-2265.

Case: Your customer, Mrs. Jessica Silvers, has contacted you regarding the damaged office desk that was delivered to her. As service manager, inform her that the damage occurred in transit from the warehouse and offer to send her a replacement of the desk. If Mrs. Silvers accepts this offer, she will receive the replacement within three weeks. At the time of delivery, the damaged desk will be picked up. However, if Mrs. Silvers is not satisfied with this arrangement, you can make an alternative offer of a desk of comparable quality and style. Ask Mrs. Silvers to contact your office with her decision. The telephone number is 800-239-5000.

ORGANIZE YOUR IDEAS

1. What is the most important point that you need to tell Mrs. Silvers?

_____

_____

_____

2. What would you want to include in the opening sentence?

_____

_____

_____

3. What specific details would you include in the body of the letter?

_____

_____

_____

4. What would you say in the closing statement to indicate your desire to serve Mrs. Silvers?

_____

_____

_____

Case Study 3: Promotional Letter

Read the case that follows and compose the letter.

Case: Send a form letter to prospective customers inviting them to apply for your store's credit card, Buying Unlimited. Invite them to complete the enclosed application form to enroll in your membership program. Inform them that new subscribers will receive a $50 merchandise check that is applicable to any purchase made. An additional advantage for credit card holders is a 2 percent cash bonus for the total amount of their annual purchases.

Case Study 4: Reply to an Inquiry

Read Case Study 4; Organize your ideas before writing, then compose the letter.

Case: Anthony Torres was given a rain check for stackable wall units that were unavailable. Mr. Torres is concerned that his rain check will expire and will not be honored and that he will not receive the merchandise at the sale price. As manager of the store, reply to Mr. Torres's letter, reassuring him that the merchandise will be sold to him at the sale price when it is received in the store. You may want to mention that the delay in filling the orders has been caused by the slow shipment from the manufacturer. Address the letter to Mr. Anthony Torres, 1301 Palma Drive, Houston, TX 77000-5487.

Challenge Level Case

Case Study 5: Information Letter

Read Case Study 5; then compose the letter.

Case: This letter is in response to customers of Bailey's Department Store who are concerned with the release of personal information. They want to be sure that their files are not distributed to outsiders.

Jan Williams, president, would like you, her assistant, to prepare a letter to be sent to all Bailey's customers to assure them that no personal information is sold or distributed to anyone outside the firm. Bailey's has taken steps physically and electronically to maintain the privacy of all personal information of their customers.

Be sure to remind your customers that Bailey's Department Store provides quality namebrand merchandise at reasonable prices. Thank them for their loyalty.

Case Study 6: E-Mail Memorandum

Read Case Study 6; then complete the e-mail memo.

Case: David Roche, executive vice president of Bailey's Department Store, is planning to hold a storewide inventory sale in July. He needs to meet with department managers to discuss the strategy for this sale. Some of the questions to be addressed are: What merchandise is to be put on sale? What type of discount should be offered? What type of promotional campaign will be used? What type of advertising—newspapers, home flyer, and/or TV—will be adopted? How long should the sale run?

Mr. Roche expects each one of the department managers to have a proposed plan based on these questions. Their input is important for the success of the sale. The meeting will be held on May 1 in the conference room.

Compose an e-mail memorandum to be sent to department managers. The subject of this e-mail is "Planning Meeting for July Inventory Sale."

 ## Activity G   Report Writing Power: Periodic Memo Reports

Introduction: Periodic Reports

Periodic reports, one of the most common types of reports in business, often take the form of **memo reports.** They are prepared at regular intervals, such as monthly, quarterly, or annually.

The sales report is an example of a periodic report. To present data effectively in a report, tables and charts are often included. Sideheadings also contribute to the orderly flow of information.

Writing Pointers—Periodic Memo Reports

■ Sales and financial reports are commonly written in memo form.

■ Analysis of business operations can be reported internally in memo format.

■ Periodic reports are prepared at specified times (i.e., quarterly, monthly).

■ Headings highlight major ideas.

■ Charts and tables help the reader visually understand data.

■ Statistical data is presented in table form.

■ Informational statements should interpret data for the reader.

■ Bulleted statements are used where clarification is essential for understanding.

■ Reports are concise and clear.

Model Periodic Memo Report

TO: Michael Carpenter, Vice President
FROM: Rose Dimitri, Sales Manager
DATE: Current Date
SUBJECT: Fourth-Quarter Sales

Purpose identified

Year-End Results

Data presented

Our firm continues to show modest sales growth for the current fiscal year. From the beginning of the year, the sales increased by 33 percent. In the fourth quarter, sales increased 10 percent over the previous quarter. The following table shows a comparison of the sales figures for the past four quarters of the year. It is apparent that there is a pattern of growth.

Table format for clarity of statistical information

Quarter	$Sales	Percent of Increase/Decrease From Previous Quarter
Fourth	$418,000	+10.0%
Third	380,000	+22.5%
Second	310,000	− 1.6%
First	315,000	+ 3.0% (from previous year)

Heading orients reader to content

Analysis

The fourth quarter increase in sales reflects an upward trend that began during the third quarter. A number of factors contributed to this turnaround:

Bulleted statements used for clarity

• Increase in seasonal buying of clothing
• Early start of cold weather during the fall months
• Increase in promotional activities
• Consumer interest in our classic, casual apparel
• Five percent decrease in general and administrative expenditures

The lower sales figure during the second quarter was unexpected. One of the reasons was the poor sales throughout the retailing industry due to a weak economy. With colder weather during the fall months, the demand for heavy-weight outerwear increased. Our new jeans collection in a variety of fabrics was introduced in September, and it has been very popular among our customers.

Interpretation of
data clearly stated

During the past three months, we have refocused our advertising strategies to portray a brand image that identifies with high-quality merchandise. Newspaper advertising and mail-order flyers have been redesigned to illustrate to shoppers that we offer a versatile, yet classic style of clothing.

In addition, implementation of cost-saving procedures in shipping and distribution of merchandise has realized a 5 percent decrease in expenditures. With the use of a more sophisticated computerized system, our inventories have decreased and our delivery schedules are being met.

Conclusions

Sales projections in the retailing industry are very promising for next year; therefore, with our present plans, we should be able to continue to show an increase in profitability. We have moved forward as a company in building customer loyalty.

Case Study 1: Memo Report

After reading the case, respond to the questions that follow to help you organize your ideas, then compose the periodic memo report. Address the memo to Mark Cohen, Vice President, from Eugene Dinsmore of the Assessment Team.

Case: Bayport, Inc., is a well-known catalog retailer. It offers an extensive line of women's clothing, footwear, and accessories. The clothing appeals both to the working woman and to the individual with a casual lifestyle. The semiannual catalog is the major medium used to advertise Bayport's merchandise, and seasonal flyers focus on specific items popular at various times of the year.

A review of the firm's operations was made to determine the catalog business and sales trends for the past three years. This resulted in the implementation of the following changes. First, a refocus of the firm's marketing strategies included the redesigning of its semiannual catalog with greater use of graphics and color to highlight merchandise. Second, a line of home merchandise directed at the needs of the working woman was introduced. Among the items were bath products, linens, and time-saving kitchen utensils. Third, a concerted effort was made to provide good customer service, including seven-day mail-order service.

The catalog circulation, which increased 22 percent over the past three years, was 50,000 copies for the current year; 45,000 and

41,000 for each of the previous years. The largest increase occurred this year when the changes were implemented. The number of active catalog customers who made at least two purchases a year doubled over the past three years to 20,000 customers. For each of the previous years, the number of customers was 12,000 and 10,000 correct respectfully.

The net sales during the three-year period also showed gains, especially during the current year with $1.6 million; net sales were $750,000 and $600,000 in each of the previous years.

As a member of the assessment team involved in the review, prepare a report of the firm's catalog business over the past three years and an analysis of the sales trend for the same period. Use a table to present the catalog and sales data for the past three years.

ORGANIZE YOUR IDEAS

This is your guide to writing your memo report. These questions follow in sequential order to help you develop the process of writing this memo.

1. What is the purpose of this memo report?

    _____

2. What is the subject line?

    _____

3. What is the best way to show a three-year comparison of Bayport's catalog business?

    _____

4. What are the three categories you would use in column 1 of the table?

    1. _____

    2. _____

    3. _____

5. What are the four column headings in the table?

    1. _____   3. _____

    2. _____   4. _____

6. How would you clarify important information that relates to a specific item in the table?

    _____

7. After completing the table, what is the sideheading of the next section?

    _____

8. What specific areas would you discuss in this section?

_____

9. What three specific areas of change affected sales?

    1. _____

    2. _____

    3. _____

10. How would you incorporate in your report the listing of the three areas of change?

_____

Case Study 2: Memo Report

The Corner Store, a specialty home furnishing retail chain with 150 stores nationwide, has undertaken a five-year expansion program. Prepare a memo report to the Executive Board reviewing the firm's progress to date. For clarity, the use of tables is recommended.

Case: Over the past year, the Corner Store's total sales for the geographic areas of the country were as follows: West Coast, 35 stores, $6.3 million; East Coast, 20 stores, $4.5 million; South, 5 stores, $675,000; Midwest, 10 stores, $1.2 million. The total increase in sales from the previous year was 3.5 percent, a small increase when compared to projections.

As part of the expansion plan, a study has been completed that evaluated the following areas: (1) analysis of sales, (2) review of product offerings, and (3) strategies for future growth.

The store brand name of towels and linens is very popular in all the stores. Customers also like the coordinated sets of sheets, bedspreads, and window furnishings. The bathroom products that sell in stores on the West and East Coasts are the best sellers. In the Midwest, sheets and pillows are excellent sellers; in the South, accessory items for the bathroom are very popular. The weakest sales in all stores are curtains and drapes. Customers have requested that the stores carry more accessory and gift items for the home.

Another area of expansion that needs to be considered is online shopping. Many of the competitors have Web pages, and marketing studies show that retailers need to offer Internet services to survive.

Store displays lack a trendy image. A design consultant could make recommendations for better store layouts and displays of merchandise.

Over the next two years, the focus should be on improving sales in the existing stores rather than on rapid expansion of new stores. The opening of new stores should be limited to three in the West, five in the East, three in the South, and two in the Midwest.

The projected sales for the company should be a 10 percent increase for each of the next two years. An added line of house gifts and accessories should be considered; the slow sellers, curtains and drapes, should be discontinued unless these items are part of coordinated sets.

After the two-year period, stores not meeting the sales goals should be closed. Within five years, the Corner Store should have increased sales.

ORGANIZE YOUR IDEAS

Here is a guide to writing your memo report. The questions follow in sequential order to help you develop the process of writing this memo. Remember to include a side heading for each of the sections.

1. What is the purpose of this memo report?

   _____

2. What is the subject line?

   _____

3. What is the best way to show the breakdown of sales for each geographic area?

   _____

4. What column headings would you use in a table?

   _____

5. How should the best-selling items be listed?

   _____

6. List the recommendations you would make to improve the firm's sales.

   _____

   _____

   _____

   _____

   _____

7. What is the most effective way to list these recommendations?

   _____

Activity H   Surfing the Web

Introduction

The Internet has changed the way we access data, research information, and communicate globally. With its enormous, timely wealth of information, the Web is one of the most important tools used by individuals. In today's world of communications, it is important that you become adept at using the Internet to retrieve information whether for personal, business, or academic use.

In Chapters 7-12, Activity H will give you an opportunity to explore Web sites to obtain information and data relevant to a variety of situations.

Research buying a car

When purchasing a major item, the buyer needs to research the product for its quality, performance, features, and durability. Comparison shopping with other similar brands is also important in the buying process.

In this assignment, you will use the Internet to research buying a new car. You may choose any brand or auto style you want. You are to search for the following items and write a one-page summary of your findings.

■ Brand name and model of the auto

■ Special features of the car

■ Changes made from previous year's model

■ Price; special promotions

■ Comparison of a similar car from another manufacturer

■ Review of car by independent agency, e.g. *Consumer's Report, Buyer's Guide*

■ Reason for buying the specific auto

Tip: You may research the information by either using a search engine, such as Yahoo, or Google and clicking on to a link for new model cars or going directly to the car manufacturer's Web site.

⁘ Cultural Communication

Germany:

■ Compete with each other on quality of products and services.

■ Need to provide logical arguments and examples when presenting a proposal.

■ Problem-oriented, time-managed way of conducting meetings.

■ Expect every detail of a proposal to be examined carefully before a decision is made.

■ Avoid showy advertisement of a product.

■ Maintain close relationships between managers and workers.

See www.executiveplanet.com

Self-Assessment
English Power

Directions: Insert commas where required. If no comma is needed, write C (Correct) in the space provided.

_____ 1. The retail chain is opening stores in Atlanta Tucson and Spokane.

_____ 2. Salespersons who exceed their quotas will receive a bonus.

_____ 3. Ann Ryan our marketing analyst will meet with the firm's executives in Chicago Illinois.

_____ 4. Shopping online is a convenient fast way to purchase merchandise.

_____ 5. The applicant who had computer knowledge was offered the job.

_____ 6. Our Portland Oregon office will more to Tucson Arizona.

_____ 7. On May 1 2007 the food market opened its first superstore.

_____ 8. The new automobile models that are manufactured in the United States are popular with consumers.

_____ 9. The new book *Organic Menus* is a best seller among individuals interested in natural foods.

_____10. The dollar stores which carry discounted items can be found in most malls.

Directions: Revise the following sentences so that they are parallel in construction.

11. The fashion show was chic, creative, and had appeal.

_____

12. Some of the topics at the seminar were online selling, discount merchandise, and buying through catalogs.

_____

13. In retailing, computers are used to control inventory, recording sales, and to register buying trends.

_____

14. The marketing analyst is responsible for analyzing trends and to design promotional programs.

_____

15. The mail order catalog was designed to advertise the latest trends, offering discounts, and gave fashion tips.

_____

Editing Power

Directions: Edit, format, and proofread the following unarranged letter for errors; key it correctly.

Mr. Ralph Torres, 162 Marathon Avenue, Phoenix, AZ 58203-3310

Our firm is committed to offer it's customers quality merchandise. Your dissatisfaction with the sneakers, that you purchase two month ago, has come to my attention.

The style of sneaker that you choose is primarily for walking. It is my understanding that you were interested in a good running shoe. As you know sneakers are manufacture according to specifications related to the primary function of the item. The Apex brand is one of the finest on the market. it is regrettable that the sneaker is not giving you the service you expected.

We would like to accommodate you. However the sneakers shows wear so, that we cannot refund the entire cost of the item. We will give you an 50% discount on another pair of sneaker. We are confident that you will find this offer acceptable, and invite you to continue to shop with us. Sincerely yours, Marsha Kaplan, Store Manager

Writing Power

Directions: After reading the case, draft a letter.

Send a form letter to all the customers of Norton's, an upscale department store, announcing a spring sale for the month of May. The sale will be on all brand-named home items. Among the sale items will be linens, towels, dinnerware, cookware, and china. Customers using the Norton's rewards card will receive an additional 20 percent off each item. Let the customers know that this sale is in appreciation for the preferred customers who shop at the store. Letter is sent by Stephen Rice, Store Manager.

> "Leaders don't force people to follow—they invite them on a journey."
>
> —Charles S. Lauer

CHAPTER 8

Check-In with the Semicolon

CORPORATE SNAPSHOT

HILTON HOTEL CORPORATION is the most recognized name worldwide in the hospitality industry. It is known for its fine accommodations and quality service. The Hilton chain includes four-star hotels, mid-priced accommodations, extended-stay facilities, resorts, and convention properties. Names such as Waldorf-Astoria in New York City, Hampton Inns, and Homewood Suites are easily recognized by business and leisure travelers.

Hilton Hotels are committed to preserving the environment. Through its Outreach Project, the firm participates with the community in planting trees, cleaning beaches, and restoring natural resources. Within the company, the goal is to reduce, reuse, and recycle. Programs have been implemented to reduce water usage, conserve electricity, and recycle products. The hotels also encourage their guests to conserve and reuse items.

In all aspects of the business operations, diversity is a priority. The corporation has adopted diversity principles into all phases of its business, including employment, training, management, marketing, purchasing, and advertising. It is management's belief that diversity has strengthened the organization.

Source: *http://www.hiltonworldwide.com*

WHAT YOU WILL LEARN IN THIS CHAPTER

- To punctuate independent clauses not joined by a conjunction
- To punctuate independent clauses in which either clause has an internal comma
- To punctuate independent clauses in which the second clause is introduced by a conjunctive adverb
- To correct dangling and misplaced modifiers
- To punctuate a series of items that contains internal commas
- To develop a business vocabulary in the **HOSPITALITY INDUSTRY**
- To proofread and edit correspondence and reports
- To compose a letter of inquiry
- To compose a letter of response to an inquiry
- To compose a letter of complaint
- To compose an interoffice memorandum
- To compose an internal business proposal
- To compose a promotional letter
- To write an e-mail memo
- To search the Internet

EVENTS COORDINATOR: Plans, organizes, and implements public and corporate events; provides supportive services to clients; oversees the daily operations of an event or conference; works for a hotel, convention center, or government tourist agency.

Skills: college degree in marketing, hotel management, detail-oriented, work under pressure to meet deadlines, organizational skills, interpersonal.

FRONT DESK CLERK: Registers and assigns accommodations for guests, makes room reservations, transmits messages to guests, assists visitors with local activities, handles check-out process.

Skills: on-the-job training, hospitality courses at community college, interpersonal, oral communications.

CONCIERGE: Assists clients with personal services, offers information on available business services, makes reservations to restaurants and entertainment functions, facilitates travel or other hotel accommodations.

Skills: on-the-job training, hotel management courses at community college, interpersonal and people-oriented skills.

Activity A   Language Arts Recall

SEMICOLON USAGE

In chapter 5, you learned that a comma is used before a conjunction that joins two independent clauses.

Example: We have landscaped our property, **and** these illustrations will show you our new appearance.

Rule 8.1: When there is no conjunction between two independent clauses, use a semicolon.

Example: We have landscaped our property; these illustrations will show you our new appearance.

Rule 8.2: When there is a comma in both or either one of the independent clauses in a compound sentence, place a semicolon before the conjunction.

Example: To introduce a new product, you need to determine the target market; and you have to plan your marketing strategies.

Rule 8.3: When items in a series contain internal commas, use a semicolon to separate items.

Example: Popular ski resorts are located in Killington, Vermont; Aspen, Colorado; and Hunter, New York.

> **Rule 8.4:** When terms such as *for example, namely,* or *for instance* introduce a list of items, use a semicolon before the term and a comma after it.

Example: Hotel chains are expanding their consumer markets; **namely,** resorts, health spas, and convention facilities.

> **Rule 8.5:** When two independent clauses are connected by a conjunctive adverb (connecting word), use a semicolon before the conjunctive adverb and a comma after it.

Examples of conjunctive adverbs: *however, nevertheless, furthermore, otherwise, thus*

Example: Your health club membership expires this month; **however,** renewals at the discount rate will be extended for two weeks.

 Check for Understanding

Directions: Review the following sentences for differences in punctuation, then answer the questions that follow.

1. You will receive a 20 percent discount at any of our hotels, and there is no cancellation charge.

2. You will receive a 20 percent discount at any of our hotels; there is no cancellation charge.

3. You will receive a 20 percent discount at any of our hotels; furthermore, there is no cancellation charge.

4. If you will make your reservation 30 days in advance, you will receive a 20 percent discount at any of our hotels; and there is no cancellation charge.

QUESTIONS

1. Compare sentences 1 and 2. Why does the punctuation differ?

2. Why does sentence 3 have both a semicolon and a comma?

3. Why is there a semicolon instead of a comma before the conjunction "and" in sentence 4?

(Answers are given below.)

Answers to "Check for Understanding"

1. Sentence 1 has a conjunction that joins two independent clauses. In sentence 2, there is no conjunction; therefore, a semicolon is used.

2. The conjunctive adverb "furthermore" connects the two independent clauses.

3. There is a comma in the first independent clause.

Building English Power: Commas and Semicolons

Directions: Insert commas and semicolons where required and then key correctly.

1. For hotel reservations you can call your travel agent or you can dial our toll-free number. (6.5, 8.2)

2. Hotels in major cities offer complimentary features in their weekend packages for example continental breakfast health club and free parking. (8.4, 7.1)

3. Popular vacation resort areas include San Juan Puerto Rico Cancun Mexico and Hilton Head South Carolina. (8.3)

4. A great way to visit new areas is to stay at bed-and-breakfast inns they are informal and friendly. (8.1)

5. The conference room has been reserved for our June meeting plans for the luncheon are incomplete. (8.1)

6. The convention activities will be held in Scottsdale Arizona in addition local tours will be offered. (7.9, 8.5)

7. For your information a layout of the Conference Center is attached and a brochure about our facilities is enclosed. (6.5, 8.2)

8. Registration for the conference will take place in the hotel lobby and the exhibit area which is rather large will be held on the mezzanine floor. (8.2, 7.2)

9. We unfortunately cannot accommodate your group during the week of May 15 but our facilities are available the following week. (6.5, 8.2)

10. The members of the Executive Board after visiting several hotels met to discuss future convention sites but they were unable to reach a decision. (7.2, 8.2)

11. Reservations must be guaranteed with a credit card otherwise rooms are held only until 4 p.m. (8.5)

12. Our hotel chain combines quality accommodations fine service and good value moreover these hotels are highly rated by travel agents. (7.1, 8.5)

13. A block of 20 rooms has been held for your company conference you are reminded of our 48-hour cancellation policy. (8.1)

14. We offer a special weekend rate however reservations must be made two weeks in advance. (8.5)

15. Our hotels are located at the following airports: London England Milan Italy and Tokyo Japan. (8.3, 7.9)

16. We will fly to Atlanta on Thursday morning therefore you can schedule an afternoon meeting. (8.5)

17. The article appeared in the July 10 2007 issue of *Leisure Living* and it was distributed to our travel agents. (8.2, 7.8)

18. The hotel chain is expanding into the vacation market namely timesharing ownership resort living and cruises. (8.4, 7.1)

19. The new suburban trains are fast and efficient they will be popular with the commuters. (8.1)

20. The general manager will visit the hotel locations in Memphis Tennessee New Orleans Louisiana and Jacksonville Florida. (8.3)

Activity B   Building Word Power

Directions: The words that follow are commonly used in the field of hotel management. From this list, select the word or phrase that correctly completes each statement. Refer to the personal dictionary in the Appendix for the meaning of each word.

amenities   directories
complimentary   gourmet
concierge   implemented
consolidation   partition
continental breakfast   projections

_____ 1. A business trend in recent years has been the _____ of companies, which means that firms join together to eliminate duplicate departments and services.

_____ 2. Hotels offer guests many _____ so that they receive extra services such as free breakfasts and health club privileges.

_____ 3. _____ dining offers customers specialty foods often prepared with delicate sauces and seasonings.

_____ 4. Studies on future trends often present _____ based on the research findings.

_____ 5. New security measures were _____ after the accident in the lobby.

_____ 6. In many hotels, a(n) _____ copy of the local newspaper is delivered to guests.

_____ 7. The large room was divided by a(n) _____ to make two smaller rooms.

_____ 8. At airports, the traveler can find posted lists of hotels with their locations and rates on billboard-type _____.

9. Some hotels offer guests a(n) _____, which usually includes coffee and a roll.

10. The _____ assists guests in booking shows and sports events.

On the Alert

- *compound adjectives*—A one-thought modifier that describes a noun or pronoun is hyphenated.

    Example: check-in system, family-oriented clients, 24-hour access, three-night stay

- *numbers*—Numbers from one to ten are written as words except if other numbers above 10 appear in sentence.

    Example: ten meeting rooms; 10 meeting rooms hold 50 people

- *"well" words*—Use a hyphen to join the word well when used with another word to form an adjective before a noun; otherwise, it is not hyphenated.

    Examples:

    Our **well-furnished** rooms are popular. (hyphen)

    Our guest rooms are **well furnished.** (no hyphen)

Activity C   *Industry Perspectives: Hospitality Today*

Directions: Using appropriate revision marks, proofread and key the report below. The title of this report is "The Focus of Today's Hospitality Industry."

Rule Reference	
	HOSPITALITY INDUSTRY IN TODAY'S MARKETPLACE
	Today's hospitality industry is complex and diverse. It
7.1	is affected by social cultural political and economic
6.3	changes. With a global economy conditions in one part of
	the world can have positive or adverse affects
	throughout the industry. In such a changing climate, the
	companies need to be prepared for any swing in business.

6.3   As a service business the hospitality industry's emphasis is placed on the individual. Employees are in direct daily contacts with clients from multinational cultures. It is critical for the workforce to be aware of other cultures and the necessity to be respectful of

6.5   differences among people. Hotel chains therefore have made a commitment to promote diversity both within the organization and in the marketplace.

3.1   The hotels in this highly competitive field faces

8.1   well informed, consumer-oriented buyers they demand high quality at good value. One of the most important assets for this consumer-directed business is goodwill. The brand name must reflect a company image of consumer satisfaction and excellent service.

TRENDS IN THE HOTEL BUSINESS

Trends in the hotel business show an increase in leisure- and family oriented clients. To meet the demands of this class of clientele, hotels offer free

7.1   breakfast, free local telephone calls, and indoor pools

8.5   in addition room suites that accommodate families are more readily available. Very often the hotel is in the

8.1   proximity of restaurant chains or shopping malls, this convenience can be a drawing card for the hotel.

8.4   Vacation packages continue to be popular namely resorts,

7.1   health spas, and tours.

6.3   To continue to attract the business traveler hotels are adding business centers with 24-hour excess. These centers offer free usage of fax and copying equipment.

6.1

The international market is a new source of business for hotels. As the global market expands they must redirect their marketing strategies to these types of clients. To maintain goodwill, staff need retraining in

2.3, 6.5

knowing the customs and preferences of foreign visitors.

Did you find these errors?

14 commas
4 semicolons
2 subject–verb agreement
2 word usage
2 hyphenated words

Activity D **Editing Power**

Task A: Edit, format, and proofread the following unarranged letter. Use proofreaders' symbols to mark the errors, then key the letter correctly. Remember to insert paragraphs.
Address this letter to Mr. Stuart Hall, 105 Los Gatos Boulevard, Sacramento, CA 95813–3223. It is from Mr. Carlos Ramirez, Convention Manager. The subject of the letter is "Facilities for Annual Convention." (See model letter in Appendix B.)

We have recieved your inquiry about holding an annual convention at Royale Americana Hotel. We are pleased that we will be able to accomodate your group. Concerning our facilities they are the finest in the area and our convention rates are competitive. We have ten meeting rooms that hold a maximum of 50 people each and have noise proof partitions that allow for expansion. For the conference rooms the latest sound equipment is available. Our guest rooms are spacious and well furnished. The three gourmet restaurants that we have on the premises cater to different tastes however light snacks are served at our Oak Bar. We also offer our guests recreation amenities namely an indoor pool health spa and free movies. A walkway connects our hotel

to a major shopping mall with boutique shops and well

known retail stores. A computerized check-in system is

used and our guests are greeted in the lobby with

"smart-card" keys and a conference packet. A brochure

price list and layout of our facilities is enclosed for

your review. I am sure you will find Royal Americana

Hotel the ideal sight for your convention.

Challenge Task B: Edit, format, and proofread the following unarranged rough-draft memorandum for all errors; key it correctly.

Send this memorandum to all hotel managers from J. Edward Holmes, General Manager. The subject is a "Review of Fire and Emergency Procedures." Use current date.

Recent events in the passed few weeks force us to review

the ⟨fire and emergency⟩ procedures in each of our hotel. I request that you

meet with your staff to discuss these ~~fire and emergency~~

procedures currently being used. All emergency equipment

should be inspected ⟨and tested⟩ for proper functioning. Since we are

committed to having state-of-the-art systems in all of

our hotels you need to determine whether the equiptment

should be updated or replaced. If you have any

recomendations please outline them for our review and

include pertinent data to support these suggestions. At

a staff meeting discuss with the employees the need

for ⟨sensitivity and⟩ awareness of situations that may occur in the day-

to-day operations at your hotel. You may find that some

in-house training should be given to the employees so

that they will be well prepared in case of an emergency.

During these training sessions clearly define the roll

stet of ~~key~~ individuals in your organization who are

responsible for implementing emergency procedures. A written report on the suggestions and procedures should be submitted to my office by teh end of the month.

Activity E   Writing Practicum

Introduction: Misplaced Modifiers

Modifiers are words that show a relationship with other words in the sentence. To be certain the meaning is clear, modifiers must be placed close to the word(s) they modify. **Misplaced modifiers** make the meaning of a sentence unclear and can even change the meaning of a sentence because the modifiers are too far removed from word(s) to which they relate.

EXAMPLES

Misplaced:	Many of the larger hotel chains give a packet to their guests **containing a room key and local information**.
Meaning?	Does the writer mean that guests who have a room key and local information get a packet?
Correct:	Many of the larger hotel chains give to their guests a packet **containing a room key and local information**.
Misplaced:	**To reward employees for excellent service**, an incentive program has been created by management.
Meaning?	Is the incentive program rewarding the employees?
Correct:	An incentive program has been created by management **to reward employees for excellent service**.

EXERCISE 1   MISPLACED MODIFIERS

Directions: Correct the following sentences for misplaced modifiers. Change or delete inappropriate words. Use the blank lines provided.

1. The hotel visitors saw the golf course riding the jitney.

   _____

   _____

2. Mr. Smith left his briefcase in the hotel room containing his wallet, his passport, and his important papers.

   _____

   _____

3. Ms. Garcia met a relative she hadn't seen since childhood in the hotel lobby.

_____

_____

4. The new hotel was built in 1996 by Gutierrez Construction Co. and managed by Mr. Bright at a cost of $2 million.

_____

_____

5. The office clerk made a reservation for a room with double beds for Mr. and Mrs. Robert Jiminez with a private bath.

_____

_____

6. The Belle Convention Center has excellent facilities and good restaurants for the convenience of its guests with shuttle service to and from the airport.

_____

_____

7. Telephone reservations for prospective hotel guests are accepted on a space-available basis.

_____

_____

8. The dress code for dinner is formal for men with jackets.

_____

_____

9. Picture the landscaped beachfront vacation spot at the Waterfront Inn with its rocky shoreline.

_____

_____

10. We have deluxe hotels at two airports used by business travelers; namely, Chicago O'Hare and Los Angeles International.

_____

_____

11. The small hotel within walking distance of the shopping district is a charming place.

_____

_____

12. Spas for stressed individuals are ideal.

_____

_____

13. The concierge recommended a short distance from the hotel a restaurant to the guests.

_____

_____

14. The beach resort gave a complimentary night to its guests.

_____

_____

15. The resort offers its guests, nestled in the mountains, a relaxed vacation.

_____

_____

DANGLING MODIFIERS

An introductory phrase should modify the subject of the independent clause. When it does **not**, it is a **dangling modifier**.

Examples:

Incorrect: **While dancing in the nightclub,** the fire alarm went off. (The italicized phrase does not modify a word.)

Correct: **While dancing in the nightclub,** we heard the fire alarm go off.

OR

While we were dancing in the nightclub, the fire alarm went off.
(The phrase modifies subject "we.")

Incorrect: **Reading on the terrace,** the noise from the highway disturbed me.

Correct: **While I was reading on the terrace,** the noise from the highway disturbed me.
(Changed the phrase to an adverbial clause.)

EXERCISE 2 DANGLING MODIFIERS

Directions: Rewrite the following sentences by correcting any "dangling" words or phrases.

1. I saw riding the hot-air balloon a spectacular view of the countryside.

   _____

2. While traveling in the Southwest, her family was touring Europe.

   _____

3. Hidden in the basement for the past 40 years, the owner of the sculpture decided to sell it.

   _____

   _____

4. While a guest at the hotel, the president arrived in town.

   _____

5. Visiting the seaside village many times, plans were drawn for a summer cottage.

   _____

6. Raining for three days, the visitors left the national park.

   _____

7. While getting ready for the staff meeting, the report was completed.

   _____

8. After a 10-hour flight, fatigue set in.

   _____

9. With its breathtaking scenery, the people of New Zealand welcome visitors.

_____

10. Preferring the beaches to the mountains, the Carribean was our choice.

_____

EXERCISE 3 MODIFIER ERRORS

Directions: Rewrite the following paragraph that was taken from the brochure of a new hotel management school. Clear up any confusion created by misplaced modifiers. You may have to add words for clarity. For ease of checking revisions, each sentence has been numbered.

(1) Anyone who has studied at the Acme School of Hotel Management for a matter of minutes can learn to make quick decisions in the field of hotel management. (2) Located in a thriving and bustling downtown metropolitan area, our students benefit from internships at nearby hotels. (3) Well-trained and professional, our workshops and seminars are led by leaders in the hotel industry. (4) Our brochure, which includes itemized costs and course descriptions, on request will be free of charge.

EXERCISE 4 MODIFIER ERRORS

Directions: The following paragraph is taken from a travel diary. Rewrite it, clearing up confusion created by misplaced modifiers. Insert extra words where needed for clarity. For ease of checking revisions, each sentence has been numbered.

(1) Arriving at our hotel, members of a Bird Watchers' Convention had been checked into our room. (2) Apologizing, we were led to another room by the desk clerk on the first floor. (3) The dining room was crowded with people eating with binoculars and discussing the local migrating population. (4) There were other guests among the bird watchers who were hard to spot. (5) Rising early to spot the birds, we were awakened by the devotees each morning. (6) Eventually giving in, the bird-watching excursions intrigued us, and we decided to join in on the fun.

Letters of Inquiry

Letters of inquiry request information. The different types of inquiries are:

- request for appointments and reservations
- request for purchases
- general request

All types of inquiry letters should give the reader the necessary information for a quick and complete response.

Writing Pointers

LETTER OF INQUIRY

- Request specific information (for example, facilities).
- Give all dates, location, and time when requesting appointments.
- State special services that you may need.
- Use questions to obtain information.

LETTER OF RESPONSE TO AN INQUIRY

- Start with an upbeat tone.
- Consider reader a prospective customer.
- Give exact information requested.
- Highlight positive points.
- Express appreciation for the inquiry.
- Show potential benefits.
- Offer to provide further assistance.

LETTER FORMAT

- Use number or bullet format to focus on important facts or to list important points. (See Appendix B.)

Model Letter of Inquiry

Date

Ms. Cheryl Casey
Vice President Sales
Sun Hotels
1401 Biscayne Boulevard
Miami, FL 33100-8312

Dear Ms. Casey:

Positive opening related to hotel services

Many of our employees choose your hotel chain while traveling on business. They find that at each of your hotels, the service is outstanding and the staff always helpful. In addition, you offer many amenities that our people need when away from the home office.

Specific rationale and facts given for a response

Request for specific information

It is important for our personnel to be able to work effectively when they are conducting business out of town. Therefore, we are considering using your hotel chain whenever our employees are on business. Last year, our staff booked a total of five hundred nights with your chain. We are interested in working out an agreement to receive discounts on room reservations for our personnel.

Request for a reply

I would be happy to meet with you to discuss such an arrangement. Please call me at 407-932-6654.

Sincerely yours,

Marcia Keane
General Manager

ri

Date

Mr. and Mrs, Bert Latham
2205 Sunset Drive
Austin, TX 78700-3521

Dear Mr. and Mrs. Latham:

Welcome to the Bay Inn!

Upbeat tone

Our beautiful resort overlooking the Peconic River is a wonderful vacation spot. The highly rated Bay Inn has once again received the Traveler's Magazine Award for Outstanding Service.

Highlights important features

To help you plan your vacation, we have enclosed our resort brochure describing our amenities and area attractions. Within minutes from the Bay Inn, there are gourmet restaurants, boutique shops, and recreational theme parks. Our concierge is always ready to answer questions and to assist you in planning local activities.

Cordial closing

We invite you to book with us and enjoy a memorable vacation. Feel free to call us at 800-237-4100 or visit our Web site at www.bayinn.com.

Further assistance offered

Sincerely yours,

Ellen McCool
Manager

ri
Enclosure

Activity F   Writing Power: Composing Correspondence

Case Study 1: Response to a Letter of Inquiry

After reading the case, respond to the questions, on page 191 that follow, which will help you organize your ideas before beginning to compose the letter. Then draft the letter to Mr. and Mrs. Donald Russell, One Poplar Drive, Salt Lake City, UT 84119–0050.

Case: As a reservation representative at the Cameo Bay Club, a resort hotel, send a response to Mr. and Mrs. Donald Russell on their inquiry about your resort. Cameo Bay Club is a luxurious resort with many amenities. In your letter, you may want to mention some of the benefits Mr. and Mrs. Russell would enjoy as guests at the Cameo Bay Club. Remember to enclose a brochure and price list.

ORGANIZE YOUR IDEAS

1. What is the most important point you want to make to Mr. and Mrs. Russell?

_____

_____

2. What would you include in the opening sentence?

_____

_____

3. What are some of the benefits that the Cameo Bay Club offers?

_____

_____

_____

4. What would you say in the closing statement to get Mr. and Mrs. Russell to book a reservation?

_____

_____

_____

Case Study 2: Letter of Inquiry

Read the case, then answer the questions that follow. Use bullet format to highlight important points.

Case: As the administrative assistant to Ms. Betty Ryan, you are writing a letter inquiring about facilities for a three-day meeting. We plan to hold this meeting on June 5 to 7 at the Greenpoint Hotel. Find out what the rates are for a conference room. We will have approximately ten people. We also need five double guest rooms that are nonsmoking. What will these rates be? Please check the cost of a coffee cart for both the morning and afternoon. You also need to find out if an overhead projector and screen are available. Send the letter to the attention of Sales Department, Greenpoint Hotel, 22 River Road, Seattle, WA 98109–0900.

1. What is the most important point you want to make to the sales representative at the Greenpoint Hotel?

   _____

   _____

2. What would you include in the opening sentence?

   _____

   _____

3. What specific details would you include in the body of the letter?

   _____

   _____

   _____

4. What would you say in the closing statement to get an immediate response?

   _____

   _____

Case Study 3: Complaint Letter

Read the case that follows; then write a letter of complaint to Mr. Roy Foley, general manager at the hotel, 1125 Magnolia Drive, New Orleans LA 70100–2435.

Case: You were a guest at the Traveler's Hotel in New Orleans for three nights. During your stay, the air-conditioning unit was not functioning properly, which made the room uncomfortably hot. When you complained to the main desk, you were assured that it would be taken care of immediately. After repeated complaints, no service person came until the third day of your stay. The excuse was that the hotel was short of service personnel. The main desk offered no solution.

Case Study 4: Memorandum to Staff

Read the case that follows; then compose a memorandum to the hotel staff informing them of the holiday project to collect toys for needy children in the community.

Case: As the administrative assistant in the Human Resources Department, draft a memorandum to the hotel staff announcing a holiday project to collect toys for needy children in the community. The drive will run for three weeks in December, during which time the toys will be collected and displayed in the main lobby of the hotel.

The staff is being asked to adopt a slogan for the drive; therefore, try to be creative when appealing to your coworkers to contribute a toy for a worthy cause.

Send the memo from your manager, Gregg Simms.
(See the memorandum format in Appendix B.)

Challenge Level Case

Case Study 5: Promotional Letter

Read the case study; then compose the letter.

Case: Ken White, program director of Pathways to Diversity, is writing to Gerald Simpson, Vice President of Human Resources, about promoting a new employee training program for the development of positive attitudes toward cultural diversity. Mr. White points out the importance of offering such a program, especially in the hospitality industry where employees deal with diverse clientele. Employees must be good team members who respect each other and their customers. Pathways to Diversity includes in-service workshops and seminars. The workshops are case-oriented, discussing diverse customs of people in different parts of the world, sensitivity training to avoid conflict, and appreciation for other cultures.

A staff representative will gladly meet Mr. Simpson to make a formal presentation on the program. Compose a letter for Ken White. Mr. Simpson's address is Economy Lodge International, One Park Row, San Antonio, TX, 752 60-0011. Include subject line: "Pathways to Diversity Program."

Case Study 6: E-Mail Memorandum

Read the case study; then write an e-mail memo.

Case: Write an e-mail memo from Lori Reynolds to Gerald Simpson, Vice President of Human Resources (Gsimpson@Menzahotel.com). Lori Reynolds would like to meet with Gerald Simpson to discuss the possibility of starting a child day-care center on the premises of the Menza

Hotel. A growing problem at the hotel is the increase of employee tardiness and absenteeism. The loss of man hours is costly to the firm. Many of the employees work nontraditional hours. As a result, it is difficult to find qualified help to take care of children. Lori's staff in Human Resources has researched the problem and has proposed a plan. She believes that a day-care center would be beneficial to the company by increasing productivity. There would also be an improvement in employee morale if parents can visit their children during lunch or dinner breaks.

The subject of this e-mail is "Day-Care Center Proposal."

 Activity G   Report Writing Power:
Internal Business Proposal

Introduction: Business Proposals

A business proposal, which is commonly used in business and government, defines a need or problem and recommends solutions. The major purpose is to persuade readers to improve a product, to accept a service, to purchase equipment, to change procedures, or to solve a problem. A proposal can be initiated outside the organization or by internal personnel.

Writing Pointers

- Write an internal proposal in memo format.
- Know the purpose of the proposal.
- State the need or problem.
- Give details of need or problem.
- Present all necessary information to support your proposed plan.
- Provide accurate and complete data.
- Offer a persuasive solution to the need or problem.
- Discuss any staffing or budgetary needs.
- Use sideheadings to help readers focus on a particular point.
- Use tables or charts to present figures or percentages.
- Avoid first-person approach.
- Stress the benefits of the proposed plan.

Model Internal Proposal

TO: Members of the Town Council

FROM: Lois Branson, Council Representative

DATE: Current Date

Introduces
topic

SUBJECT: PROPOSAL TO ESTABLISH A VISITORS' BUREAU

Purpose
identified

With the major goal of the Town Council to form a partnership between business and local government for the purpose of enhancing the economic and social quality of life of Greenport, the opening of a Visitors' Bureau would be a first step in realizing such an undertaking.

BACKGROUND INFORMATION

Specifies details of problem

In recent years, many of the surrounding towns and cities have begun to revitalize their downtown areas and have been competing for new businesses and increased tourist trade. To remain competitive, Greenport must take steps to consider a master renewal program. To spearhead the program, we propose the establishment of a Visitors' Bureau. Such a bureau would work with the hospitality industry, local retailers, and service businesses in coordinating events, contacting media, and promoting Greenport as a "fun place to visit."

States accurate data

Presently, the hotel room occupancy in Greenport is only 65 percent. In the past year, two well-established retail businesses have closed. Over the past five years, there has been a decline in the number of business conferences and trade shows held in Greenport. This decline has had a negative effect both on the hospitality industry and on service businesses, such as restaurants, catering establishments, delivery services, auto rentals, and health facilities.

Stresses benefits of proposal

BENEFITS OF A VISITORS' BUREAU

With an increase in business and leisure trade, there would be job opportunities for local residents, added tax revenues, increased patronage at restaurants, higher hotel occupancy rates, and an overall positive outlook by our citizens. A Visitors' Bureau would have a direct impact on the economy of the city. As a government-sponsored agency, it would have the clout to meet with industry and encourage new businesses to consider Greenport. The bureau could cooperate with the hospitality industry to sponsor events, fairs, and tour packages. As a clearinghouse for tourist information, a Visitors' Bureau would be the ideal agency to advertise the benefits of working and visiting Greenport.

COST OF ESTABLISHING A VISITORS' BUREAU

Discusses costs of proposal

The cost of establishing a Visitors' Bureau would be minimal. For two years, the program could be initiated on an experimental basis. It is also recommended that local businesses and the hospitality industry help to defray some of the costs. The following are projected expenses:

Shows columnar format for clarity

Office space	Use of vacant space now available in Town Hall
Administrative expenses	One full-time administrator (salary: $25,000 per year) One part-time assistant (salary: $8 per hour)
Telephone/fax	$100 per month
Publication	In-house printing ($3,000 per year)

TASKS OF VISITORS' BUREAU

Discusses role of organization

Initially, the major goal of the administrator of the Bureau would be to make immediate contact with the hotels, motels, and local businesses in the city to form a partnership in promoting Greenport. After frank discussions of the needs of these establishments, some programs could be started. Among possible activities are the following:

Uses bulleted statements for clarity and conciseness

- Encourage specialty and craft shops to locate in downtown area.
- Sponsor a community fair.
- Offer hotel and restaurant packages to tourists.
- Advertise the amenities of Greenport.
- Publish brochures and maps on local attractions.
- Act as a liaison between government agencies and possible new industry.

RECOMMENDED ACTION

Requests action

We need to take action on this matter. Our Town Council should invite the business leaders of the community to an open meeting to receive reaction to the proposal. After this meeting, the Town Council would appoint a chairperson to work with a temporary planning committee to lay the groundwork for the formation of a Visitors' Bureau.

Case Study 1: Business Proposal

After reading the case, respond to the questions that follow to help you organize your ideas, then compose the business proposal.

Case: You are the manager of the Omni Hotel and have observed over the past three years the increase in foreign guests who stay at the hotel. Further study showed that during the current year, 40 percent of the guests were foreign visitors. They represented 25 percent of business travelers and 15 percent of tourists. A further breakdown showed that 15 percent of all guests are Hispanic; 15 percent, European; and 10 percent, Japanese.

The hotel personnel at the reception desk, department supervisors, and service employees speak English only. There is a growing problem of miscommunications between hotel staff and foreign guests. This has caused misunderstanding, poor guest perceptions, and frustrations of staff. There have been unnecessary confrontations and disagreements between clients and staff.

Because of this problem, you are submitting to Ms. Lori Battle, Vice President of Operations, a proposal that addresses the situation and offers recommendations. First, all future employees in supervisory capacities and staff in front-desk operations should be bilingual or with multicultural backgrounds.

Second, an educational program should be initiated to offer language courses in Spanish and Japanese. All personnel should have the opportunity to take a course of their choice. As a pilot program, a 12-week course with classes meeting twice a week could be offered. This course should focus on everyday language that would pertain to hotel communications. In addition, a sensitivity training seminar that discusses the different social attitudes and behaviors of foreigners should be given to all hotel employees.

Third, pamphlets that explain hotel services, amenities, and local tourist information should be available in various languages.

The benefits of the proposed plan would be greater customer satisfaction, especially among foreign guests. Better communications and understanding is the best way to appeal to former guests to return to the hotel. The Omni Hotel would continue to maintain its fine reputation among travel agencies and individual clients as a customer-friendly place to stay when visiting the city. The nominal cost of initiating an education program would be returned in increased revenues.

To run the program, you would need a conference room at the hotel, a language teacher, and textbooks. The fee for a teacher would be approximately $50 per hour for classes of 10 individuals. The cost of the textbook is $25 per book. A speaker on multicultural customs and attitudes can be brought in for about $500 per two-hour session.

Let management know that if the Omni Hotel is to remain competitive, it must meet the needs of its clients. Recommend that the program start within six months.

ORGANIZE YOUR IDEAS

To help you write an effective internal proposal, respond to the following questions below before composing it.

1. What would you use for the subject line in this proposal?

   _____

2. What facts should be included under the side heading "Background Information"?

   _____

3. What are the two major points that you would indicate under the benefits of the proposed program?

   1. _____

   2. _____

4. How would you present the key points of the plan?

   _____

5. What are the important points of the proposed plan?

   _____

6. How would you feature the cost of the program?

   _____

7. What information would you include in your answer to question 6?

   _____

8. What would you state in your final paragraph?

_____

_____

Case Study 2: Business Proposal

To remain competitive, the management of Hotel Gemini is exploring the possibility of offering weekend, three-day, or five-day promotional packages. Write a proposal in which you recommend a package deal. You may opt to offer only one of the three packages. In preparing the proposal, use your own experience, refer to newspaper ads for ideas, and be creative.

The following are some facts that may help you develop the proposal.

- Hotel Gemini is located in the center of the city near museums, sports facilities, theaters, exclusive shopping, and restaurants.

- Hotel bookings are low on weekends and during the months of January, February, and March.

- Hotel clients are 60 percent businesspeople and 40 percent tourists.

- The rate for a double room is $150 per night. A 15 percent discount is available.

- The hotel has a gym and health spa.

- Packages might include theater, concert, and sporting event reservations as well as restaurant and shopping discounts.

ORGANIZE YOUR IDEAS

In this case study, the following questions are only guidelines. Feel free to add your own creative ideas to the promotional package you decide to offer.

1. What sections will you include in the proposal?

_____

_____

2. What is the need of the proposal?

_____

_____

3. Which package do you expect to use?

_____

_____

4. What will you include in your package deal?

_____

_____

5. How will the hotel benefit from this offer?

_____

_____

Activity H *Surfing the Web*

Cross Culture Communications

Global communications mandate that we have an understanding of other people's culture and thinking. Cultural awareness and sensitivity are very important when doing business with foreign companies. Miscommunications and misunderstandings can result in costly errors to a firm.

This assignment will help you better understand other cultures. You are asked to choose a country and read about the diverse differences as compared to American customs.

■ Go to the search engine Google.

■ Key in Cross Culture Communications.

■ Scroll to Country Profiles—Doing Business Etiquette, Protocol and Language; click on the link.

■ Click on the name of a country of your choice.

Directions: Read the information on the country you have chosen. Write a one-page report; include the following:

■ role of family in the culture

■ important differences in the customs or behavior of the people

■ business meeting etiquette

■ dress etiquette

■ business negotiations

Self-Assessment
English Power

Directions: Insert commas and semicolons where needed. Key sentences correctly.

1. We drove three hours to the resort in the mountains it had a magnificent view.

2. The ship was due to arrive on Friday however it was delayed by stormy weather at sea.

3. Our tour included a side trip to Athens Greece consequently there was an additional charge of $200.

4. The new book *America's Best Bed and Breakfast Places* is a bestseller the author is appearing on the talk shows.

5. To ease the overcrowding during the rush hours they are adding commuter trains but the weekend schedule will remain the same.

6. After sightseeing for a full day we were tired yet we still went to see the play.

7. We are staying at four-star hotels in the capital cities of Lisbon Portugal Madrid Spain and Rome Italy.

8. As you know you can save money by booking hotels on the travel websites however the hotels you prefer may not be listed.

9. A relaxing vacation is river cruising moreover the food is gourmet with a local flavor.

10. Membership dues in the vacation club will increase next year however you will receive additional services.

Directions: Rewrite the following sentences by correcting any dangling and misplaced modifiers.

11. On the agenda for the meeting, club membership fees are to be discussed.

_____

12. Reading the report on outsourcing, we were surprised on its impact on the economy.

_____

13. Making reservations on the Internet, the customer received confirmation immediately.

_____

14. Reading the travel brochure, we decided to go whitewater rafting.

_____

15. Changing plane reservations, the traveler was charged a $50 fee.

_____

16. The company is planning an introductory offer for the cruise ship, Star, with a 10 percent discount.

_____

17. We stayed at the hotel which had a beautiful view with a five-star rating.

_____

18. The airline for senior citizens was offering a package tour to South America.

_____

19. The hotel air conditioning with the hot, humid weather was inadequate.

_____

20. Booking on the Internet appealed to the customer for a reduced price.

_____

Editing Power

Directions: Edit, format, and proofread the following unarranged letter. Supply missing parts and paragraphs; key it correctly. Address the letter to Mr. and Mrs. Ralph Pinzar, 101 Brook Creek Lane, Philadelphia, PA 19005-2001.

Our resort Villa Mare Beach Club in beautiful Naples Florida is an exclusive timeshare property which is a vacationer's dream. You can spend your time on the championship golf course at the white sandy beach or at the tennis court. Our resort offer a wide range of activities yet your privacy is always valued. Our program has a flexible time schedule you choose the weeks you want to vacation at the resort. Furthermore you can request a change to any one of our ten other sites. Among the choices are Palm Desert California Sedona Arizona Las Vegas Nevada or San Pedro Island Texas.

We invite you to visit us at Villa Mare Beach Club for a three night stay in our luxurious one bedroom suite. You are welcome to use all the facilities the cost to you is only $150. What better way to enjoy a short vacation and explore the possibility of owning a timeshare! A detailed brochure package will be mailed to you. We hope to hear from you shortly at 800-352-6009 or visit our website, www.villamare@aol.com. Sincerely yours, Gene Adamson, Property Manager.

Writing Power

Directions: After reading the case below, draft a letter. Use a positive tone.

Edna Farber is writing an inquiry letter to Mr. Juan Esposito, manager of the Empire Hotel, One Court Street, New York, NY 10004-2344. She received a letter stating that within two weeks she would receive a $300 refund for her two-day stay at the hotel. It is one month since the notification, and she still has not received the refund. Ms. Farber is inquiring about this delay and is asking Mr. Esposito to look into the matter.

➤ Cultural Communication

India:

- Workforce has highly trained engineers, technical personnel, and scientists.
- Outsourcing from other countries is a major business endeavor.
- Building relationships is a prerequisite to doing business.
- Present and exchange business cards, an important business practice.

See: www.executiveplanet.com

"TEAMWORK: Simply stated, it is less me and more we."

—Heartquotes.net

CHAPTER 9

Marketing Possessives

*C*ORPORATE SNAPSHOT

Ben & Jerry's. In May 1978, two childhood friends, Ben Cohen and Jerry Greenfield, opened an ice cream parlor business in a renovated gas station in Burlington, Vermont. This site was chosen in a college town without an ice cream shop. Ben & Jerry's soon became known not only for its unusual ice cream flavors but also as a community-oriented business committed to respect the environment.

The firm's mission statement focuses on the use of wholesome ingredients in its products and the improvement of the quality of life both locally and nationally. Business is only done with dairy farmers who do not give growth hormones to their cows. The company partners with nonprofit organizations to open ice cream shops that provide job training and employment opportunities to disadvantaged persons.

The company founders insist that "Business has a responsibility to give back to the community."

Source: *http://www.benjerry.com*

WHAT YOU WILL LEARN IN THIS CHAPTER

- To apply possessives correctly
- To recognize correct use of the apostrophe
- To develop a business vocabulary in **MARKETING**
- To write for clarity
- To proofread and edit correspondence and reports
- To compose bad news correspondence
- To compose promotional letters
- To compose a memorandum
- To write an e-mail
- To compose an external business proposal
- To search the Internet

Job Snapshot

MARKETING ANALYST: Develops and monitors marketing campaigns, designs promotions, plan and executes marketing programs, forecasts trends.

Skills: college degree in marketing, detailed-oriented, computer, communication.

PUBLIC RELATIONS SPECIALIST: Builds and maintains positive relationship for an organization or business with the general public, drafts press releases, prepares speeches for company executives, prepares visual presentations for community and business partnerships.

Skills: college degree in communications, internship, creative writing, outgoing personality.

DESKTOP PUBLISHER: Formats and combines text with charts and visual graphics, etc., produces publication-ready copy, performs writing and editing tasks, completes page layouts.

Skills: knowledge of electronic publishing technology, computer, detail-oriented, ability to meet deadlines.

Activity A **Language Arts Recall**

Possessive Case, Use of Apostrophe

Possessive words indicate ownership. The apostrophe is used to show possessive case.

> Example: the customer's needs (the needs of a customer)
> the manager's report (the report of the manager; the report belonging to the manager)

A *possessive* word is a *noun* and may be a person, place, or thing. It may be singular (one person, place, or thing) or plural (two or more persons, places, or things). A possessive noun is usually followed by another noun.

> Example: company's product (singular)
> consumers' lifestyles (plural)
> Ramon's store (singular)

SINGULAR AND PLURAL NOUNS

> **Rule 9.1:** Form the possessive case of a regular singular noun that does not end in "s" by adding an apostrophe plus "s" ('**s**). This rule also applies to plural nouns that do not end in "s."

> Examples: buyer's territory (s)   men's clothing (pl)
> child's toy (s)   children's toys (pl)
> manager's policy (s)

Rule 9.2: Form the possessive case of a singular noun that ends in "s" by adding only an apostrophe. However, if an additional syllable is pronounced after the "s," then add an apostrophe plus "s" ('**s**).

Examples: The Hasting**s**' plan
business'**s** boss'**s** Jones'**s**
(Note: A new syllable is formed in pronunciation; therefore, add '**s**.)

Rule 9.3: Form the possessive case of a plural noun that ends in "*s*" or *es* by adding an apostrophe after the "s."

Examples: customer**s**' businesse**s**' compani'**es**'

COMPOUND NOUNS

Rule 9.4: If the compound noun does not end in "*s*," add an apostrophe plus an "s" ('**s**) to the end of the word. Form the possessive of a compound noun that ends in "s" by adding only an apostrophe.

Examples: vice president'**s** office (office of the vice president)
vice president**s**' meeting (meeting of the vice presidents [pl.])
sister-in-law'**s** gift (gift of the sister-in-law)
sister**s**-in-law'**s** gifts (more than one sister-in-law; therefore, form the plural of the word first and then add '**s** at the end of the compound noun)

JOINT OWNERSHIP AND SEPARATE OWNERSHIP

Rule 9.5: To show joint ownership (ownership of the same thing by two or more persons), add an apostrophe plus an "s" to the last person's name. Ordinarily, if the name ends in "s," add only an apostrophe.

Examples: Carmen and Rosa'**s** boutique shop (Both women own the shop.)

Frank and Jame**s**' company (Both men own the same company.)

Rule 9.6: For individual ownerships, add an apostrophe plus an "s" after each of the names.

Example: Lisa'**s** and Mario'**s** pet shops are located in the South. (two pet shops, each separately owned)

PERSONAL PRONOUNS

Rule 9.7: Do not use apostrophes in the possessive form of personal pronouns.

Examples: his, his; her, hers; your, yours; our, ours; their, theirs; its

Note: "It's" is a contraction meaning "it is."

INDEFINITE PRONOUNS

> **Rule 9.8:** Some indefinite pronouns have regular possessive forms.

Examples: one's; other's, others'; anybody's

> **Rule 9.9** Use apostrophe for possessive abbreviations.

Examples: FDIC's, c.o.d.'s

OTHER USES OF THE APOSTROPHE: CONTRACTIONS

An **apostrophe** is used to show the omission of a letter in a word, a **contraction**. It is suggested that in formal writing, contractions be avoided. Some of the more frequently used contractions are:

can't—cannot	let's—let us
couldn't—could not	we're—we are
doesn't—does not	who's—who is
don't—do not	won't—will not
it's—it is	
isn't—is not	
hasn't—has not	
haven't—have not	

Other meanings for the apostrophe include:

- *measurements*—meaning ft. ex. 3′ (3 ft.)

- *omission of years in date*—'08 (year 2008)

Note: do not add apostrophe for *plurals* in *numbers*—in the 1990s, temperature is in the 70s.

Check for Understanding

Directions: Review the words in the columns; then answer the questions that follow.

1. **Column A**   **Column B**

   territory of a salesperson   salesperson's territory (singular possessive)

   complaint of a customer   customer's complaint

   product of a company   company's product

   Question: What similarity appears in the words in Column B?

   _____

2. **Column A**   **Column B**   **Column C**

   child   children   children's plural possessives

   man   men   men's

   alumnus   alumni   alumni's

Questions: What is the difference in the word form between Column A and Column B?

_____

How are plural possessives formed in the irregular nouns?

_____

3. Column A   **Column B**

boss   boss's (singular possessive)

Congress   Congress' **s**

business   business' **s**

Question: How is the singular possessive formed when the word ends in <u>s</u>?

_____

4. Singular   **Plural**   **Plural Possessive**

business   businesses   businesses'

buyer   buyers   buyers'

class   classes   classes'

Question: How is the plural possessive formed when the word ends in <u>s or es</u>?

_____

Building English Power: Possessives

EXERCISE 1   POSSESSIVE NOUNS

Directions: Use the apostrophe (') to form the possessive of the following nouns. The first column gives the singular phrase. Form the singular possessive and the plural possessive of each one.

Phrase	**Singular Possessive**	**Plural Possessive**
policy of the firm	firm's policy	firm's policies

1. bonus of the employee _____

2. report of the committee _____

3. representative of the company _____

4. profit of the business _____

5. gift of the mother-in-law _____

6. export policy of a country _____

7. testimony of the eyewitness _____

8. toy of the child _____

9. fee of the attorney _____

10. salary of the executive _____

EXERCISE 2   CONTRACTIONS

Directions: In the following sentences, change the contractions to the full words.

_____ **1.** It's time to review the staffing needs for next year.

_____ **2.** Since we have prior commitments, we can't attend the seminar.

_____ **3.** Who's responsible to record the minutes of the meeting?

_____ **4.** They haven't appointed the new chairperson of the committee.

_____ **5.** We won't support the tax bill in its present form.
(Note: In this sentence, its is in the possessive form.)

EXERCISE 3   REVIEW OF POSSESSIVES

Directions: Insert an apostrophe or 's where necessary. Then key each sentence.

1. The firm decision to introduce video disks in its marketing plan will affect the advertising department. (9.1, 9.7)

2. Management met to discuss the use of telemarketing to increase the businesses sales. (9.2)

3. A multimedia approach provides opportunities to meet many readers and listeners needs. (9.6)

4. David and Emily proposal to study the advantages of direct mailing was given to the marketing research group. (9.5)

5. The applicant with five years experience in fashion display was offered the department manager position. (9.3, 9.1)

6. Franchises offer an individual the opportunity to be ones own boss. (9.1)

7. The Jones and Burns companies are merging to increase their productivity. (9.2, 9.6)

8. Salespersons attitudes often determine customers decisions to purchase merchandise. (9.3)

9. Competitors prices are influencing the sales policies of the firm and its subsidiaries. (9.3, 9.7)

10. The women and men departments are being reorganized to include designer clothing. (9.1, 9.6)

11. We bought three similar CDs for our brothers-in-law birthdays. (9.4)

12. The store is offering a 10 percent discount off the manufacturer suggested retail price. (9.1)

13. Trucks are a popular means of transporting goods because merchandise can go directly from the shipper place to the customer business. (9.1)

14. The library new electronic information center will offer access to business periodicals. (9.1)

15. Although Jared has the advantage of better locations for his shops than Eric, each of Jared and Eric repair shops has a good reputation for fast and satisfactory service. (9.6)

16. It was not anyone fault that the shipment was delayed. (9.8)

17. Subscribers will be able to visit the newspaper Web site to read its editorial page. (9.1, 9.7)

18. The HMO ruling affected the patient insurance coverage. (9.1 9.9)

19. I sat in my boss seat at the men basketball game. (9.1, 9.2)

20. Lori and Donna presentation on e-marketing was well received by the firm sales staff. (9.1, 9.5)

Activity B   *Building Word Power*

Listen to customers; take action to resolve problems. Don't "pass the buck."

The words that follow are commonly used in the field of marketing. From this list, select the word or phrase that correctly completes each statement. Refer to the personal dictionary, if necessary.

commission	network marketing
entrepreneur	rebate
feasibility	standalone
franchise	subsidiary
franchisee	supplement
franchiser	telemarketing

_____ 1. Independent owners acquire a(n) _____, which is a legal contract to own and operate a well-established business according to the regulations of the parent corporation.

_____ 2. You, the _____, bought the licensing rights to own and operate the Pizza Delight store in San Diego.

_____ 3. Salespeople in the automobile industry receive a small base salary plus _____ on their total sales.

_____ 4. The term _____ often refers to computers that are not interconnected with large systems; for example, personal computers.

_____ 5. Some large corporations have _____ companies that they control.

_____ 6. Many people have a second job to _____ their income.

_____ 7. _____ is a popular trend in which sales are made over the telephone.

_____ 8. _____, also known as multilevel marketing, is a selling approach in which individuals sell products privately through contacts and recommendations.

_____ 9. The owner of the local flower shop is an example of a(n) _____ in our economic system.

_____ 10. The firm that sells franchise rights is referred to as the _____.

_____ 11. The company is studying the _____ of introducing voice-activated disks as a workable approach in selling.

_____ 12. To promote sales, the automobile manufacturer is offering a $500 _____ on new cars.

On the Alert

- *geographic locations*—should be capitalized when referring to a specific region

    Example: West Coast; Northeast *BUT* travel north; southeast of Hartford

- *ASAP*—abbreviation for "as soon as possible," a common term used when shipping merchandise

Activity C **Industry Perspectives: Marketing and Public Relations**

Directions: Using appropriate revision marks, proofread, correct, and key the report below. The title of the report is MARKETING AND PUBLIC RELATIONS FOR THIS DECADE.

Rule Reference

7.1

Marketing is the tool used to inform the public of a

product, service, organization or idea. Good marketing

strategies translate into successful selling of

merchandise or ideas. Marketing and public relations

9.1	work hand-in-hand to maintain an organization positive image in the marketplace.

PUBLIC RELATIONS

	The task of a public relations agency is to convey
7.1	credibility, develop goodwill and enhance an
9.1, 9.7	organization's or individuals image. It's work can vary
	from product publicity to corporate publications. The
3.1	clients of a public relations firm includes corporations,
	charitable organizations, government agencies, performers
7.1	and politicians. Organizations and public figures are
	very sensitive to the image that they portray in the
7.1	public eye. Identifying with a brand name, a logo or a
	jingle is important when marketing a product or service.
	Promoting a singer or electing a politician is similar to
9.1	advertising a product. It's the PR firms responsibility
	to portray a positive image of the client.

MARKETING TOOLS

6.3	In this world of technology e-mail is used to sell goods
	and services. This media is popular with retailers since
	it gives them an opportunity to build good customer
6.5	relations which translates into sales. Furthermore
	e-mail is fast and less costly compared to other means
6.6	of advertising such as television. Some firms send
9.7	e-mail newsletters to there customers as a way to keep
	in touch and promote products or services.
	One of the most powerful marketing tools for firms is
9.3	the Internet. Companies Web sites are a convenient means
	for individuals to shop. Orders can be placed from the

9.8, 9.1	comforts of ones home or at an individual leisure. The travel and hospitality industries use the Internet to offer discounts and vacation package deals.
9.3	Another marketing strategy to meet busy shoppers
3.1, 6.5	demands are the mail-order business. Once again it is a easy way to purchase an item without the hassle of
6.3	shopping at a mall. To be successful a mail-order firm must offer quality merchandise and good service. Since
6.1	the catalog is the prime means of advertising it often
7.4	resembles a fashion magazine, that is well designed displaying attractive photographs of products. This marketing strategy attracts the potential customer to order merchandise.

It is apparent that a effective marketing plan is essential to the success of a product brand or image of an individual.

Did you find these errors?

11 commas
 9 possessive
 2 subject-verb agreement
 2 word usage (a, an)

Activity D **Editing Power**

Task A: Edit, format, and proofread the following unarranged memorandum. Use proofreaders' symbols to mark the errors, then key the memorandum correctly. Remember to insert paragraphs.

Send this memorandum to the sales representatives from Eric Choy, Vice President. The subject is fax software.

Errors
- commas
- semicolon
- word usage
- possessives

Because of complaints from sales representatives we are now considering alternative procedures to eliminate time wasted while waiting to use a standalone fax machine. One suggestion is the feasibility of using fax soft ware to

transmit documents directly from the desktop PCs. Studies
show that users of this type of software have increased
there productivity sales representatives can save an hour
of each workday. You no longer waste valuable time that
could be spent contacting a perspective client. General
computer Company will present it's software at a meeting
scheduled for Monday June 19. Please clear your calendar
to attend. After this session we shall expect the sales
forces reaction before a decision is made.

Challenge Task B: Edit, format, and proofread the following rough-
draft letter for all errors, then key it correctly.

Address this letter to Mr. Brian Price, Vice President at The Clothing Loft, Inc., 1150 Dogwood Lane, Tulsa, OK 74101–7562. This letter is
from Muriel Ryan, General Manager. Use current date.

We will be happy to meet with you and your staff in
exploring the possibility of offering our ~~consultant~~
expertise to your firm. Anderson & Andersons reputation
as a consulting firm in the direct marketing field is
well-known.

(Insert A)

The direct marketing business can be a successful
profit-making venture. However the management skills in
running this type of business is crucial. We ~~would~~ *will* help
you define a plan ~~which could~~ *that will* work for you. After your
staff identifies your consumers market we will design
the most effective promotional program to built a
consumer base. We also will explore with you ~~the~~
effective ways to sell through catalogs which have shown
sales increases in the passed few years.

Insert A   Our staff representatives are specialists and we have
been in the field for more than 25 years. We will be
For your reference,

happy to forward a clients list to you. Please call my

office to arrange for a meeting date.

Activity E   *Writing Practicum*

Redundancy (Repetitive Words)

At times we tend to be wordy and use unnecessary words to express a thought. Often when speaking we use colloquial terms or repetitive words which are not as noticeable as in formal writing. The following words are examples of redundancy, which should be avoided in writing:

Unnecessary Words	Concise Writing
a total of 10 items	10 items
at the present time	now
a whole lot	a great deal
12 midnight	midnight
consensus of opinion	consensus
due to	because of, caused by
due to the fact that	since
in spite of the fact	if, even though
in regard to	about, concerning
in the event of	if
repeat again	repeat
refer back	refer
period of three days	three days
reason was because	reason was that
there is no doubt that	no doubt
have got to	must
you all	all of you
we are in receipt of	we have received
would of, should of	have

EXERCISE 1   REWRITE CONCISELY

Directions: From the previous list, select the word(s) that complete the sentence in a concise manner. Rewrite the sentence in the space provided.

1. Due to the bad weather our plane arrived at 12 midnight.

    _____

2. In a period of three days, we shipped a total of 1000 lbs. of food.

    _____

3. In the event of another bad hurricane season, we shall be forced to raise the insurance rates.

_____

4. In spite of the fact that we cut the budget by 20 percent, we still face a deficit.

_____

5. We request that you refer back to last month's statement and check the purchases.

_____

6. We are in receipt of your check to cover the $100 balance.

_____

7. Please repeat again the instructions.

_____

8. You have got to call a meeting to get a consensus of opinion on the proposed advertising campaign.

_____

EXERCISE 2   SENTENCE REWRITE FOR CLARITY

James Wolf is an independent distributor for the Indigo Vitamin Corporation. The following are the poorly written sentences from a letter he sent to prospective customers. Follow the instructions for correcting each sentence. Rewrite these sentences and put them into paragraphs. (Refer to chapters 4 and 5 for review of active voice.)

Instructions

1. Use active voice; rearrange sentence

2. Concise writing; eliminate wordiness
3. Reverse order of sentence for a clear explanation of Indigo Vitamin System
4. Use active voice; rearrange sentence
5. Use introductory phrase in sentence for clarity

6. Rearrange sentence beginning with introductory clause

7. Rearrange order; start with "you" for emphasis

1. Personal health and appearance are strongly emphasized by most people in their daily living.

2. However, schedules which are very busy don't always enable individuals to get the nutrients they need.

3. The combination of vitamins and minerals essential for a healthy body is the nutritionally balanced Indigo Vitamin System.

4. Furthermore, a weight-management program that includes daily exercise, proper diet, and stress control is encouraged by the Indigo Vitamin System.

5. I am so strongly committed to the Indigo Program after following it for one year that I have become an independent distributor of its nutritional line.

6. Please contact me if you wish to order any of the exceptional products with which you are impressed by the enclosed brochure.

7. An independent distributor could be you after using the products for a trial period.

8. Change position of nonrestrictive clause in sentence 9. Emphasize "you" 10. Begin with introductory clause	**8.** As an independent distributor, which would give you a good income, you would represent an outstanding product line. **9.** Items are discounted on all purchases you make personally. **10.** You will receive the training support needed to provide customers with superior service whether you are a beginner or a veteran salesperson.
11. Delete unnecessary words; change word order 12. Change to present tense; make stronger positive closing statement; add words as needed	**11.** Health that is good is the key to a successful and productive life. **12.** If you accepted our invitation, you can try the Indigo Vitamin Program that may change your lifestyle.

Bad News Letters

Two formats can be used to convey bad news: the direct or indirect approach.

In the **direct** approach, the reader is informed of the bad news immediately. The correspondence is courteous and direct. This approach is often used when the receiver needs to be informed in a direct, firm manner; for example, announcing a rate increase or rejecting a contract. It is not designed to promote goodwill.

The **indirect** approach delays the bad news or rejection by buffering it with a more positive opening and offering reasons for the news. The reader is then better prepared to receive the bad news. Use words that do not disturb the reader, but still deliver the message. You may also offer a suggestion or alternate action to soften the situation. This approach attempts to preserve customer goodwill; therefore, it is a more acceptable strategy.

Writing Pointers

ANNOUNCEMENT OF BAD NEWS (INDIRECT STRATEGY)

- Open with positive statement about product, service, or customer.
- Provide objective information.
- State reason for change in policy or delay in delivery.
- De-emphasize the bad news.
- Offer alternative solution.
- Ask for cooperation or understanding.
- End with a positive statement; look forward to continued business.

PROMOTIONAL LETTER

- Capture reader's attention.
- Explain the sales campaign.
- State the duration of the offer.
- Offer some incentive for quick customer response.
- Indicate contact person, if possible.

LETTER FORMAT

- For letters addressed to companies, the salutation is either "Gentlemen" or "Ladies and Gentlemen."

TO: Sales Staff

FROM: Peter Lewis
             Sales Director

DATE: (current date)

SUBJECT: Delay in the Delivery of Apex Notebook Computer

Indicates news directly and clearly to staff

Explains reasons for delay

The Apex Notebook Computer, a new addition to our line of computers that was targeted to be shipped on November 1, has been delayed. A slight modification in the design is causing this problem, and the new shipping date will be January 15. Unfortunately, we have lost the important holiday market.

Suggests alternatives

You should contact your accounts and explain the delay in shipment. Remind them that our policy is to offer the highest quality product; therefore, we had no alternative in the matter. Since this delay undoubtedly will have an adverse effect on your customers' sales, our firm is willing to offer a compromise. We shall give a 15 percent discount off the original contract price to compensate for any losses, and you may need to offer some incentives to keep the order.

Positive, upbeat closing

Demonstrates support and confidence in staff

I am confident that you will be able to rectify this matter with your clients and continue to maintain a good business relationship with them. A formal letter will be sent to our customers from this office. Feel free to call me for any further information.

ri

Date

Mr. Roy Bentley
Central Computer Store
100 Central Avenue
EL Paso, TX 79900–6375

Dear Mr. Bentley:

Opening positive statement about product
Buffers bad news
Gives reason for delay

Our firm prides itself on giving superior quality products to its customers. Unfortunately, a slight modification is required in the design of the Apex Notebook Computer, the latest addition to our line of quality computers. Therefore, our new shipping date is January 15. To maintain our firm's commitment to excellence in our products, we have no other alternative for this change in delivery date.

Demonstrates empathy	We realize the delay comes before the holiday season, which is a crucial marketing period. To compensate for any losses, we are giving you a 15 percent discount on your order. Our sales representative will contact you personally to offer any assistance that you may need.
Offers solution by compensating for loss	
Positive closing	We apologize for this inconvenience; however, we are confident that as a loyal customer you understand the situation.

Sincerely yours,

Peter Lewis
Sales Director

ri

Activity F   Writing Power: Composing Correspondence

Case Study 1: Bad News Letter

Case: Prepare a letter to your customers informing them that there will be a 10 percent price increase on all printers as of the coming year. You need to explain that we are facing higher manufacturing costs as well as shipping fees. Remind them about our quality product. Use the indirect approach.

The form letter will be signed by Ms. Emily Prince, who is the vice president of sales for Arrow Electronic Corporation, 115 Midland Drive, Toledo, OH 43600–2432.

ORGANIZE YOUR IDEAS

1. What positive statement would you make in your opening sentence?

_____

2. What type of statement would you make preceding the announcement of a price increase?

_____

3. How would you convince your customers that this price increase was the lowest amount the company could assess and still maintain a quality product?

_____

4. What would you say in the closing statement to keep the customer's loyalty?

_____

Case Study 2: Bad News Informational Letter

After reading the following case, respond to the questions which will help you organize your ideas before beginning to compose the bad news letter. Then draft the letter. Use the indirect approach.

Case: This form letter will be sent to Computer-Op customers signed by Richard Thompson, President. Computer-Op is announcing to customers that it plans to close all the branch stores on December 31 (current year). Explain that the reason for the closings is the result of higher costs in employee benefits, rent, and supplies. Management attempted to cut costs by reducing inventory and operating expenses. They did not want to decrease services to their customers. Computer-Op has always offered quality products at moderate prices. Therefore, the firm made the decision to close some of its stores. The main store at One Park Terrace will remain open and will carry a complete line of computers and office equipment.

ORGANIZE YOUR IDEAS

1. What is the most important point you want to make?

   _____

   _____

   _____

2. What would you say in the opening sentence?

   _____

   _____

   _____

3. Where in the letter would you mention the bad news of store closings?

   _____

   _____

4. What is your alternative solution?

   _____

   _____

   _____

5. What would you say in the closing statement to end on a positive tone?

_____

_____

_____

Case Study 3: Memorandum to Sales Staff

After reading the case below, draft the memorandum.

Case: Your general manager, Walter Parks, asked you to prepare a memorandum to all sales representatives. It should inform them about the annual three-day sales meeting. This is to be held at the Midway Hotel in Los Angeles, California, from April 1 to 3. The 15 percent decrease in sales this past year is a major concern of management, and it will be the major topic discussed. What are the reasons for the decline and what is the impact on the firm? The sales representatives will be expected to talk about sales figures for the year, projected income for the next year, and plans to attract new customers. They will be asked to give input on ways to improve company service and product line.

Case Study 4: Promotional Letter

Read Case Study 4, organize your ideas before composing the letter.

Case: You are working for a new car dealership in your local community, and your employer has given you the task of composing a promotional letter to be sent to prospective buyers. Discuss the line of cars you are promoting, highlight special features, and offer customers an incentive. Appeal to customers' emotions and interests. You may want to refer to automobile ads in your local newspaper for ideas.

Challenge Level Case

Case Study 5: Promotional Letter

Read the case study; then compose the letter.

Case: Mr. Larry Torres, President of Peabody Communication, Inc., is writing a promotional letter to Mr. Richard Deveroux, Vice President of Public Relations, ABC Products, One River Road, Boston, MA 02241. The letter describes the services of Peabody Communications, Inc., a marketing consultant firm specializing in media communications. This company custom-designs marketing plans for both small businesses and multinational corporations. Staff members are experienced in marketing research. They study the target market that is suited for each product line. The analysts then propose a comprehensive package of online marketing and print media to promote the brand of products. They handle the entire promotional campaign. Mr. Torres invites Richard Deveroux to discuss a successful communication program for ABC Products.

Case Study 6:   E-Mail

Draft an e-mail to José Rodriguez (jose@electronicgraphics.com) from Mark Price, Vice President of Operations, informing him that the project to install a Web page for Loral Products has been postponed. Communicate to Jose that his proposed Web site was impressive. The graphics were creative. Mark Price liked the idea of including a column on health information that would be a drawing card for customers. However, explain to José that there has been a slowdown in sales. Even with a projected net sales increase of 20 percent a year, the budget director at this time has placed a freeze on all new projects. Therefore, the plan to implement a Web site will be delayed. As soon as there is an improvement in the economy, the firm intends to initiate a Web page. Tip: Use a closing sentence that offers a positive solution.

Include your own subject line.

Activity G   Report Writing Power: External Business Proposal

An **external business proposal** is prepared by a firm or an individual outside a company. It is more formal than a memo proposal, which is prepared internally. The external business proposal contains many of the same parts of a formal report. Projected costs are generally included. It does not include an index or bibliography that is usually found in a formal report. The executive summary is optional.

A **transmittal letter** frequently accompanies the business proposal. This letter introduces the reader to the text of the proposal. Include a brief statement that describes the objective of the proposal and persuades the reader to take action. End the letter with a request for approval and offer assistance.

One of the main purposes of the proposal is to sell an idea; therefore, the text should reflect this goal.

Writing Pointers for External Business Proposals

Components of an external business proposal are presented in a formal structure.

- ■ Letter of transmittal
- ■ Cover page
- ■ Table of contents
- ■ Body
  Summary—overview of plan
  Purpose—goal of proposal
  Need or problem—discuss situation
  Benefits of proposal
  Description or design of plan
  Projected costs—be as specific as possible
- ■ Conclusions or recommendations

Model Transmittal Letter to Accompany an External Business Proposal

Current Date

Ms Debra Miranda
President and CEO
Renaissance Department Store
109 Blossom Drive
Savannah GA 31400–3522

Dear Ms. Miranda:

Subject: Proposal for the Expansion of the Renaissance Department Store's Web site

Highlights important aspects of proposal

As you requested, enclosed is the "Proposal for the Expansion of the Renaissance Department Store's Web site." The online retail business has become increasingly popular among shoppers who have limited free time. Studies show that online shopping will increase revenues for retailers.

Persuades reader to take action

Our proposal presents a positive plan that will result in added sales for Renaissance. The present Web page is inadequate to meet the needs of the consumer. Redesigning the Web page to include a personal shopper service will enable Renaissance to remain competitive in retailing.

Requests approval

With your approval, we will be able to implement the plan immediately. If you have any questions, please call me.

Sincerely yours,

Joel VanderMeer
Retail Marketing Consultant

ri

Enclosure

TITLE PAGE

PROPOSAL FOR THE EXPANSION
OF THE
RENAISSANCE DEPARTMENT STORE'S WEB SITE

Submitted to
Debra Miranda, President and CEO
Renaissance Department Store
Savannah, GA 31400–3522

Submitted by
Joel VanderMeer
Retail Marketing Consultant

Current Date

(Page Break)

CONTENTS

(Page Break)

PROPOSAL FOR THE EXPANSION
of the
RENAISSANCE DEPARTMENT STORE'S WEB SITE

SUMMARY

Gives overview
of plan

Online retail selling is a major source of revenue for department stores. The purpose of this proposal is to redesign Renaissance's Web site so that it offers expanded services. The prime focus of the Web site will be the personal shopper service.

PURPOSE

The purpose of this proposal is to expand the Renaissance Department Store's Web site so that it will enhance customer service and increase the market share of online buying. Since the Internet plays a major role in retail selling, the firm's Web page must not only attract shoppers but also appeal to repeat customers. To achieve this objective, the Web page will include a personal shopper feature.

PROBLEM

The present Web site is basically an online catalog that features the store brand clothing line, cosmetics, and accessories. Online purchasing is not a dominant part of the firm's present marketing policy. It accounts for only 10 percent of total sales.

In comparison with other retailers' Web sites, it is apparent that competitors have the advantage. They feature free gifts, periodic sales, free delivery, and customer discounts. Information on the latest fashions are frequently given on the Web sites as well as tips on budgeting. The Web page is used by competitors as an integral part of their marketing program.

BENEFITS OF THE PROPOSAL

The proposed addition of a personal shopper service to Renaissance's online shopping offers hassle-free shopping for busy people. The human contact of a personal shopper makes the shopping experience more individual. Experienced personnel who are familiar with the latest clothing line and accessories will assist the customer in making a purchase without wasting time in the store. Customers will be more satisfied with their purchases, thus lowering the percentage of returned merchandise.

Sales would increase because shopping is easier and less stressful. A more positive image of Renaissance's Department Store would develop as more unique services are provided.

DESCRIPTION OF THE PROPOSAL

When customers make online purchases, they will be referred to a personal shopper. This employee, who is a knowledgeable salesperson, will assist the shopper in making wise decisions. Each customer who uses Renaissance's Web site will have a personal profile outlining the shopper's clothing size, style, color preferences, and previous purchases.

The Web page might also include other information about merchandise; for example, suggestions on clothing accessories and wardrobe coordination, which would be of interest to shoppers, and beauty questions and answers related to cosmetics, which would appeal to women clients. This added service expands the Web site from a catalog approach to an informative fashion magazine.

Initially, the present staff of personal shoppers would handle this new service. They are the best qualified individuals to introduce the program because of their experience. Additional staff will be hired as the need arises.

PROJECTED COSTS

The proposed changes would not be costly because the present staff, with assistance from the consultant, could redesign the home page. Software development to update the Web site, however, would cost approximately $25,000.

As an incentive to increase sales, a bonus program for the personal shoppers could be introduced, such as awarding a sum of $10 for every customer who purchases more than $500 annually.

A 20 percent increase in sales is anticipated during the first year of the proposed plan. This increase may result in the hiring of new personnel at the salary of $30,000 that is presently paid to a personal shopper.

The consultant's fee to oversee the implementation of the plan will be $10,000.

CONCLUSION

Brief statement summarizing proposal

Redesigning the Web site will undoubtedly increase the number of customers who use online shopping, thus creating more business for Renaissance. The Web is a key element in enabling Renaissance to remain competitive in retail marketing.

Case Study 1: External Business Proposal

In this chapter, you are required to prepare an external business proposal. Follow the writing pointers that appear at the beginning of this chapter. You will find a model of an external business proposal in this chapter to use as a guide. The following are suggested topics you may use in developing the proposal. However, feel free to write a proposal on a topic of interest to you or with which you are familiar.

You will need to research the project to support your statements and plan of action. Be specific and provide details of the design and implementation of the plan.

SUGGESTIONS

■ Imagine that you are a consultant who has been hired by your college to submit a proposal on one of the following topics: improvement of procedures, development of curriculum, expansion of college offerings, updating equipment, or establishing programs that will reach out to the community.

■ Think of a procedure that you would like to introduce or change at your place of work. Assume that you are an outside consultant when writing the proposal.

 ## Activity H Surfing the Web

BEST CORPORATE CITIZENS

Corporations have an ethical and social responsibility to its employees, community, and shareholders. In recent times, companies have been under scrutiny related to business practices that impact on everyone.

In this assignment, you will read about some of the best corporations in the United States that are recognized as organizations with high business standards.

- Go to the Yahoo Web site.
- Key in Business Ethics' Names 100 Best Corporate Citizens.
- Click on the site.

DIRECTIONS:

- Read the information on the selected companies
- Identify the criteria for choosing the companies
- Record the names of five companies on the list
- Choose one company and go to its Web site
- Write a one-page summary on the selected company; include the following:
  - general information on the firm
  - products or services
  - outstanding features or information
  - community or social programs
  - career opportunities

Cultural Communication

Japan:

- Emphasis in the society is on harmony and group loyalty.
- Proper etiquette and protocol is important; be punctual.
- Establish one' credentials; use of business cards.
- Non-verbal communications include:
  - Use professional title.
  - Bowing is the common greeting; avoid touching.
  - Eye contact is not used.
  - Avoid idle conversation.

See www.executiveplanet.com

Self-Assessment
English Power

Directions: Insert an apostrophe, where necessary, correct word form, if needed; key each sentence.

1. Our company marketing strategy is to focus on the various foreign country social customs.

2. Smith and Travis clothing store will carry a new line of men accessories.

3. The editor-in-chief report showed increased readership in the newspaper Web site.

4. Lady handbags are very trendy among today shoppers.

5. The children tv show will promote exercising and natural foods.

6. Our major city traffic problems will be the main topic at the national mayor conference.

7. Jones article defends the economy slow growth.

8. Lets discuss the environmental issues facing the decade of the 2000.

9. NYC famous logo is "the big apple."

10. David and Lisa sports cars are popular among their friends.

Editing Power

Directions: Edit, format, and proofread the following unarranged letter. Correct possessive case and other grammatically errors. Supply missing parts and paragraphs: key it correctly. Send this letter to Pete Mulligan, president of Basis Services, Lower Hatch Street, Dublin 2, IRELAND (Note: In an address, foreign countries appear in all caps on a separate line.) This letter is written by Christine Taylor, Vice President.

My staff and I welcomed the opportunity of meeting with you in boston. We were pleased with your firm offer of contracting our billing and payroll operations to your company in Dublin. We understand that the advantage of labor cost savings are substantial. Furthermore, we will be able to transfer our employees to other areas of our organization where they are needed. We hope to benefit from these individuals talents. However we have some concerns. Our billing department services 2,000 customers

each month. We must meet our clients deadlines. We must
be assured that these bills are mailed prompt. Also, we
offer our employees a number of benefits. Each employee
salary has numerous deduction. The present software
program is tailored to calculate each individual
deductions, such as federal and state taxes, 401k with-
holdings, health premiums and stock option withdrawals.
We must be assure that the accounting procedures will be
satisfactory to meet our company requirements. I shall be
meeting with our executive staff to discuss your
proposal. You will hear from me within one week. I am
confident that we shall be able to reach a agreement.

Writing Power

Directions: After reading the case below, draft a memorandum.

Mr. Joseph Samuelson, Vice President of Marketing at Brown's Corporation, is sending a memorandum to the sales staff informing them
that the firm is opening a branch in Singapore. The office will be managed by Sam Cheng who has been in the San Francisco public relations
department for the past five years. Sam has had previous experience in
dealing with companies in Asia. His responsibility will be to develop
strategies to market Brown's best-selling seltzer brand. Samuelson is
pleased that the firm is expanding into this key Asian city.

> "No problem is insurmountable. With a little courage, teamwork,
>
> and determination, a person can overcome anything."
>
> —B. Dodge

CHAPTER 10

Traveling with Colons and Pronouns

WHAT YOU WILL LEARN IN THIS CHAPTER

- To apply correct pronoun usage
- To apply correct colon usage
- To develop a business vocabulary in **TRAVEL AND LEISURE**
- To proofread and edit correspondence and reports
- To compose a memorandum
- To compose a response to a request
- To compose a letter of notification
- To compose a claims letter
- To compose a response to a claim
- To write an e-mail
- To prepare a formal report
- To search the Internet

*C*ORPORATE SNAPSHOT

SOUTHWEST AIRLINES. In the 1970s, a dream was born. A little three-jet airline started business in the Southwest. Its mission was to offer the highest quality consumer service. Southwest Airlines pledged to provide safe, affordable, reliable, timely, and courteous air travel. The skeptics doubted that a small regional airline that offered low fares could compete against the industry giants.

Thirty years later, Southwest has proved to the industry that its way of doing business is successful. Today it is one of the largest domestic commercial airlines and has remained faithful to its pledge of commitment to the customer. The airline pioneered senior discounts and ticketless travel. The fleet of planes is new and roomy with an uplifting interior decor giving a message that flying is fun.

Southwest has become a model for many of the new discount airlines.

Source: *http://www.southwest.com/about_swa*

TRAVEL AGENT: Assesses client's travel needs and offers possible arrangements; advises customers on vacation sites, transportation, hotels, and tours, researches possible vacation packages and tourist areas.

Skills: usually works for a travel agency, specialized courses at two-year colleges, on-the-job training, personal travel experience, computer, interpersonal skills.

TRAVEL COUNSELOR OR CLERK: Plans itineraries which include points of interest, accommodations and restaurants; offers travel suggestions and best auto routes.

Skills: employed by membership organizations such as auto clubs, specialized courses, computer, knowledgeable in all sectors related to travel, interpersonal skills.

RESERVATION AGENT: Works for large hotel chains, airlines, or car rental companies; answers phone or e-mail inquiries, quotes room or transportation rates, suggests best package deals, makes reservations.

Skills: computer, knowledge of in-house reservations system, interpersonal skills.

Activity A A-1 Language Arts Recall

COLONS

Colons appear at the end of an independent clause when followed by a list or an explanation.

Rule 10.1: Place a *colon* after the phrase *as follows*, the *following*, or *as detailed below* after an independent clause that is followed by a list or an explanation.

Example: Travelers are interested in touring **the following countries:** England, Spain, and Australia.

Rule 10.2: Place a colon between the hours and minutes when the time is expressed in figures.

Example: The plane leaves at **1:30** p.m.

Rule 10.3: Use a colon after an independent clause that introduces a quotation of three or more lines.

Example: Here is the advice given to travelers in the new edition of *The Travel Guide*:

Charter flights are often the least expensive way to travel on transcontinental routes. A traveler must be willing to adjust to the limited flight schedule of the chartered airline.

> **Rule 10.4:** Place a *colon* after a salutation in business correspondence.

Example: **Dear Ms. Johnson:**

COLONS, PRONOUNS

A **pronoun** is a word that is used to replace a noun. The form of the pronoun depends on its use in the sentence (subjective, objective, possessive).

Rule 10.5:

Subjective	Objective	Possessive
subject of verb	object/indirect object of verb	shows possession
apposition to subject	object of preposition	
predicate pronoun (follows verb **to be**)	object of infinitive	
I, we	me, us	my, mine, our, ours
you	you	your, yours
he, she, it	him, her, it	his, her, hers, its
they	them	their, theirs
who, whoever	whom, whomever	whose

Examples:
Subjective
   I plan to visit Europe; but **they** will take a cruise. (subject of verb)
   The new tour guides, Marie and **he**, will meet the group at the airport. (apposition)
   It was **she** who recommended the video of the vacation resort. (predicate pronoun following verb *was*).

Objective
   We shall visit **him** at the hotel. (object of verb)
   The company offered **them** a discount on the car rental. (indirect object)
   The bank manager will speak **to him** about the vacation loan. (object of preposition)

Possessive
   Larry gave **his** e-mail address to the airline representative. (possessive)

 Check for Understanding

Directions: Read the sentences and complete the questions that follow.

1. **We** went hiking at the state park.

2. The new employees, Sue and **he**, will receive training on the new computer.

3. The most popular tour guide is **she**.

4. The tutor will read to **her**.

5. The volunteers will teach **them** water sports.

6. **Your** brochure on cruises will be mailed next week.

QUESTIONS

a. What form of the pronoun appears in sentences 1, 2, and 3?

_____

b. Give the reason why the pronoun **we** is used in sentence 1?

_____

c. Give the reason why the pronoun **he** is used in sentence 2?

_____

d. Give the reason why the pronoun **she** is used in sentence 3?

_____

e. What form of the pronoun appears in sentences 4 and 5?

_____

f. What form of the pronoun appears in sentence 6?

_____

Answers to "Check for Understanding"
a. subjective   b. subject of verb   c. apposition   d. predicate pronoun   e. objective
f. possessives

Activity A A-2 Language Arts Recall: Who, Whom, That, Which

Interrogative and **relative pronouns** are similar in nature. An **interrogative pronoun** is used in a sentence that asks a question.

Examples: who, whom, what, which, whoever

What can we do to promote tourism in the state?

Who has been appointed to head the Tourist Board?

A **relative pronoun** introduces a dependent clause within a sentence. The pronoun refers back to the noun in the independent clause. The form of the pronoun (who, whom) is determined on how it is used within its own clause.

The most frequently used relative pronouns are *who, whom, that, which*. **Who** and **whom** refer to people. **That** and **which** usually refer to things.

Note: To help you determine whether to use *who* or *whom*, re-arrange the sentence and substitute a personal pronoun for *who* or *whom*.

- To determine if the pronoun **who** should be used, substitute *I, we, he, she, or they*.

- To determine if the pronoun **whom** should be used, substitute *me, us, her, him or them*.

Rule 10.6: In a direct question, the pronoun **who** is used in the sentence. (subjective case)

Example: *Who* signed up for the trip to the Canadian Rockies?

Check: *She* signed up for the trip to the Canadian Rockies.

(S*he* is the substitute for the pronoun *who*.)

Rule 10.7: In an interrogative sentence, the pronoun **whom** is used if it appears in the objective case.

Example: **Whom** did you sign up for the trip to the Rockies?

Check: You signed **him** for the trip to the Rockies. (*Him* is the substitute for the pronoun *whom* in the objective case.)

Rule 10.8: The pronoun **who** is used as the subject of a verb in a subordinate clause.

Example: Blanca is the client **who** is planning a trip to Canada. (*Who* is the subject of the verb is *planning* in the subordinate clause. *Who* relates back to client.)

Rule 10.9: The pronoun **whom** is used as the object of a verb or a preposition. (objective case)

The pronoun **whom** is used as the object of a verb or a preposition. (objective case)

Example: The applicant **whom** I interviewed for the position was willing to work overtime.

(*Whom* is the object of the verb *interviewed* in the subordinate clause.)

Check: I interviewed **her** for the position. . . . (*Her* substitutes for pronoun *whom*.)

Example: Do you know anyone with **whom** we can discuss the use of the Internet in advertising tourism for our state?

(*Whom* is the object of the preposition *with*.)

Check: We can discuss . . . with *him* the use of the Internet. . . . (*Him* substitutes for *whom*.)

> **Rule 10.10:** *That* and *which* are relative pronouns. *Which* refers to things; *that* refers to people or things. Always use *which* when introducing a nonrestrictive non-essential clause; *that* is generally used to introduce a restrictive essential *clause*.

Examples: The European tour, **which** was scheduled for next month, was canceled. (nonrestrictive)

The island **that** he visited was beautiful. (restrictive)

> **Rule 10.11:** Use the possessive form of the pronoun when it precedes a verb ending in **ing (gerund)**.

Examples: I approve **your writing** the summary report. **Her winning** the tournament was a surprise.

 Check for Understanding

Directions: For each of the following sentences, indicate the reason for using *who* or *whom*.

1. *Who* will plan the itinerary for the club members?

   Reason: _____

2. *Whom* did you write to for a travel guide?

   Reason: _____

3. The frequent flyer mileage credits will be given to those travelers *who* accumulate 30,000 miles.

   Reason: _____

4. The tour director *whom* we have used in the past is an expert in archaeology.

   Reason: _____

5. The screening committee was to recommend three candidates from *whomever* they interviewed.

   Reason: _____

(Answers are below.)

Answers to "Check for Understanding"
1. subject of verb
2. object of preposition
3. subject of verb
4. object of verb
5. object of verb *interviewed*

Building English Power: Pronouns and Colons

EXERCISE 1   PRONOUNS (RULE 10.5)

Directions: For each of the following sentences, select the correct form of the relative pronoun in parentheses and write it in the space provided.

_____ 1. The supervisor and (he, him) have organized the city tour.

_____ 2. Travel agents use (their, theirs) Internet to search low-priced airfares.

_____ 3. Please send (they, them) a revised itinerary.

_____ 4. The firm will send a refund to (he, him).

_____ 5. They will open the main office for (we, us) to hold the meeting.

_____ 6. (He and I, Me and him) are flying business class to California.

_____ 7. The committee asked John and (she, her) to make a presentation at the conference.

_____ 8. Are (they, them) going to the annual state fair?

_____ 9. Lori gave (she and I, her and me) maps for the trip.

_____ 10. (Me and her, She and I) will meet the group at the rail station.

EXERCISE 2   WHO AND WHOM, THAT AND WHICH

Directions: For each of the sentences that follow, select the correct form of the relative pronoun in parentheses and write it in the space provided.

_____ 1. We are offering a discount to members (who, whom) renew their subscriptions before April 1. (10.8)

_____ 2. To (who, whom) do we mail the check for the tickets? (10.9)

_____ 3. It is not everyone (who, whom) can qualify for membership to the travel club. (10.8)

_____ 4. The young lady (who, whom) I met at the country inn was the editor of the travel magazine. (10.9)

_____ 5. The couple (who, whom) I met at the hotel is from your home town. (10.9)

Still Puzzled? See *Writer's One Key* Home Page: Pronouns Agreement, Reference, and Case. Click on any of the following:

How can I select the correct case? (p. 13) Which case is correct when *and* connects pronouns? (p. 14) How can I match case in appositives? (p. 15) When should I use *who, whoever, whom, and whomever*? (p. 17) (On this page, you will be able to click on to "additional exercise") What case should I use with infinitives and *ing* words? (p. 19)

Need more exercises? Go to toolbar and click on Practice and Assess; do exercises on pronouns (lines 4, 5, 6) Pronouns: Agreement, Reference, and Case Additional Exercise.

_____ 6. (Whoever, Whomever) they appoint director of the travel agency will have five assistants (who, whom) will report to him or her. (10.9, 10.8)

_____ 7. (Who, Whom) shall we consider as our representative to the trade show? (10.9)

_____ 8. The travel guide, (which, that) I purchased yesterday, has detailed city maps. (10.10)

_____ 9. We are interviewing ten applicants, many of (who, whom) have more than five years' experience (10.9)

_____ 10. The suggested itinerary for the tour will be planned by (whoever, whomever) you select. (10.9)

_____ 11. The new travel agent (who, whom) I met today came from Florida. (10.9)

_____ 12. I do not remember to (who, whom) I sent my trip map. (10.9)

_____ 13. The travel club members (who, whom) have paid their dues are entitled to a free vacation kit. (10.8)

_____ 14. He is one of the tourists (who, whom), I believe, lost his luggage at the airport. (10.8)

_____ 15. Does anyone know (who, whom) is planning to attend the travel agents' seminar? (10.8)

_____ 16. Snowboarding and skiing are two sports (that, which) are popular in Colorado. (10.10)

_____ 17. Amy and Ted (who, whom) celebrated their fiftieth anniversary left for Europe. (10.8)

_____ 18. (Whoever, Whomever) you recommend for the panel discussion will be approved by us. (10.9)

_____ 19. I will send the $100 deposit (that, which) is required to reserve the hotel room. (10.10)

_____ 20. (Whoever, Whomever) is speaking to the group will clarify the misunderstanding. (10.11)

EXERCISE 3   USE OF COLON AND OTHER PUNCTUATION

Directions: Correct and key the following sentences. Be sure to express time in figures, using a.m. or p.m.

1. We plan to leave for the airport at ten past three in the afternoon with (whoever, whomever) is available at that time. (10.2, 10.9)

2. (Who, Whom) is interested in touring the following cities London Milan and Athens? (10.6, 10.1, 7.1)

3. Tourists (who, whom) are planning to travel by car should review the following checklist get car tuneup obtain roadmaps get sightseeing information and carry emergency supplies. (10.1, 10.7, 7.1)

4. The manufacturing executives will visit their plants as follows Bangkok Thailand Jakarta Indonesia and Kobe Japan. (10.1, 8.3)

5. (Who, Whom) has scheduled the afternoon tour for one fifteen? (10.6, 10.2)

Activity B   *Building Word Power*

The words that follow are commonly used in the field of travel and leisure. From the list, select the word or phrase that correctly completes each statement. Refer to the personal dictionary, if necessary.

Wear business attire on the job; avoid trendy, informal clothes which are worn at social activities.

accrues	itinerary
budget	liaison
cost conscious	no-frills
diversified	nominal
emerging	preliminary
extended-stay hotels	priority
globalization	segments
instantaneously	strategies

_____ 1. As lifestyles change, different types of vacation packages are _____ to meet consumer demands.

_____ 2. When planning a tour, be sure to have a(n) _____ that outlines in detail your accommodations, special events, and daily activities.

_____ 3. A(n) _____ that projects spending and income is an important aspect of managing money.

_____ 4. Many people are sensitive to the price of items. These individuals are described as being _____.

_____ 5. For a(n) _____ fee, which is relatively low, you can purchase liability insurance when renting a car.

_____ 6. There are travel agencies that specialize in targeting certain _____ of the market.

_____ 7. A successful vacation requires _____ planning before taking the trip.

_____ 8. The safety of an area is a major _____ in choosing a vacation site.

_____ 9. With today's fax machines, information is transmitted _____; and the message is received within minutes.

_____ 10. There are _____ ways to travel so that people have many choices when planning a trip.

_____ 11. _____ is a term often used to describe businesses that interact and work jointly with foreign firms.

_____ 12. A(n) _____ refers to an individual who brings people and organizations together for a special purpose.

_____ 13. Under the frequent flyer plan, a traveler who _____ the prescribed minimum number of miles can receive a free ticket.

_____ 14. To improve sales, businesses develop different _____ or plans to reach their goals.

_____ 15. The new low-fare, _____ airlines do not offer passengers free meals.

_____ 16. If families prefer more homelike accommodations for a few weeks, they should consider _____.

On the Alert

- *an (indefinite article)*—used before words beginning with vowels and before silent "h."

    Examples: **An** ideal city; *an* honorable man

- *chose (verb, past tense)*—selected

    Example: They **chose** a travel package to Hawaii.

- *choose (verb, present tense)*—to select

    Example: Many Americans **choose** the national parks for their vacation.

- Hyphenate compound adjectives that precede a noun.

    Example: **toll-free** number

- Do not add a decimal point or zeros to whole-dollar amounts.

    Example: **$40**

- Use the dollar symbol ($) when expressing exact amounts of money; do not write out the word "dollars" when the dollar symbol is used.

    Example: **$50,000**

TRENDS

Activity C   *Industry Perspectives: Travel Industry*

Directions: Using appropriate revision marks, proofread and key the following report. The title is EMERGING TRENDS IN THE TRAVEL INDUSTRY.

Rule Reference

6.3

7.1

3.4

The travel industry is greatly affected by the economy and the world situation. In recent times the uncertainty of the marketplace his increased competition within the industry. Companies compete for the consumer dollar by offering discount prices, travel perks and attractive vacation packages. Everyone recognize that the Internet has become a very important means of doing business.

7.1

10.8

CHANGES IN MARKETING STRATEGIES

Marketing strategies have shifted to accommodate the globalization of our economy, the diversified population from countries worldwide and the changing demands of consumers. Airlines and hotels attempt to accomodate the client whom needs to conduct business and keep in touch with the home office. Excess to high speed computers and fax machines are readily available.

7.1

10.8

Hotels, airlines, car rental agencies and tour companies use the Internet to offer attractive programs for the leisure traveler whom may be interested in low-cost package deals.

7.7

As competition remains high, low-fare no-frills airlines have become popular among vacation travelers. Some hotel chains offer free breakfasts and snacks to

10.8	attract patrons whom prefer this type of convenience.
10.10	Extended-stay hotels now offer suites which accommodate
9.1, 10.5	families. In todays market, whomever offers the best
	deal will get the business.

CHANGES AFFECTING THE TRAVEL BUSINESS

6.3	In the travel industry the following are some of the
	emerging trends that are affecting the way business is
10.1	conducted.

7.1	• The Internet has become a favorable way of booking air fights hotel accommodations and car rentals.
	• Many airlines and hotels use the Internet to offer discount rates.
10.8	• Cruises have become popular for individuals whom prefer a sea vacation with entertainment.
3.6	• A increased number of travelers enjoys touring historic places or specific geographic areas of interest.
10.10	• The changes which are occuring in the travel industry will benefit the traveling consumer
10.8	whom wants quality service at the best price.

Did you find these errors?

10 commas
1 colon
8 pronouns
1 possessive
1 spelling
2 subject/verb agreement
1 word usage
1 article
1 typographical

Activity D *Editing Power*

Task A: Edit, format, and proofread the following unarranged form letter. Use proofreaders' symbols to mark the errors, then key it correctly.

Use "Dear Customer:" as the salutation. The letter concerns additional travel privileges, and it is written by Edward Lawson, General Manager.

Errors

- ■ pronouns
- ■ commas
- ■ spelling
- ■ subject-verb agreement
- ■ capitalization
- ■ hyphen
- ■ typographical

In an effort to offer our customers additional travel priviledges we are pleased to announce our new frequent flyer plan with Executive Airlines. Whenever you arrange a tour or make plane reservations through us you will recieve bonus air miles based on the number of miles flown and type of land arrangements. Anyone whom accrues 25,000 miles can apply for a free round trip ticket in business class to any U.S. city served by executive Airlines. If you have a minimum of 10,000 miles you will be able to get a cash discjount on one of our regularly priced tickets. This new policy offers our customers a greater insentive to take more vacations. An added amenity for our customers is our new priority reservations system. This computer4ized service allows you to call our toll free number for reservations. Our representatives are on call seven days a week for vacation information and suggested travel packages. Whomever wishes to take advantage of this frequent flyer plan need only to fill out the enclosed application form. There is no charge to enroll in the frequent flyer plan. Why not join the thousands whom have already taken advantage of this offer.

Challenge Task B: Edit, format, and proofread the following rough-draft letter for all errors; key it correctly. Address this letter to Ms. Colleen Burke, National Retailing Association, 100 Pine Street, Pittsburgh, PA 15218-7622. This letter is from Mr. Arnold Black, Director.

In response to you letter of June 15 we are pleased that you are intrested in holding the National retailing Convention in Charleston ^(South Carolina). Our staff is ready to assisat you wil arrangement from hotel availability to conference facilitites. Charleston is a ideal city to hold a convention. ~~Charleston~~ *it* is more than a historical sight.

Charleston
~~It~~ offers a variety of attraction, such as cultural events sports and fine beaches. Our staff is knowledgable in arranging ~~any~~ *all* types of meetings. We will coordinate transportation to and from *the*^airport *and*^shuttle services with in the city. Mr. Gary Scott whom is our liaison coordinator will work with your group in planning ~~all arrangements~~ *the convention.* He ~~can also~~ *will* make suggestions for ~~the most efficient ways to facilitate your meetings~~ *group tours entertainment and local events.*

Mr. Scott will contact you next week for preliminary discussion. we are delighted to have you with us and hope to work with you in the near future. *Thank your for chosing charleston as your convention city;*

Activity E   Writing Practicum

EXERCISE 1   POINTING AND LIMITING ADJECTIVES

The adjectives *this, that, these,* and *those* point out a noun and indicate whether the noun is singular or plural. The adjective must agree with the noun. To be an *adjective*, it must be *followed by a noun*; otherwise, it is a pronoun.

Examples: **This** travel agency is rated high. (adjective, singular, followed by noun)

Those maps are too old to use. (adjective, plural, followed by noun)

These are the tools I need. (pronoun, plural, followed by verb)

That is the proper route. (pronoun, singular, followed by verb)

Directions: Rewrite each of the following sentences so that the correct pointing adjective is used. You might have to change the pronoun or adjective, add an "s" to the noun, or eliminate a word.

Example:

Incorrect: Them there cruise ships leave for foreign ports daily.

Change: Change "them there" to "those."

Correct: Those cruise ships leave for foreign ports daily.

1. Those kind of package tours are inexpensive.

   _____

2. That there tour guide was well informed.

   _____

3. That cruises cater to senior citizens.

   _____

4. Please ask them there travel agents to come to the tourism convention.

   _____

   _____

5. Are these type of flights eligible for frequent flier miles?

   _____

6. This here brochure describes a very exciting trip to the Galapagos Islands.

   _____

   _____

7. I can't decide between this accommodations and that there luxury rooms.

   _____

   _____

8. That countries which are in the news because of terrorism show a sudden drop in tourism.

   _____

   _____

9. This bellhop over there took such good care of my luggage that I gave him a big tip.

_____

_____

10. These kind of side trips are available for nominal fees after you pay for the total package.

_____

_____

EXERCISE 2   WRITING SENTENCES FOR CONCISENESS AND CLARITY

Concise sentences use only words that are essential to the meaning. Avoid unnecessary words and those that are repetitious (redundant). Generally, wordiness hides ideas; conciseness promotes clarity.

Directions: Revise the following sentences to eliminate wordiness.

1. At this point in time, people prefer shorter vacations.

2. Because of the fact that there was an increase in the airfare, we decided to take an auto trip.

3. In the event of a strike, the airline will offer passengers a refund.

4. For the most part, individuals still prefer to discuss vacation plans with a travel agent.

5. As per your request, the travel brochure for Alaska has been mailed to you under separate cover.

6. We acknowledge receipt of your payment for your European vacation tour.

7. I am writing this letter to tell you that I am unable to attend the seminar next week.

8. I wish to thank you for your support and help.

9. In spite of the fact that we have sent you numerous reminders, we have not received your check for the overdue balance in the amount of $500.

10. We are sending you our check in the amount of $100 in order to reserve the meeting room.

EXERCISE 3   WRITING PARAGRAPHS FOR CONCISENESS AND CLARITY

Read the following two paragraphs to assess their conciseness and clarity. Using proofreaders' symbols, delete unnecessary words. Key each paragraph.

PARAGRAPH 1

Are you planning to take a trip and vacation this summer? Now we are happy to tell you that there is a fast, efficient way of doing this.

TripSaver™ is a new software package that will without a doubt help you plan your trip and make all arrangements. This package, believe it or not, will map out and indicate a road and route, give you suggested side trips, and give you an approximate estimated driving time. This software program will also offer overnight accommodations and lodgings for you to stay at. If you want a quick, fast, short, and scenic way to travel, use TripSaver.

PARAGRAPH 2

We are very pleased to let you know that if you join our club, Five Star Travel Club, you will receive an opportunity to take a vacation at the low price of $199 for each member of your family.

Our club, Five Star Travel Club, offers its members low and greatly reduced rates in airfare, hotel accommodations and good sleeping quarters, and car rentals. Our destinations include exotic Hawaiian resorts to cosmopolitan U.S. cities.

To be eligible for these inexpensive, cheap vacations, all you have to do is to join our club today. Fill out the enclosed card, and we will bill you for the $25 membership fee.

Writing Pointers

RESPONSE TO SPECIAL REQUEST LETTERS

- Convey to readers your thorough knowledge of the topic.
- Express enthusiasm about the topic.
- Emphasize important features.
- Enclose literature, if available.

LETTER OF NOTIFICATION TO CUSTOMER

- Notify customer of situation (changes in price, service, or policies).
- Open with positive statement if news is bad.
- Include benefits of product or service.
- Indicate reasons for changes.
- Express appreciation for past business.
- Suggest alternatives.
- Maintain goodwill.

CLAIMS LETTER

- Be specific in your claim.
- Give a clear explanation of the problem.
- Provide specifics: dates, costs, locations.
- Appeal to the firm's reputation of fairness.
- Suggest a solution or adjustment.
- Use a courteous closing.

LETTER OF RESPONSE TO CLAIMS

- In the opening sentence, deliver the good news or positive response to claim.
- In the body of the letter, explain the problem and/or give a solution.
- Use a pleasant closing; express confidence in future business relations.

Date

Mr. and Mrs. Laurence Charles
3641 Magnolia Boulevard
Savannah, GA 31400–4732

Positive
opening

Dear Mr. and Mrs. Charles:

B & E Tours has enjoyed a wonderful reputation in providing exciting tours to out-of-the-way places. Travelers who enroll in our tours have memorable experiences that remain with them forever.

Notify customer
about change

Reason for
change

We are disappointed to inform you that the High Road to the British Isles and the Treasures of the Amazon tours have been canceled this year. Interest in these two tours has been minimal, and they could not be offered at this time.

Suggest
alternative

Maintain
goodwill

We know you have expressed an interest in these two tours; therefore, we have enclosed a brochure with other possible itineraries you may find interesting. We hope to hear from you soon so that we can help plan your next exciting trip.

Sincerely yours,

Julia Fisher
Tour Coordinator

ri
Enclosure

Date

Mr. Wayne Reed
Manager
Leisure Tours, Inc.
3000 Northern Parkway
Philadelphia PA 19100-3200

Dear Mr. Reed:

Positive
opening

I have been looking forward to the spring tour to Ireland planned by your agency. It included all the places that I wished to visit.

Explanation of
problem

Last week I was informed that I need to undergo major back surgery. The recovery period will be lengthy. Therefore, I need to cancel my booking with you.

| Appeal to firm's reputation | I am aware that the deadline for a refund has passed. Your travel firm has a fine reputation in accommodating its clients. In view of this unforeseen serious situation, I hope you will consider refunding to me the full amount of $2,000. |

Solution

Courteous closing

Please let me know what action your firm will take.

Sincerely yours,

John McCulley

ri

Date

Mr. and Mrs. Stephen Vargas
10 Seneca Drive
Naples, FL 34101-5650

Dear Mr. and Mrs. Vargas:

Positive response

We, at Holiday Cruise Line, are committed to offer our clients pleasurable and carefree vacations. Your letter expressing dissatisfaction with our staff services was disconcerting.

Discuss problem

All personnel who work for our cruise line receive extensive training in all phases of cruise travel. The claim that your luggage was damaged while being delivered to your cabin is an unforeseen situation. In reviewing the ship,s records, we notice that you did not report this incident to the ship's purser. Therefore, we cannot verify that our baggage employees mishandled the luggage.

Give solution

Maintain goodwill

In the spirit of goodwill to you as a loyal client, a check for $100 is enclosed. We trust that this meets with your approval and look forward to serving you in the future.

Sincerely,

Tina Bolton, Manager
Customer Services

Ri
Enclosure

Activity F   Writing Power: Composing Correspondence

Case Study 1: Memorandum to Staff

After reading the following case, respond to the questions that follow, which will help you organize your ideas before beginning to compose the memorandum; then draft it.

Case: Linda Billings, sales manager, has been asked to notify her staff of the revised travel expense policy, which becomes effective immediately. All travel arrangements will be made through XYZ Travel Agency. Hotel accommodations must be booked at midrange rates, airline reservations cannot go beyond business rate, and meal expenses cannot exceed $50 per day. Indicate that these restrictions are being made to reduce expenses.

ORGANIZE YOUR IDEAS

1. What is the subject of the memorandum?

   _____

   _____

2. What would you include in the opening sentence?

   _____

   _____

3. What specific details would you include in the body of the memorandum?

   _____

   _____

   _____

4. What would you say in your closing statement?

   _____

   _____

Case Study 2: Letter of Response

Read the case, then answer the questions that follow.

Case: As an employee of the local Convention and Visitors Bureau, you receive a letter from Mr. and Mrs. Joseph Barnes at 14 Sterling Drive, Stamford, CT 06900–3412, requesting information about your town or city. Send a response highlighting the interesting points about your town or city. You may want to include popular sites, historical places, festivals, sports, and cultural events. You should also enclose a brochure that describes in detail the town's hotel accommodations, restaurants, tours, and transportation facilities. Warmly welcome the Barneses to your city.

ORGANIZE YOUR IDEAS

1. What is the most important point in responding to the inquiry?

   _____

   _____

2. What would you include in the opening statement?

   _____

   _____

3. What specific details would you include in the body of the letter?

   _____

   _____

   _____

4. What would you say in the closing statement to encourage tourism to your city?

   _____

   _____

Case Study 3: Form Letter of Notification

Read the case, and compose the letter.

Case: Compose a form letter to be sent to those individuals whose subscriptions to *Vacation Get-A-Way* magazine are ending. There is an increase in the subscription rate to $24 for 12 issues. The rate increase is due to higher costs of paper and production. This rate is still 50 percent lower than the newsstand price. Use the indirect approach to give the bad news of a rate increase by mentioning the positive features of the magazine. Subscribers are excited about the feature columns that are written by experts in the field. Informative articles discuss foreign vacation cities, cruise tours, and scenic worldwide places. In future issues, a food and shopping section will be included. To renew, use the postage-paid form. The salutation should read Dear _____: (the subscriber's list will be used to address individual names). Lara Hung, Managing Editor, will sign the letter.

Case Study 4: Bad News Claims Letter

Read the case; then compose the letter

Case: Write a letter on behalf of Sara Hong to the attention of Customer Services, Express Airlines, LaGuardia Airport, New York, NY 11105-3002. On May 1 (current year) Sara Hong flew from Chicago to New York City on Express Airlines flight 630. Her luggage was badly damaged. It was ripped on the side and could not be repaired. This was a new 23-inch piece of Sports brand luggage; the retail price was $125. Sara would like to be reimbursed the full amount for the damage so that she can replace this piece of luggage.

Challenge Level Case

Case Study 5: Response to a Claims Letter

Read the case; then compose the letter

Case: Compose a letter in response to Ms. Sara Hong's claim for reimbursement of $125 to cover the cost of her damaged luggage. Express Airlines will reimburse her for the damages. The company is implementing new baggage handling procedures so that such problems will not occur in the future. Mention to Ms. Hong that Express Airlines is committed to satisfy its customers. End on a positive note expressing confidence in serving her in the future. Address the letter from Ted Wells, customer advisor, to Ms. Sara Hong at 550 Thornhill Road, Great Neck, NY 11420-1834.

Case Study 6: E-Mail

Read this case; then complete the e-mail to Jim Lange.

Case: Send an e-mail to Jim Lange (jiml@yahoo.com) notifying him that the cruise tour on September 1 (current year) through the Panama Canal has been canceled because of a lack of bookings. Suggest an alternate tour of the Caribbean ports or a refund of his $500 deposit. Express the apologies of Leisure Tours, Inc.

Activity G   Report Writing Power: Formal Reports

Introduction

For an in-depth review of the research process related to preparing formal reports access *Writer's OneKey*:

■ Go to home page toolbar: Click on Research.

■ Click on Research Navigator.

■ Click on keywords: The Research Process

■ Click on keywords: Finding Sources

Formal reports usually deal with complex issues that may involve research and analysis of data. In business, it may be necessary to find the causes of a problem before solutions can be suggested. This requires an in-depth report so that management is fully informed of the situation before taking action.

Students often are required to prepare reports and term papers. Before writing a report, you need to focus on the central theme of the paper. Is the report one of persuasion, informational, inquiry, or resolution of a problem? Often you must initially collect data, analyze the information, and draw conclusions based on the facts. Depending on the topic, data can be gathered from primary or secondary sources.

The Internet has become an important tool to research information. There is such a vast amount of data online that you need to be sure that the sources are reliable. Is the information accurate, current, and credible? Also, is the author reliable and respected in the specific field of inquiry?

Plagiarism

Refer to *Writer's OneKey* on the topic of "Plagiarism."

■ Go to home page toolbar: Click on Research.

■ Click on Research Navigator.

■ Click on keywords: Understanding Plagiarism

It is easy to retrieve information and download a document on the Internet. Copying words verbatim or paraphrasing someone else's ideas as your own is **plagiarism**. This is a serious infraction in the publishing world.

It is easy to avoid this violation by using proper reference documentation as presented in the style manuals. Cite the author and source whenever you:

■ quote an individual's writing, speech

■ present facts, data, statistics

■ paraphrase someone else's ideas

This chapter will review the components of a formal report and illustrate a model of an informative report.

Steps in Writing a Report

The steps in writing a report follow:

1. Prepare an outline (a plan to help focus the purpose and structure of the report).

2. Gather data.

   Primary sources: surveys, telephone interviews, experiments
   Secondary sources: published materials, newspaper articles, government documents, online resources

3. Sort and analyze data.

4. Draft the report.

5. Rewrite if needed

6. Proofread and edit the draft copy for the final text. (Rewriting sections of a report is at times necessary).

7. Use proper documentation (preferred style manuals are the *MLA Style Manual* and *The Chicago Manual of Style*). To ensure proper format refer to a style manual.

In the MLA document style, the source immediately follows the citation in the report.

Example: In 2003, worldwide online sales were about $80 billion (U.S. Bureau of Statistics, 10).

The complete reference appears in Works Cited.

The Chicago style uses footnotes or endnotes.

Example: . . . $80 billion.[1]

The complete reference appears in a footnote or in endnotes.

Writer's OneKey

For additional information on the proper way to document a reference source using MLA, APA, or *Chicago Manual of Style* refer to *Writer's OneKey*.

■ Go to home page toolbar: Click on Research.

■ Click on Research Navigator.

■ Click on keywords: End Notes & Bibliography.

Parts of a Formal Report

There are different types of formal reports. Some reports, such as the sample in this chapter, are informative and use secondary sources to collect data. It is essential to obtain the latest data and relevant information before writing the report. There are many sources of secondary information. The library is an excellent source to examine newspapers, periodicals, government publications, and electronic databases. The Internet is another essential source to obtain current news, industry trends, and company-related data. Many companies offer helpful Web sites.

Some business and academic reports require research that uses primary sources; such as interviews, surveys, and experiments. This type of firsthand data lends support to analytical and scientific findings. Remember, one must always give credit to the source of data or a cited quotation.

Based on the type of report, sections may differ; however, most reports include the following categories:

- Title Page
- Table of Contents
- Text
  - Introduction
  - Body
  - Findings
  - Analysis
- Conclusions and Recommendations
- Endnotes, if applicable
- Appendix, if applicable
- Bibliography or Works Cited

Writing Pointers—Formal Report

- Report facts.
- Refrain from personal opinions.
- Document all quotations or statistics with footnotes, endnotes, or textnotes.
- Refer to an updated style manual to format references correctly.
- Place endnotes on a separate page at the end of the report. Key endnotes in the order in which the notation numbers appear in the text.
- Include side headings for clarity.
- Use visual aids, if necessary, to clarify information to reader.
- Prepare report free of errors in acceptable style.

Model Outline

Twenty-First Century Traveling

I. Introduction
   A. Travel in the early part of the twentieth century
   B. Recent developments in travel

II. The Years Beyond 2000
   A. Reasons for explosion in travel industry
   B. Travel expenditures
   C. Predictions for leisure travel
      1. out-of-way places
      2. eco-travel
      3. health/wellness tourism

III. Impact of Technology
   A. Online travel market
   B. Use of Internet by airlines & hotels
   C. Discount rates available to consumers

IV. Redesign of Airline Terminals
   A. Business centers
   B. Children's play facilities
   C. Shopping and restaurants
   D. Transportation

V. Conclusions

Model Formal Informational Report

Title Page

TWENTY-FIRST CENTURY TRAVELING

Submitted to
American Travel Association
New York, NY 10021–3523

Submitted by
(Your name)

Current Date

Table of Contents

Text

TWENTY-FIRST CENTURY TRAVELING

Introduction
Informational
report

What a difference a century makes! Travel in the early part of the 1900s was often an arduous task. A cross-country trip on the railroad took over a week. The means of transportation from Europe to the United States was by steamship. As air travel expanded in the mid-1900s, business and leisure trips to Europe and the Far East became more accessible.

With the new millennium, the popularity of the Internet directly impacted the travel industry. Major changes were in store for both the traveler and the provider.

THE YEARS BEYOND 2000

Side heading to
focus attention

The explosion in the travel industry has resulted from booming economies, easy access to global communications, and speed in reaching a destination.

Secondary source

Travel expenditures in the U.S. alone have increased dramatically over the past five years. There has been an increase of $100 billion in spending

Endnote notation

to $652.9 billion in 2006.[1]

Text provides
information to
support topic of
report

Travel experts predict that out-of-the-way places such as Asia and Africa will be popular with the adventurous. Travelers who are interested in the environment will be attracted to eco-travel tours that visit natural, unspoiled areas.

The health/wellness tourism trend has been growing for some time. With a revived economy, more individuals are opting to combine a wellness holiday at a spa with other activities such as cooking classes, archeological study tours, and cultural activities.

IMPACT OF TECHNOLOGY

Facts explain
side heading

The rapid growth of technology has had a dramatic influence on the travel industry. The Internet has become the major means of accessing travel information. It has not only opened a new world of unknown sites; but individuals can now book tours, purchase airline tickets, and reserve hotels

Endnote notation
documents facts

rooms at discounted rates. In 2005, approximately 32.1 million households used the Web to book leisure trips.[2]

Through the Internet, airlines and hotels have found that they have a direct distribution system to the consumer, simultaneously cutting costs and offering customers attractive package deals.

THE REDESIGN OF AIRLINE TERMINALS

Informative side heading

Presents information related to side heading

Example supports text information

In the past, accommodations and services at airports were often unpleasant. To improve this situation, airline terminals are undergoing complete renovations. The new designs allow passengers to carry on business or personal activities in a pleasant, safe environment. Business centers equipped with data ports, computers, and fax machines can be found in the larger airports.

Airline terminals are becoming family-friendly by offering play facilities for children. At Chicago O'Hare, there is an interactive climbing experience created by the Children's Museum.

Shopping is big business at airports. Brand name stores along with boutiques have opened up attractive places to shop at competitive in-town prices. For meals, passengers have choices from upscale restaurants to fast-food eateries.

Transportation to and within the airport is also undergoing major changes. Monorails connect downtown cities to airline terminals so those travelers can bypass traffic congestion.

CONCLUSION

Concluding statement of report

The travel industry will continue to face challenges during the next decade. Companies that are innovative and sensitive to the needs of the present-day savvy traveler will be the leaders of the future.

ENDNOTES

Chicago Style reference notations

1. TIA Research Travel Forecast Summary, Travel Industry Association of America, Washington, DC. Available from <http://www.tia.org/Travel/forecasts.asp.>
2. Trends 2005: Travel Web Sites, www.forrester.com/find research/results. (August 10, 2006)

Case Study: Formal Report

In this chapter, you are required to prepare a *formal report*. Follow the "Writing Pointers" and guidelines given in this chapter. Use the model of a formal informative report in this chapter as a guide. Suggested topics you may use in developing this report follow. However, feel free to write a report on a topic of interest to you or with which you are familiar.

You will need to research the project to support your statements.

SUGGESTIONS

■ Choose a locale of interest to you. This may be a city, state, country, or historic or vacation site. Research the topic and gather the data to be used in writing an informative report.

■ Compare two types of cruise lines that would include an analysis of the company, number of passengers served over a period of time, facilities, types of cruise ships, services on board the ship, types of tours, and prices. Some of the data could best be displayed in tables.

■ Write an historical report on a mode of travel (automobile, railroad, air).

Activity H   Surfing the Web

Travel Arrangements

In the corporate world, an employee of a firm may be asked to travel for business. In some firms, travel arrangements are made in-house. However, it is advantageous for an individual to be informed of the place to be visited and the available travel options to the particular destination. In this way, the employee will be able to discuss intelligently the travel plans. The Internet is an excellent source of reference for an individual to use for business or personal bookings.

In this assignment, you will use the Internet to familiarize yourself with the possibilities in planning a trip. You are to plan a one-week vacation trip. You can choose a particular city, state, or resort area. In the planning, you will obtain the following information.

- Choose the location or resort.
- Give reason for you choice.
- Describe briefly the area.
- Outline the area's attractions.
- Check flights and choose a round-trip flight.
    - airport of destination/return
    - dates of trip
    - name of airline
    - flight time
    - airfare
- Select hotel or resort.
    - name and location of hotel
    - type of room
    - amenities
    - price per night
    - hotel rating
- Choose car rental, if needed.

    Tips: There are a number of ways to research the information:

- Use search engines—Yahoo or Google.
- Check discount travel Web sites for low-priced flights, hotels, car rentals, vacation packages—Travelocity, Expedia, Cheaptickets.
- Choose Web sites of individual hotels or resorts.
- Refer to Web sites of individual airlines, car rental agencies.
- Select Web sites of individual cities to obtain area information.

Self-Assessment
English Power

Directions: In each sentence that follows, select the proper form of the pronoun and write it in the space provided.

_____ 1. Rob and (I, me) will go snorkeling with the swim club on the weekend.

_____ 2. I think that (we, our) leaving for the trip in the morning is a good idea.

_____ 3. (Who, Whom) would you recommended to monitor the ticket booth?

_____ 4. The chaperones, Claudia and (he, him) will referee at the Special Olympic games.

_____ 5. Luis Diaz (who, whom) we have hired in the past has experience organizing activities on cruise ships.

_____ 6. The hotel chain plans to expand (its, it's) services overseas.

_____ 7. The applicant (who, whom) I interviewed has been assigned to our travel department.

_____ 8. The airline ticket (that, which) was issued by South Airways is nonrefundable.

_____ 9. (Me and him, He and I) plan to skydive in the Southwest.

_____ 10. (Who, Whom) provides the transportation to the crafts fair?

Editing Power

Directions: Edit, format, and proofread the following unarranged letter. Supply missing parts and paragraphs; key it correctly. There is one sentence with a misplaced modifier that you need to correct. Address this response letter to Ms. Sara Kinsley, 10 Old Country Road, Nyack, NY 10940-2300; subject; Bus Tour to Northern New England.

We welcome for your church group your inquiry about a bus tour throughout northern New England. Our four day tour through Maine New Hampshire and Vermont is a very popular one that would interest your organization. The tour travels through the rugged coastline of Maine to the mountains of New Hampshire and on to the lakes of Vermont. Among the interesting destinations which you will visit are.

- quaint shops and galleries in Camden Maine
- breathtaking mt. Washington in New Hampshire
- scenic lake champlain in Vermont

To customize a tour we require a minimum of 20 people. We are enclosing a informative brochure it describes the trip in detail. The total cost include accommodations most meals and cultural sights to visited. You will have your own guide whom will handle all arrangements, just sit back and enjoy. We invite you to book with us. We shall be happy to plan a tour to meet your groups interests. Feel free to call for an appointment at 800-440-8000. Sincerely, Marie O'Donnell, Travel Agent

Writing Power

Directions: After reading the case, draft a letter to Mr. and Mrs. Sam Braslow, 10 Fieldstone Drive, White Plains, NY 10540-0988.

The couple had booked a one-week vacation to the Sands Point Resort in the Bahamas. The resort has been damaged in the latest tropical storm. The resort is offering to exchange the week to its other luxurious resort in Palm Desert, CA. This five-star resort offers the same amenities including an 18-hole golf course and dining in four gourmet restaurants. If the couple declines the offer, you can suggest a complete refund. However, encourage them to vacation in California. The letter is to be signed by Leon Wilhelm, General Manager.

➤ Cultural Communication

Korea:

- They generally show great respect for elders, bosses, authority figures.
- Follow protocol; saving face is important.
- Don't promote one's personal achievements.
- People are more important than profit motive.
- They need to develop trust.

See www.culturalsavvy.com

"If your failing to plan, you are planning to fail."

—Tariq Siddigue

Best Places to Live

THROUGHOUT the United States, many communities have been recognized as best places to live. What criteria determine a desirable town or city?

Among the factors to consider are job and income growth, educated workforce, affordable housing, good educational facilities, cultural and sports activities, low crime rate, community involvement, and a vision for the future. The following communities are samples that have been cited as great places to live.

Portland, Oregon: The citizens are proud of their city's transformation from a timber town to a high-tech hub. Keen city planning has given rise to an urban metropolis incorporating natural environment, transportation, parks, and neighborhoods. Within an hour of the city, its residents can be on a mountain, at the beach, in the desert, or in the natural forest.

Anchorage, Alaska: As a tent city in 1957, Anchorage exploded in the 1970s with the construction of the Trans-Alaskan Pipeline. No longer dependent on the oil industry, Anchorage has a diversified economy and a steady increase in population. Tourism has become the major industry for this city known as the "crossroads of the world." Its residents on one hand can enjoy Anchorage's cosmopolitan lifestyle; on the other, they take pleasure in the incredible natural wonders of the surrounding areas.

Sugarland Run, Virginia: This small town with a population of under 30,000 was listed as a top-ranked place to live. Sugarland Run is horse country close to the Potomac River and Washington, DC. Newcomers are attracted to the area. It has good employment opportunities, fine schools, and affordable housing options. At the same time, the population is within a short drive of the cultural life of the capital.

Sources: *http://money.cnn.com/best/bplive/portland.html*
http://money.cnn.com/2003/12/08/pf/bplive 03_east/index.htm
Frontier Airlines Magazine, May–June, 2004

CHAPTER 11

Governing Quotations

WHAT YOU WILL LEARN IN THIS CHAPTER

- To apply quotation marks correctly
- To apply correct punctuation when using quotation marks
- To develop a business vocabulary in **GOVERNMENT**
- To review prepositions and puzzling words
- To proofread correspondence and reports
- To compose community public relations letters
- To compose an informational letter
- To compose a citizen's complaint letter to a government official
- To compose a personal complaint letter to a government official
- To compose a reply to a citizen's request
- To write an e-mail memo
- To compose a news release
- To compose minutes of meetings
- To search the Internet

ASSESSOR: Values properties for tax purposes, maintains database of every parcel of real estate within a given jurisdiction, writes reports of assessed properties.

Skills: state license required, appraisal courses given at community college, computer.

COURT AND MUNICIPAL CLERKS: Perform clerical duties, prepare docket of court cases, set up agendas for town council meetings, keep fiscal records, collect municipal fees.

Skills: on-the-job training, computer, clerical skills.

COURT REPORTER: Records and transcribes verbatim legal proceedings, conversations, and meetings where the spoken word is legal proof.

Skills: state license may be required, court reporting courses at community college or business school, communication skills.

Activity A   Language Arts Recall

Quotation Marks

Quotation marks indicate a speaker's exact words. Quotation marks are used at the beginning and end of the quoted phrases or statements. This is called *direct speech*.

Note: Quotation marks are not used for a paraphrase or a restatement of a quotation, called *reported speech*. Paraphrases are often introduced by the word *that*.

Rule 11.1: Use quotation marks around a person's exact words.

Example: Mr. Eric Johnson stated, "Satellite discs will be a hot issue at the next meeting." (direct speech)

Mr. Johnson said that a discussion on satellite discs will be on the agenda next month. (paraphrase/reported speech)

Note: A comma usually precedes a quotation. The first word of the quotation is capitalized.

Rule 11.2: Use quotation marks around each segment of the quotation when there is an interruption. Note that the first word of the second segment of the quotation begins with a lowercase letter unless it is a proper noun. Set off the interrupting expression with commas.

Example: "We need to call a meeting," the town supervisor said, "to discuss zoning procedures for commercial development."

Rule 11.3: Use single quotation marks for words or titles quoted within a quotation.

Example: The guest speaker asked, "Has anyone read the pamphlet 'Tips for the Consumer'?"

Rule 11.4: Use quotation marks around the titles of complete but unpublished works, such as reports, manuscripts, programs, and booklets. However, underline or italicize the titles of complete published works, such as books, magazines, and newspapers.

Example: You will want to read the report "The New Direction of Government Spending" that appeared in *The Daily Record*.

Rule 11.5: Use quotation marks around titles that represent parts of published works, such as chapters in a book, lessons, and articles.

Example: The chapter "Community Volunteerism" that is found in the best seller *Government Update* is very informative.

PUNCTUATION AT THE END OF QUOTATION MARKS

Rule 11.6: When a sentence ends in a period or comma, the period or comma is always placed inside a quotation mark.

Examples: Mary Kelly stated, "A major construction project on our main highway will begin at the end of the year." He said, "I found the article entitled 'Controlling Floods'."

Rule 11.7: Colons and semicolons are always placed outside the quotation mark.

Example: The flyer read, "The conference fee is $59"; however, the special group rate was not mentioned.

Rule 11.8: Question marks and exclamation points are placed either inside or outside the quotation marks depending upon the meaning of the sentence.

Place a question mark or exclamation point inside the quotation marks when it applies to the sentence that is within the quotation marks.

Example: The professor asked, "Is there a difference in earnings between union and nonunion workers?"

When the question mark or exclamation point applies to the entire sentence, it goes outside the quotation mark.

Example: Did Ramon say, "The unemployment rates in the various sections of the country are decreasing"?

Check for Understanding

Directions: Change each of the following sentences from reported speech to direct speech.

Example: The town clerk announced that she will run for the office of town supervisor.

Rewrite: The town clerk announced, "I will run for the office of town supervisor."

1. The mayor stated that there must be a reduction in municipal spending.

   Rewrite: _____

   _____

2. Our county legislator asked about ways in which government spending can be reduced.

   Rewrite: _____

   _____

3. The congresswoman commented that legislation will be enacted to assist single parents.

   Rewrite: _____

   _____

4. The guest speaker wanted to know if anyone read the pamphlet on government programs.

   Rewrite: _____

   _____

5. The repaving of Main Street will begin on Monday, according to a statement by a spokesperson of the traffic department.

   Rewrite: _____

   _____

(Answers are given below.)

Answers to "Check for Understanding"

1. The mayor stated, "There must be a reduction in municipal spending."
2. Our county legislator asked, "How can government spending be reduced?"
3. The congresswoman commented, "Legislation will be enacted to assist single parents."
4. The guest speaker asked, "Did anyone read the pamphlets on government programs?"
5. "The repaving of Main Street will begin on Monday," said a spokesperson for the traffic department.

Building English Power: Quotation Marks

Directions: Insert quotation marks and other punctuation where needed.

1. The town supervisor stated If you have any suggestions on ways in which we can improve the town please contact my office. (11.1, 11.6, 6.1)

2. Property taxes will increase by 10 percent stated the controller unless we reduce spending. (11.2, 11.6)

3. Are you interested in the newly formed civic association asked my neighbor. (11.1, 11.8)

4. The judge suggested that a community service program could be an alternative means of punishment for minor offenses. (11.1)

5. The notice read as follows A public hearing to discuss housing will be held on April 15 2007 at Town Hall. (11.1, 10.1, 7.8)

6. You an active civic leader are invited to attend the meeting on Thursday stated the council president. (11.1, 11.6, 7.5, 1.4)

7. I asked Have you seen the article titled federal budget that appeared in the Tribune Herald last week. (11.1, 11.3, 11.4, 11.5, 1.6)

8. Did the community leader say We need to have greater recreation facilities for our youth. (11.8)

9. Do you plan to attend the program called multicultural interaction that is being sponsored by the Community Development Department. (11.4, 11.1)

10. As you know commented the congresswoman we are introducing legislation to give financial assistance to college students. (11.2, 11.6, 6.1)

11. My friend asked Have you read the article The Role of Government in the 1990s. (11.1, 11.3, 11.5, 11.8)

12. With the changes in traffic patterns announced the legislator we need to revise our noise ordinance. (11.2, 11.6)

13. Is it possible that the trial will be postponed asked the lawyer. (11.8)

14. In honoring the town resident Jim O'Connor the mayor said Jims dedication to his neighbors has helped our quality of life. (11.1, 11.6, 7.6, 6.3, 9.1)

15. The civic association member asked Why were the beautification plans for Main Street postponed until the spring. (11.1, 11.8)

16. The chapter Ensuring Clean Water in the newly published book *Save Our Environment* reviews a number of suggestions to improve our drinking water. (11.4, 11.5)

17. Mr. Ryan said Government works better in cooperation with its citizens. (11.1)

18. The student said I cannot find the article entitled Protecting Open Space. (11.3, 11.6)

19. The committee chairperson asked What progress has the task force made on evacuation plans for the town. (11.8)

20. The governor commented We need to abolish the state sales tax; however, some of the legislators disagreed with the suggestion. (11.7)

Activity B   Building Word Power

The words that follow are commonly used in the field of government. From this list, select the word or phrase that correctly completes each statement. Refer to the personal dictionary, if necessary.

Avoid personal business during office hours; use of cell phones and the Internet should be limited for emergencies.

alternative	legislation
assessment	legislator
budget	multicultural
bulk	municipal
commissioner	ordinance
diminished	stalled
fiscal	town council

_____ 1. The _____ year for our town ends in July; therefore, all monies allocated must be spent before that date.

_____ 2. The town is sponsoring a(n) _____ fair featuring ethnic foods and entertainment that represents the many different nationalities in our community.

_____ 3. The main function of Congress is to vote on new _____; that is, to pass proposals that become laws.

_____ 4. Legislation was _____ in the Senate because the members could not reach a majority vote; therefore, the law did not pass.

_____ 5. The rate of inflation has _____ greatly in the past decade. It has declined to its lowest point.

_____ 6. Both individuals and government need to have a(n)_____ so that they can plan for expenditures based on their income.

_____ 7. The first woman in our community elected as _____ was assigned to chair the Planning Board.

_____ 8. The _____ is made up of legislators who are elected to govern the community.

_____ 9. In this year's budget, the city must increase monies for _____ services, such as fire and police.

_____ 10. The mayor offered a(n) _____ plan to raise taxes, which differed from the town council's recommendation.

_____ 11. The new recycling program requires that newspapers be packaged in _____ rather than disposed of individually.

_____ 12. The town board passed a new _____ that prohibits loud noise after 11 p.m.

_____ 13. The traffic _____, a public official, is responsible to the mayor for the progress of the bridge construction.

_____ 14. The official value, or _____, of your house is based on the current market value.

On the Alert

■ *residents (plural noun)*—people who live in a place

Example: The town **residents** will vote on the school budget.

■ *residence (noun)*—place to live

Example: The governor of New Jersey has an official **residence** in Trenton.

■ One-thought modifiers (compound adjectives) are hyphenated before the noun.

Example: well-known public figures

■ "Cannot" is always written as one word.

■ *time of day*—When written in lowercase letters, the abbreviations "a.m." and "p.m." are separated by periods with no spacing within.

Example: 10 a.m.

■ Seasons are generally not capitalized unless they are personified.

Examples: 1. The annual convention will be held in the **spring.**

2. Each October, **Autumn** spreads its leaves across the earth, draping it in color.

TRENDS

Activity C *Industry Perspectives:*
Famous Quotations Reflecting
American Attitudes

Rule Reference

Directions: Using appropriate revision marks, proofread and key the report below. The title is FAMOUS QUOTATIONS REFLECTING AMERICAN ATTITUDES.

6.3

7.1

Over the years there have been many changes in our

society—politically socially and economically—which have

come about through changing attitudes and beliefs. The

following quotations from well known public figures

reflect their thinking during the decades from the 1940s

to the present.

THE DECADE OF THE '40S

Franklin D. Roosevelt, in the 1940s, stated in one of

11.1

his annual messages to Congress We have come to a clear

realization of the fact that true individual freedom can

11.1

not exist without economic security and independence.

THE DECADE OF THE '60S

6.3

In the 1960s Martin Luther King's famous speech at the

11.4

Lincoln Memorial, I Have a Dream, gave the following

10.1, 11.1

message I have a dream that one day this nation will

rise up and live out the true meaning of its creed, 'We

11.1

hold these truths to be self evident that all men are

created equal'

6.3, 1.7

THE DECADE OF THE '80S

9.1, 11.4

During the 1980s americans were concerned with the

countrys ability to meet global competition. Business

11.1, 9.1   Week reported The nations ability to compete is

             threatened by inadequate investment in our most

11.6   important resource: people".

             THE DECADE OF THE '90S

             During the 1990s, the country became concerned about

             protecting its environment and natural resources. Helen

1.4   hayes captured the feelings of those Americans who love

11.1   nature in one of her poetic statements. It read All

             through the long winter I dream of my garden. On the

             first warm day of spring, I dig my fingers deep into

             the soft earth. I can feel its energy, and my spirits

11.6   soar.

             THE NEW MILLENIUM

9.1   The new millenium brought to the forefront Americas

             sensitivity to the cause of diversity and women. U.S.

             Supreme Court Justice Ruth Bader Ginsberg reflected this

11.1   attitude when she said I expect to see the day when

             women serve the cause of Justice in numbers fully

             reflective of their talent. That day, when bias,

11.1   conscious or unconscious, is no longer part of the

             scene, has already dawned in some places.

             Did you find these errors?

             11 quotation marks
             9 commas
             2 hyphens
             1 spelling/typographical
             1 colon
             2 capitalization
             3 possessives
             1 underscore or italicize
             3 other punctuation

Activity D Editing Power

Task A: Edit, format, and proofread the following unarranged memorandum, then key it correctly. Remember to insert paragraphs.

Errors

- quotation marks
- commas
- capitalization
- colon
- word usage
- dates

TO: Civic Association Leaders, FROM: Paul Turner, SUBJECT: BUDGET HEARINGS. You are cordially invited to participate in the 20xx budget process. There will be two public meetings to discuss the budget proposal. The first meeting will be held on thursday October 15 20xx at 7 p.m. at City hall. The following departments will make their presentations Department of public works Parks and Recreation, and Planning and Zoning. The second meeting which will be held on november 1 at 7 pm will include the following departments police fire and purchasing. At these meetings the public will have an opportunity to ask questions on any item of the budget. In the passed people frequently have asked How come we were never informed about local issues. I firmly believe that local residents must be knowledgeable about there community. As I have stated previously public involvement is vital to effective functioning of government. I look forward to working with you as we begin to prepare for the next fiscal year.

Challenge Task B: Edit, format, and proofread the following handwritten form challenge letter for all errors; key it correctly. Remember to insert a salutation and closing.

Many of the Greenfield residents have asked about my future in government now that my fifth term on the Town Council has ended. Over the passed few years I have watched our wonderful community slide backwards. Our taxes have doubled in five years yet our community services has diminished drastically. Greenfield has lost many of its experienced and competent employees. They felt that there voice was not being heard in the decision-making process. Important community projects that can increase our tax base has been stalled in committee. Recently, a local real estate agent commented Greenfield's property values are declining. Private citizens are heard asking Where is our leadership? During the past few months I have talked with many of you who share my vision of getting Greenfield back on track. Therefore I have decided to seek the office of Town Supervisor. With your help, I am confident that we once again can make Greenfield a great place to live. Please feel free to call me at my office (992-6000).

Activity E **Writing Practicum**

Prepositions

A preposition is a word that connects a noun or pronoun to another word in a sentence. A preposition does not usually stand by itself. It makes no sense. Following are some examples of commonly used prepositions.

about	down	over
above	during	regarding
after	except	through
around	for	to
at	from	toward
before	in	under
behind	into	until
below	of	up
beside	off	with
by	on	without

among (used with three or more persons or things)
between (used with two persons or things)

A **prepositional phrase** consists of the preposition and its object (noun or pronoun).

Examples: The committee discussed the budget **during the seminar** (noun pronoun).

The city offices reopened **after the storm.**

EXERCISE 1 USING PREPOSITIONS CORRECTLY

Directions: Complete each of the following sentences by selecting the correct preposition from within the parentheses. Check the meaning of unfamiliar words in the dictionary. Write the word in the space provided.

_____ 1. The Federal Government consists (of, in) three branches: executive, legislative, and judiciary.

_____ 2. The municipal judge noticed a discrepancy (among, between) the testimony given by the police officer and the crossing guard.

_____ 3. Rural counties deal (with, in) problems different from those of urban governments.

_____ 4. The minority does not have to agree (to, over) the majority decision.

_____ 5. The small downtown businesses asked their state representatives for help to avoid relocating (off, from) their present sites.

_____ 6. A celebration in the state capitol will be held later (in, on) the week.

_____ 7. Two-thirds of the voting members must agree (to, for) the proposed amendment.

_____ 8. Senior citizens may apply for a reduced tax assessment (on, from) their property.

_____ 9. The market value of homes like yours is based on recent sales of similar properties and also is used as a guide (for, of) new assessments.

_____ 10. The special committee argued (about, with) the terms of the contract.

_____ 11. The conservative party differed (about, from) the way community funds should be used.

_____ 12. The members of the city council could not agree (between, among) themselves about the legal wording of the ordinance.

_____ 13. The Zoning Board's report was accompanied (with, by) a video presentation.

_____ 14. The merchants were angry (at, over) the Traffic Commissioner for rerouting the downtown traffic.

_____ 15. The proposal for a community center was introduced (to, during) the meeting.

LIST OF PUZZLING WORDS

Some words are troublesome to a writer. To help you avoid making some common errors in word usage, study the following words and definitions; then complete the exercise after these words.

a lot	(adjective) a great number (slang; do not use)
allot	(verb) to assign
among	(preposition) in a group of three or more
between	(preposition) each with one other (only two)
angry	(verb) to be enraged, displeasure toward someone
mad	(adjective) violent behavior, insane
anyone	(pronoun) a person
any one	(pronoun) an individual person or thing
can	(verb) used to indicate *ability* or power to do something physically or mentally
may	(verb) used to indicate *permission* or possibility to do something
capital	(noun) official seat of government, material wealth
capitol	(noun) building which houses the legislature
council	(noun) governing body
counsel	(noun or verb) to give advice
everyone	(pronoun) everybody
every one	(pronoun) each person in a group

(Note: Spell the pronouns *anyone* and *everyone* as two words when they are followed by an *of* phrase and mean *one* of a *number of* things.)

fewer	(adjective) applies to numbers and nouns that can be counted ex: fewer students, fewer buses
less	(adjective) refers to degree or amount and used with noncountable nouns ex: less money, less time
lay	(verb) to place or put something down (always takes an object)
laid	(verb) past tense of lay
lie	(verb) to rest or recline
lose	(verb) to be unable to find; to mislay
loose	(adjective) not fastened; not close together
quiet	(adjective) calm, silent
quite	(adverb) very, positively
quit	(verb) to stop or give up
irregardless	*not acceptable usage*
regardless	(adjective) showing no regard
set	(verb) to place something somewhere
sit	(verb) to be seated
some time	(adjective–noun) period of time
sometime	(adverb) an indefinite time in the future
stationary	(adjective) standing in place
stationery	(noun) writing paper

their   (pronoun) possessive form of "they"

there   (adverb) in a place; used to introduce a clause

they're   contraction for "they are"

Did (past tense of verb *do*)

Done (past participle) needs auxiliary verb with it; never use do*ne* alone

Examples: has done, have done, will be done

               Jim has *done* his homework.

Don't (contraction for *do not*) use only with I, they, we

Example: I don't know when the job will be available.

EXERCISE 2 PUZZLING WORDS

Select the word or phrase that correctly completes each statement, then write it in the space provided.

_____ **1.** We have (fewer, less) people willing to serve on the election committee.

_____ **2.** The candidate has been given (fewer, less) time to address the TV audience.

_____ **3.** You (may, can) attend the seminar if you are a member of the organization and have made advance reservations.

_____ **4.** Only people who have the financial resources (can, may) afford to be candidates for government offices.

_____ **5.** The speaker (set, sit) the microphone on the lectern.

_____ **6.** The prospective jurors will (set, sit) in the main waiting room.

_____ **7.** You may want to get insurance in case you (lose, loose) your luggage on the trip.

_____ **8.** The (lose, loose) door handle caused the car rattle.

_____ **9.** The club was to (a lot, allot) circus tickets to the underprivileged children.

_____ **10.** The suspension of the two employees was caused by a disagreement (between, among) them.

_____ **11.** The discussion on a fare increase was held (between, among) the community residents.

_____ **12.** (Some time, Sometime) next year, I plan to take a trip to Alaska.

_____ **13.** The travel agent spent (some time, sometime) with the client in planning a vacation trip to the West Coast.

_____ **14.** (They're, Their, There) planning to publish a travel newsletter in the spring.

_____ **15.** The couple planned (they're, their, there) vacation by surfing the Internet.

_____ **16.** (Any one, Anyone) who resides in this community is eligible for a reduced parking rate.

_____ **17.** (Any one, Anyone) of our state employees is eligible for a pension after 20 years of service.

_____ **18.** A token gift was given to (every one, everyone) in attendance at the festival.

_____ **19.** (Everyone, Every one) of the candidates proposed open space legislation to maintain park land.

_____ **20.** (Regardless, Irregardless) of public opinion against a property tax increase, it was approved by the assembly vote.

_____ **21.** The librarian (lay, lie) the historical document on the table for our review.

_____ **22.** After the strenuous exercise class, my friend decided to (lay, lie) down before going to dinner.

_____ **23.** We need to (quiet, quite, quit) arguing and have some (quiet, quite, quit) time to analyze the issues.

_____ 24. The monument will remain (stationary, stationery) in the plaza.

_____ 25. I ordered personalized (stationary, stationery) with my initials.

_____ 26. There are seven elected members on the town (council, counsel).

_____ 27. The therapist will (council, counsel) the family regarding the tragedy.

_____ 28. Our (capital, capitol) building in Richmond is very impressive.

_____ 29. Washington, D.C. is the (capital, capitol) of the United States.

_____ 30. The teacher was (angry, mad) at the student's behavior.

_____ 31. We (did, done) our work.

_____ 32. It (don't, doesn't) make a difference.

Writing Pointers

COMMUNITY PUBLIC RELATIONS LETTER

▪ Stress importance of the meeting/activity.

▪ Appeal to sense of community responsibility.

▪ Impress on readers that they can make a difference.

▪ End with statement that encourages reader to become involved.

▪ Maintain support of constituents by keeping them informed of legislative actions.

Model Information Public Relations Letter to County Constituents

Date

Ms. Nora Brody
177 East Main Street
Irvington, NY 10524-3213

Dear Ms. Brody:

Demonstrates interest in community welfare

The recent survey completed by the residents of Greenburgh County revealed broad support for the preservation of open space in our communities. A clear mandate was expressed to end overdevelopment of shopping malls and large office parks in the towns.

Explains action to be taken

At the county and state levels, I intend to use the findings of the survey to enact immediate legislation to prevent the depletion of open space. Local government needs to reexamine its policies and practices with regard to zoning for building, traffic patterns, and quality of life. At the next legislative

	meeting, I will request state funds to secure parcels of land that will be used for parkland. This initiative will ensure open spaces to protect the environment for future generations.
Appeals to sense of community cooperation	
Offers to provide further assistance	As we work together, I am confident that we shall maintain the quality of life that has made Greenburgh County a desirable place to live. If you have any further concerns, do not hesitate to contact my local office at 479–3000.

Sincerely yours,

Richard L. Pearce
Assemblyman

rlc

 ## *Activity F* *Writing Power: Composing Correspondence*

Case Study 1: Informational Letter to Community

After reading the following case, respond to the questions in "Organize Your Ideas" before beginning to compose this letter. Then draft the letter.

Case: A cover form letter from Blanche Mitchell, town clerk, is to be mailed to the community leaders informing them that the revised color-coded Sanitation Schedule is enclosed. This schedule includes the following information:

■ pickup days for refuse

■ pickup days for recycling of bottles and plastics

■ listing of telephone numbers of town offices

Sanitation schedules are available in bulk at Town Hall to civic associations for distribution in their neighborhoods. In the letter, ask for the community's cooperation in maintaining a clean, healthy environment.

ORGANIZE YOUR IDEAS

1. What is the subject of this letter?

_____

2. What would you include in the opening sentence?

_____

_____

3. What specific details would you include in the body of the letter?

_____

_____

_____

4. What would you say in your closing statement?

_____

_____

Case Study 2: Public Relations Informational Letter to Town Residents

After reading the following case, respond to the questions in "Organize Your Ideas," then draft the letter.

Case: Howard Wallace, town supervisor, asked that you send out a form letter to the residents of Smithport informing them that there will be a public hearing on the needs of senior citizens. The letter will include the following information:

Agenda topics:

■ updating present programs

■ future services

■ assessment of recreational facilities

Location: Community Center
Date: Monday, May 5
Time: 7 p.m.
Transportation to the Community Center: Call 592–2916

ORGANIZE YOUR IDEAS

1. What is the main topic of the letter?

_____

2. What would you include in the opening sentence?

_____

_____

3. What specific details would you include in the body of the letter?

_____

_____

_____

4. What would you say in your closing statement?

_____

_____

Case Study 3: Informational Letter

Read the case below, then draft the letter.

Case: The town supervisor, Paul Murphy, has asked you to write a cover letter that will be attached to the proposed annual town budget. In the letter, explain that the 2.5 percent increase in taxes is the lowest in the past five years. Also, mention that there has been an increase in police and recreational services. Invite the readers to attend the town board meeting on the budget to be held on the first Monday of next month. (Insert the correct date of the meeting.) Close the letter by asking the town residents to support the proposed budget. Address the letter to the "Town Residents."

Case Study 4: Public Relations Letter to Concerned Residents

Read the case below, then draft the letter.

Case: In the city of Oakridge, the residents have voiced their concern about the lack of after-school educational and recreational services for school-age children. They fear this will result in an increase in the social problems that will arise in the community. To prevent this from occurring and to keep the community safe, one proposal suggests offering reading courses, gymnastics, and team sports at the local school from 3 to 5 p.m. weekdays.

Pauline Slater, chairperson of the City Council, is writing to the residents inviting them to an informational meeting on Tuesday, April 10, (current year), at City Hall to discuss the issue, consider possible solutions, and raise funds for such a program. The residents are being asked for their input in designing a plan. Draft a letter from Ms. Slater.

Challenge Level Case

Case Study 5: Response to Citizens' Request

Read the case study; then compose the letter.

Case: Anna Lorenzo, town supervisor, is responding to a request from the residents on Cooper Street. They want a traffic light to be installed at the intersection of Cooper Street and Brook Avenue. Numerous accidents have occurred at the site in the past year. Motorists do not adhere to the stop signs and race through the intersection. The latest casualty occurred a week ago when a 12-year-old youngster was severely hurt and remains in serious condition.

Ms. Lorenzo acknowledges the seriousness of the situation. However, it is a more complex problem. Traffic lights are under the jurisdiction of the state, and a study will need to be conducted by traffic engineers. Based on their findings, a decision will be made.

Ms. Lorenzo will petition the state to install a traffic light. In the meantime, she will request an additional police patrol be assigned to the area.

Prepare a form letter for Ms. Lorenzo. Use the salutation "Dear Resident:"

Case Study 6: E-Mail Memorandum

Read the case study; then compose the e-mail memo.

Case: Sophia Cruz, town supervisor of Pomona, is writing this e-mail to the Town Board members informing them of the meeting she held with the merchants on Main Street with regard to the revitalization plan for the downtown area. Ms. Cruz received an excellent response from the merchants with the first phase of the plan that will involve the resurfacing of the sidewalks with bricks and planting of trees. The group also agreed to redo the facades of their stores so that there would be a uniform hometown feeling. The town will pay one-half of the cost. This phase will start next summer after a design is approved. The next meeting will be held at the start of the resurfacing.

Prepare an e-mail memo. The list of Town Board members who are to receive the memo will be taken from the address book. Leave the "To" line blank.

Activity G *Report Writing Power: News Release*

A news release is a document sent to the media (newspaper, magazine, radio, and TV) to convey timely news that is of interest to readers. The content of a news release may include an introduction of new products or services, organizational or personnel changes, staff accomplishments, and firm's financial status.

A news release is an excellent way to build good public relations.

Writing Pointers for News Releases

- ■ Include a headline to identify story.
- ■ Give most important message immediately.
- ■ Be brief, specific, and to the point.
- ■ Avoid any marketing or advertising pitch.
- ■ Double space document.
- ■ Indicate the time when news can be released (For Immediate Release).
- ■ Include contact person, name, and telephone number.
- ■ End news release with # # # centered on line.

Model News Release

ALBERTVILLE TOWN BOARD
20 Fairview Road
Albertville, MD 21400–2100

Special instructions

Contact person

For Immediate Release
From: Emanuel Delgado
Director, Public Relations
(410) 832–6021

NEWS RELEASE

Title highlights topic

PURCHASE OF THE GREENWALL ESTATE

Dateline

States most important fact

Specific information

ALBERTVILLE, MD, December 10, 20xx. James Peterson, Town Supervisor, announced last night at the Town Board meeting that an agreement had been reached to purchase the Greenwall Estate for $10 million. The purchase of the property is a victory for the town and the environmentalists who feared that the beautiful park-like site would be sold to developers. The purchase was made possible through private fund-raising.

Quotation projects a personal touch

Positive closing

In keeping with the open-space policy of the town, Supervisor Peterson said, "We are committed to maintaining the quality of life for all families of Albertville. The purchase of the Greenwall Estate will assure our citizens the enjoyment of a new park for many years."

Symbol indicates end of release

# # #

Case Study 1: News Release

After reading the case, respond to the questions in "Organize Your Ideas," then compose the news release.

Case: As the assistant to the Commissioner of Environmental Services, compose a news release announcing that the town of Hartsview, New York, will adopt a recycling program for the community. Explain that such a program is essential to maintain the quality of life by reducing pollution.

The pickup schedule will be every first and third Tuesday of the month. Special containers will be distributed to each household. Include a phone number for further information.

This announcement is being made for immediate release by Larry McGuire, Commissioner of Environmental Services.

ORGANIZE YOUR IDEAS

To help you write an effective news release, respond to the following questions before composing it.

1. What title would you give your news release?

   _____

2. What information must appear in the news release?

   _____

3. Which of the following approaches would give a human interest appeal to the news release?
   a. Quote from the Commissioner of Environmental Services
   b. Lecture readers on the importance of recycling
   c. Present news on recycling from neighborhood communities

   _____

4. What other statement would you include in your closing paragraph?
   a. Citizens' reaction to recycling plan
   b. Appeal to community for cooperation
   c. End news release after explaining project

   _____

INTRODUCTION: MINUTES OF MEETING

Minutes of meetings are the written record of the proceedings of a meeting. Accurate recording is essential because minutes serve as a permanent record of decisions that were made and actions taken. Individuals who did not attend the meeting use the minutes as a resource to become familiar with the business that occurred.

Formats for producing minutes vary. However, they are uniform in requiring all topics covered to be in chronological order and to include exact quotes from participants when necessary. Read the "Writing Pointers" to learn the fine points in developing minutes of a meeting.

Writing Pointers

MINUTES OF MEETINGS

- Indicate time and place of meeting.
- List the names of those individuals who were present and absent.
- Mention whether previous minutes were read, approved, amended, or not approved.
- Record important facts discussed at the meeting. The body of the minutes should include all old and new business.
- Record verbatim resolutions and motions. Include the names of those people who introduced and seconded motions.
- Indicate the date and time of the next meeting in the closing paragraph as well as the time of adjournment.
- End with words "Submitted by" or "Respectfully submitted."
- Include the name and signature of the person who writes the minutes.

Model Minutes of Meeting

ALBERTVILLE TOWN BOARD

MINUTES OF THE MEETING
January 4, 20xx
Town Hall, 8 p.m.

Individuals in attendance	PRESENT: Town Supervisor James Peterson, Councilman Ray Adler, Councilman Edward Barnes, Councilwoman Sandra Parker, and Councilwoman Lisa Choy.
	ABSENT: Town Justice Deborah Coles
Approval of minutes	The minutes of the previous meeting held on December 4, 20xx, were approved as distributed.

OLD BUSINESS

Topics previously discussed

Town Supervisor James Peterson reported on the Open-Space Committee meeting held last week. The committee voted to study the possibility of purchasing the ten-acre vacant lot on Eastern Boulevard to be developed into a "pocket park."

Police Commissioner Reynolds discussed the duties of the newly appointed street patrol officer. This appointment was made possible as a result of a federal grant to increase police protection in communities. One of the most important duties for this police officer is to establish a rapport between the police and the merchants.

Motion made and approved

Motion was made by Ray Adler and seconded by Lisa Choy that E. R. Transport Co. be awarded a one-year contract for $35,000 to transport senior citizens to recreational and shopping centers. Motion carried.

NEW BUSINESS

Topics presented

Refurbishing the children's playground was introduced by parents of the community. The Albertville Town Board tabled the issue.

A public hearing would be held at the next meeting to discuss the adoption of new fire codes for public buildings.

ADJOURNMENT

The meeting was adjourned at 10 p.m. The next meeting is scheduled for February 15, 20xx.

Respectfully submitted,

Shirley Schuller

Shirley Schuller, Secretary

Case Study 2: Minutes of Meeting

After reading the case, respond to the questions in "Organizing Your Ideas," then compose the minutes of the meeting.

Case: You were given an assignment to cover the monthly meeting of the Student Government to be held on January 15, 20xx, at 1 p.m. at your school. Prepare the minutes of this meeting.

All the officers were present: Vicki Forsythe, Daniel Rhodes, Gloria Rockport, and Chris DeAngelis. Minutes of the previous meeting were approved.

Leslie Dunn reports that 50 students volunteered to work on the Local Disaster Committee to raise funds for the victims of the recent floods in the community. The committee plans to collect money from merchants, shoppers at the mall, and the school. Posters and flyers will be distributed throughout the neighborhood. The group will start its drive next week.

Robert Jones reports that he is representing the students at the Faculty Senate. One of the topics under discussion is raising academic standards. Subcommittees will be formed to explore various aspects of academic achievement. Each subcommittee will have a student representative.

A new topic on the agenda is Brian Scott's request that the Student Government look into the possibility of extending the hours of the Media Center. It would also help students who work to keep the Center open on Sundays.

The Political Science Club proposes that Student Government should plan a debate and invite the local candidates running for office. This will be discussed at the next meeting.

The meeting was adjourned at 2:30 p.m. The next meeting will be held the following week at the same time.

ORGANIZE YOUR IDEAS

To help you write effective minutes for the meeting, respond to the questions below.

1. What are the subheadings to use when writing the minutes of the meeting?

_____

2. What are the major topics to be reported under Old Business?

_____

3. What are the major topics to be reported under New Business?

4. What should you write in the closing statement?

Activity H   Surfing the Web

Know Your Town

To be responsible citizens, it is important to know one's community. An awareness of how local government functions, makes decisions, and implements programs will help us be knowledgeable voters.

From the Web site of your town or city, you are to summarize unique and important features of the area.

Directions:

■ Read the Web page of your town or city.

■ Write a one-page summary describing your community; include the following:

   ■ geographic location

   ■ history of community

   ■ population profile

   ■ type of government (town council, mayor, town supervisor)

   ■ types of businesses (retail, malls, offices, etc.)

   ■ special community projects

   ■ employment opportunities

⚡ *Cultural Communication*

Mexico:

■ Family is a priority.

■ Title and position of an individual are important.

■ Loyalty to superiors; management is autocratic.

■ Deadlines are flexible.

■ Cultivating personal relationships are essential in business affairs.

See www.executiveplanet.com

Self-Assessment
English Power

Directions: In the following sentences, insert quotation marks and other punctuation where needed, then key each sentence.

1. Do you plan to attend the International Folk Festival sponsored by the town asked my friend.

2. The notice read The City Commission will hold four public meetings in May to present the redistricting plan.

3. The governor warned A cut in taxes will affect aid to schools.

4. If we enforce water use restrictions now said the town clerk we shall not face shortages this summer.

5. Why do you oppose the airport expansion plan asked the state legislator.

6. A sense of community may get lost in a large city he said.

7. The newspaper headline that reads Mayor to Announce a $100 Million Project is a good attention-getter commented the editor.

8. The governor said We need a ten-year highway building plan however the legislature has been unable to draft a comprehensive transportation bill.

9. Who made the statement Water recycling has become a necessity in our environment.

10. My neighbor said The newspaper article Green Space in Our Town was very informative.

Editing Power

Directions: Edit, format, and proofread the following memorandum; supply the missing parts and paragraphs, key it correctly. Memo will be sent to the members of the Town Board from Carolyn Pepper, Town Supervisor. Use current date and subject is "Open Space Proposal."

Many of our town's residence have asked When are we going to address the need for more open spaces for parks and playing fields in this community? I believe that during this legislative session we need to draft a plan for the town.

I propose two available sights. The area on Ridge Road can be used as a public park with facilities for a children playground. The open space adjacent to Tibbets

Park could be developed into a ball field. At our

meeting next week let us lie the groundwork for this

important project. A committee need to be formed to

study the issues and make recommendations to our group.

If you have any individuals who you would suggest for

this committee, please submit the names at the meeting.

As I have said in the passed It's time for us to improve

this town quality of life.

Writing Power

Directions: Compose a letter informing the city homeowners that the City Council passed a resolution restricting the use of water for gardening. With the present drought conditions watering can take place only on Mondays and Thursdays from 5 p.m. until 8 p.m. There will be a $100 fine for the first offense for anyone using water at any other time. The fines will double each time for violators. Encourage citizens to conserve water for other purposes. Address the letter to Town Citizens; it will be signed by Mayor Tom Rizzo.

"There is no 'I' in TEAMWORK".

—www.heartquotes.net

CHAPTER 12

Help Wanted: Applying Hyphens and Numbers Correctly

CORPORATE SNAPSHOT

Kelly Services, Inc., is an international leader in providing staffing to multinational companies in 26 countries. It offers businesses temporary services, outsourcing, on-site and full-time employment, and consulting services.

The agency defines specific staffing needs of a company and coordinates a workforce that meets its daily business requirements. The contracted firm can then stay focused on its core business and not worry about employee relations. This cost-effective model is popular among many companies.

Kelly Services' commitment to diversity has won its recognition as one of the best companies in the field. Its philosophy is one of forming partnerships with companies that are controlled by minority, women, and disabled veterans. The firm's program to assist and advise these business operations has proven successful.

Source: *http://www.Kellyservices.com*

WHAT YOU WILL LEARN IN THIS CHAPTER

- To apply hyphens correctly
- To write numbers correctly
- To develop a business vocabulary in **HUMAN RESOURCES**
- To review the process of searching for employment
- To proofread and edit correspondence and reports
- To compose correspondence related to the job search
- To prepare a resume
- To search the Internet

HUMAN RESOURCES COORDINATOR: Organizes and directs administrative functions of a firm's human resources department, works with management on personnel issues, implements corporate policies related to employees, prepares data on company personnel, organizes staff development programs, deals with employee work-related issues and government regulations.

Skills: B.A. degree in human resources, business administration, professional certification available, organizational, analytical, communication, problem-solving, knowledge of labor laws.

EMPLOYMENT SPECIALIST: Works for a company or an employment agency; facilitates job placement according to company standards, conducts pre-employment screening, administers employment testing and interviews.

Skills: degree in human resources, interpersonal, communication.

ADMINISTRATIVE ASSISTANT: Performs office administrative and clerical duties, plan and schedule meetings, manages projects, prepares reports, manages mail, interacts with individuals at all corporate levels.

Skills: associate degree in office administration, communication and interpersonal skills, well organized, knowledge of office technology, multitasking.

Activity A *Language Arts Recall*

Hyphen and Number Usage

> **Rule 12.1:** Use a **hyphen** to join a compound adjective (one-thought modifier) when it precedes the word it modifies; otherwise, it is not hyphenated.

Example: Job opportunities exist in **computer-related** fields. (precedes noun it modifies).

BUT

Job opportunities exist in fields that are **computer related**. (does not precede noun it modifies).

The personnel department keeps **up-to-date** records on all employees.

BUT

The personnel department keeps employee records that are **up to date**.

The supervisor and employee will have a **face-to-face** meeting to discuss **on-the-job** training.

Note: If an *adverb* that ends in "*ly*" *precedes* the *adjective*, do *not* hyphenate.

Example: The human resources department is a **newly formed** division of the corporation. (no hyphen because "newly" ends in "ly" and is an adverb)

Rule 12.2: Use a hyphen after words in a *series of hyphenated adjectives* that modify the same noun(s). When there are two hyphenated adjectives, space once after the hyphen not linked with the noun. When there are three or more, use commas to separate them.

Examples: The **five-** and **ten-year** trends continue to show an increase in service jobs.

We will review our **one-, three-,** and **five-year** goals.

Rule 12.3: Use a hyphen after *self* when used as a prefix (*self* words are hyphenated).

Example: **Self-esteem** improves when an individual gains **self-confidence.**

Rule 12.4: Use a hyphen to join the word *well* to another word to form a modifier before a noun; otherwise, no hyphen is used.

Examples: A **well-written** resume will get positive results.

A resume that is **well written** will get positive results.

Rule 12.5: Use a hyphen in simple fractions.

Example: Of the 100 questionnaires mailed, only **one-third** replied.

Rule 12.6: Use a hyphen to link compound titles containing an "ex" and "elect."

Example: The acting **ex-secretary** joined the **president-elect** for lunch.

Note: Titles containing "vice" are not hyphenated.

Example: vice president

Rule 12.7: Use a hyphen to link compound titles in which a person or thing has two functions of a dual nature.

Example: The acting **secretary-treasurer** attended the **dinner-dance** with the **manager-supervisor**.

Rule 12.8: Use a hyphen to join a prefix to a number or to a capitalized word.

Examples: The fall semester begins in **mid-September**. Marilyn was promoted to general manager in the **mid-1990s** when she was in her **mid-30s**.

NUMBER USAGE

The following are the most common rules for expressing numbers in business correspondence.

Rule 12.9: *Word Style—Spell out*

- numbers from one through ten

    Fax five copies of the report.

- numbers beginning a sentence

    Fifty applicants mailed their resumes.

- millions and billions as part of a dollar amount

    $10 million $1.5 billion

Note: Never write the word "dollar" after the amount when the dollar symbol ($) is used.

- fractions that stand alone

    one-third

- street addresses beginning with "one" in inside address

    One Park Avenue

- time of day in formal writing

    eight-thirty o'clock

Rule 12.10: *Figure Style—Write as numbers*

- exact numbers over ten

    Fax 20 copies of the report.

- all decimals and percents (unless they begin a sentence)
  The salesperson received 10 percent commission on all sales.

Note: Write out word *percent* in correspondence.

- time of day when written with a.m. or p.m.

    8 p.m.   11:15 a.m.

- measurements, dimensions, page numbers, house numbers

    68 degrees   3″ × 6″card

    page 25   101 Broadway

- numbers in compound adjectives

    70-story building,   10-page manual

    35-hour workweek   3-year budget

- whole dollar amounts

    $50 $5,235 $25,000

Note: Do *not* add a decimal point and zeros after the whole amount.
Use a comma to separate thousands. Comma is optional with four digit amounts.($5235)

- series of items

Note: If any number in a sentence is above 10, write all numbers as figures.
We need to reorder 5 reams of computer paper, 10 disks, and 25 file folders.

Check for Understanding

Directions: Rewrite the sentences that follow by changing the *italicized* phrases into one-thought modifiers.

Example: The speaker who is *well informed* addressed the conference.
Rewrite: The *well-informed* speaker addressed the conference.

1. The manager has a commute of *40 minutes* to work each day.

   Rewrite: _____

   _____

2. The firm's plan was to hire workers who were *skilled on the computer.*

   Rewrite_____

   _____

3. The union agreed to a retirement plan that was *sponsored by the employer.*

   Rewrite_____

   _____

4. The communications company hired a consultant who was *well known.*

   Rewrite_____

   _____

5. The employee was given a leave of absence for a *short term.*

   Rewrite_____

   _____

Conclusion: Complete the following sentence.

A _____ is used to join a _____ modifier when it _____ the noun.

(Answers are given below.)

Building English Power: Hyphens and Number Usage

Directions: Punctuate each sentence correctly, inserting or deleting hyphens where necessary. Review number usage and make appropriate corrections, then key each sentence correctly.

1. Employers are interested in self motivated individuals who are well informed about the firms products. (12.3, 12.4, 9.1)

2. The regular conference fee is $20.00 dollars members have a 10% discount. (12.10, 8.1)

3. Applicants should send a follow up letter to thank the interviewer. (12.1)

4. The well known speaker Dr. Robert Reed will present a two day workshop on self assertiveness. (12.4, 7.5, 12.1, 12.3)

5. The applicants interview was scheduled for two p.m. at the company's headquarters at 1 Park Row. (9.1, 12.10, 12.9)

6. The firm budgeted $1.2 million dollars for renovation of its 50 story building. (12.9, 12.10)

7. At the conference the vice president of the firm remarked that the salesforce will be reduced by one third by mid April. (6.5, 12.6, 12.9, 12.8)

8. The new contract includes a three week vacation for employees who have been in the company for 5 years. (12.1, 12.9)

9. Home based work is a good option for part time employment. (12.1)

10. The 12 page manual will give you detailed step by step instructions for the new computer software. (12.1, 7.7, 12.2, 12.10)

11. Seventeen and eighteen year olds are encouraged to find volunteer internships to gain hands on experience. (12.10, 12.2, 12.1)

12. Entry level jobs have become more demanding with the need for higher technical skills. (12.1)

13. The president of the company is well-known in the electric utility industry. (12.4)

14. Some individuals prefer the freedom of a freelance job rather than a traditional 8 hour position. (12.1, 12.10)

15. 20 applicants were interviewed for the 3 positions as paralegals. (12.9)

16. We are voting for either a one or two year contract. (12.2)

17. The human resources director commented Only 1/3 of the applicants qualified for the position. (12.8, 11.1, 11.6)

18. We asked all supervisors to submit a 3 year plan for their departments by Friday at five p.m. (12.10)

19. The 3 million dollar grant was well-received by the newly-elected chairperson. (12.9, 12.4, 12.1)

20. Please fax me 5 copies of the plan which proposes a 35 hour workweek. (12.9, 12.10)

Activity B   Building Word Power

Do not present a negative attitude toward customers and coworkers; show an interest in the job.

The words that follow are commonly used in the field of human resources. From this list, select the word or phrase that correctly completes the statements. Refer to the personal dictionary, if necessary.

assertiveness   internship
assess   modulated
commitment   perusal
crucial   preliminary
human resources   prospective
                       teleconferencing

_____ 1. The administrative assistant has a well-_____ voice when he speaks on the telephone.

_____ 2. The meeting between the San Francisco and Tokyo offices was conducted by _____ so that both parties could discuss the issue via television.

_____ 3. The job applicant was interviewed by a staff member of the _____ department.

_____ 4. An employee who is interested in promotions within a firm should demonstrate _____ to the company.

_____ 5. In the highly competitive field of sales, self-_____ is an important trait for a successful career.

_____ 6. The manager will _____ the present procedure used in interviewing applicants.

_____ 7. In today's job market, some people accept a(n)
_____ to work with no salary for possible
future full-time employment.

_____ 8. A(n) _____ meeting was held by staff to prepare for the president's press announcement.

_____ 9. A person's integrity and honesty are _____
traits for conducting business transactions.

_____ 10. The salesperson called the _____ client regarding the future order.

_____ 11. The application is enclosed for your _____.

Activity C   Industry Perspectives: Recruiting in Today's Job Market

Directions: Using appropriate revision marks, proofread and key the
following report titled RECRUITING IN TODAY'S JOB MARKET.

Rule Reference

The changing workplace and the popularity of the

Internet has had major affects on job search and

recruitment. Other than the traditional way of looking

2.1   for a job, alternative strategies exists for both the

employer seeking qualified workers and the individual

searching for a job.

What are some things you need to know about the job

6.3   search process. After deciding on a career path you

will need to do some preliminary research about the

firms in this field. Having knowledge of the company

where you are seeking employment can be crucial in

getting a job offer. An excellent source of information

is the Web site http://www.hoovers.com.

6.3   Before writing the resume you should prepare a list of your skills, educational background, work experiences

7.1   and other related activities. Then you will decide how you plan to pursue the job search. The traditional way of searching for a job in the newspaper is being overshadowed by other alternative means. One of the methods used most is the Internet.

INTERNET JOB RECRUITING

Employers are using various channels to list job openings. Special Web sites similar to a newspaper

2.1   listing is available. Some of the popular sites are http://www.hotjobs.com; search engines, like yahoo, also post job openings. Many companies that post openings have there own web sites. The job seekers then submit their resumes online or fill out application forms on the Internet.

Another electronic service is the Internet provider that acts, for a fee, as an online employment agency. It maintains current databases of recruiters who have job openings and resumes of job seekers. Recruiters are supplied with the resumes that match their needs. Job seekers are matched only with those openings in which they qualify. This method of filling positions is faster and more efficient.

PERSONAL INTERVIEW

12.1   In the present type of job market, a face to face interview only takes place after an employer has determined which candidates qualify for the opening. At

6.3

7.1

the interview the applicant needs to be well-prepared,

be knowledgeable about the firm make a good appearance,

and have a positive attitude.

JOB FAIRS

Job fairs are popular throughout the country. It gives a

group of employers in a geographic area or in a specific

industry the opportunity to meet with perspective

applicants. At the same time, the job seekers can

evaluate the existing job market, obtain job information

7.1

on a number of firms and interact with company

recruiters.

SUMMARY

12.1

The job search is a time consuming and challenging

process. The best advise is to be prepared and to be

12.3

self confident that you are the one for the job.

Did you find these errors?

5 hyphens
6 commas
4 word usage
2 subject–verb agreement
1 punctuation

Career Planning

Career planning is a lifelong process. Individuals change careers three to five times in a lifetime. Therefore, you need to carefully assess your career goals, expectations, and capabilities before your job search begins. Whether you are an entry-level applicant or someone interested in changing careers, you need to take time to research and inquire about the career field that interests you. Then search those companies within the field to find out what are their corporate culture, philosophy, and employment demands. Employers are impressed with applicants who are knowledgeable about the particular business field as well as the individual company.

There are a multitude of books and Internet sites on careers and job hunting available to the job seeker. They offer valuable background information and data. One of the most useful resources to examine is *Occupational Outlook Handbook, 2006-2007*, published by the U.S. Department of Labor. It discusses career information, job requirements, salary potentials, and future opportunities for each career field. Refer to the Web site www.jist.com.

Some of the preliminary questions that you need to ask yourself before you begin your job search are:

- What are your interests?

- What industry would you like to work in?

- What type of organization would you feel comfortable working for?

- What are the job opportunities for the particular career field?

- What are the educational requirements, skills, and experience that are usually required in the field?

- What skills and abilities do you bring to a company?

Job Search

Job search can be a "full-time" task. There are a number of avenues that you need to explore where you may find a potential job.

- Networking with friends, relatives, teachers, former employers

- School placement offices and on-site recruiters

- Internet

- Corporate Web sites

- Classified ads in local newspapers

- Job fairs

- Government agencies

- Private employment agencies

INTERNET SOURCES FOR JOB-SEEKING INFORMATION

The Internet is a search tool that you, as a job seeker, should utilize. It offers a wealth of the latest job information. Whether you are searching for job listings, resume writing, interviewing process, or career advice, there is a Web site that will provide you with useful data.

http://www.careerjournal.com—provides career advice, daily news on jobs, employment opportunities and earnings.

http://www.careerbuilder.com—matches resume with job descriptions in database, searches jobs by categories, locations, and job types.

http://www.careerpath.com—links to local newspapers with current job listings; out-of-town resource.

http://www.hot.jobs.yahoo.com—matches applicants with employers, posts resume, searches jobs in any geographic location.

http://www.job-interview.net—reviews the interviewing process; offers suggestions to job applicants, cites questions asked during an interview.

http://www.careermag.com—provides informative career advice.

http://monster.com—searches jobs, gives career advice in specific industries, and offers resume writing service.

http://hoovers.com—offers basic information on public and private companies.

http://salesjobs.com—lists available sales positions.

http://greatplacetowork.com/best/list-bestusa.htm—Forbes' listing of 100 best companies to work for in America.

WRITING STAGE OF JOB SEARCH

In searching for employment, you will need to prepare a resume, job application letter, and a follow-up letter. Each of these categories will be discussed at length later in the chapter.

Job Interview

Another phase of job searching is the interview. There are different types of interviews. Preliminary interviews are often conducted over the telephone or Internet. At this stage, applicants are screened and a selection decision for further consideration is made by the interviewer. Then the potential candidate will be scheduled for a formal interview.

The purpose of a formal interview is for the employer to assess face-to-face whether you, the prospective employee, will be effective in the position and fit into the culture of the organization. You should be prepared to answer questions about past work experience, educational background, career goals, and knowledge about the company. At the same time, it gives you an opportunity to evaluate the firm and the job offer. It is important to give a good first impression to the prospective employer. Some points to remember:

- Dress appropriately in business attire.

- Have a positive attitude; know your personal strengths.

- Arrive promptly.

- Be knowledgeable about the firm.

- Show interest; use eye contact.

- Speak grammatically correct; avoid slang and terms such as "I don't know, uh."
- Thank the interviewer at the end of the session.
- Show interviewer a portfolio of past achievements, samples of special projects.

Job Offer

If a job is offered to you, be sure to evaluate the offer carefully before accepting the position.

- Will the organization be a good place for you to work?
- What is the organization's reputation in the industry?
- Will the work be interesting and challenging?
- What are the responsibilities and duties of the position?
- What are the chances of professional growth and advancement?
- Will you be happy in the field of work?
- What are the employee benefits?

Remember, getting the right job is important for you personally. With some preparation, the job-seeking task will be easier and successful.

Cover Letter

The **cover letter** or job application letter introduces the prospective employer to the applicant's resume. It needs to attract the reader's attention. The letter does not repeat the information on the resume. It should highlight the applicant's qualifications for the job as well as the person's strong points.

A cover letter can be written to a specific firm or organization that has posted an opening (solicited) or to firms that you believe would be a good fit for your skills and career plans (unsolicited). You should always attempt to address the letter to a specific individual.

In the opening of a solicited cover letter, refer to the source of information whether it is a newspaper ad, Internet posting, or contact. In an unsolicited letter, specify the type of work you are interested in doing.

The body of the letter should highlight your qualifications that meet the needs of the job and benefit the organization. You may also refer to academic or technical courses that you have taken and explain how they can help your work. Also, indicate how your previous work experience will be valuable to your prospective employer.

A request for an interview should appear in the closing.

Remember that in essence the cover letter is a sales letter. It should be effective and professional looking.

Designed
letterhead

LAURIE WHEELER
500 River Lane
Riverdale, NY 10471

(Current Date)

Addresses specific
person

Mr. Joseph Engers
Human Resources Manager
EGR Realty Corporation
One Park Avenue
New York, NY 10057-3200

Dear Mr. Engers:

Identifies source
and position

Your advertisement in the May 1 edition of the NEW YORK TIMES for an administrative assistant interests me.

Relates education
to job
requirements

I recently graduated with an A.S.S. degree from Bronx Community College with a major in Office Information Systems. This curriculum gave me the necessary communications, computer, and interpersonal relationship skills that will prove valuable in the position that is available in your firm.

Refers to firm's
reputation
Emphasizes
qualifications

EGR Realty Corporation has a fine reputation for its innovative approach in the real estate business. While a student, I worked at Riverdale Realtors where I became very attracted to a career in the dynamic, challenging field of real estate. You will find that I am a highly motivated person who can deal effectively with clients and staff.

Refers reader to
resume
Shows interest in
job

My resume is enclosed for your perusal. I would appreciate meeting with you to discuss my qualifications and possible employment with your company. You may reach me at 718-220-7832.

Sincerely yours,

Laurie Wheeler

Activity D *Editing Power*

Task A: Edit, format, and proofread the following unarranged letter, then key it correctly. Remember to insert paragraphs.

You, as the applicant, should send this cover letter to the attention of the Human Resource Department, Anchor Corporation, 55 Pine Street, Edison, New Jersey 08032–3387.

Please consider me as an applicant for the position of

sales representative which you advertised in The New

York Times on sunday May 16. I have chosen your company

Errors

■ commas
■ hyphen
■ capitalization
■ underscore
■ typographical
■ spelling
■ verb tense

because it is a well respected organization with a reputation for supporting employees in their professional developement. As shown in my enclosed resume you will find that my educational background has provided me with an excellent foundation for the position for which I am applying. I am skilled in the use of Microsoft office software, including Word Excel and PowerPoint. My position as an administrative assistant has enable me to develop my interpersonal and communication skills which are essential in a sales position. I will bring to the job a willingness to work and an eagerness to learn. May I have the opportunity to discuss employment possibilities with you? I would like to schedule an interview at your convenience. My telephone number is (student's telephone number).

Writing Pointers

Interview Follow-up Letter
(Refer to Activity D, Challenge Task B for example of letter content)

- Send letter immediately after interview.
- Express appreciation for the interview.
- Remind the interviewer of your interest in the job.
- Reemphasize a positive point about yourself.
- End with a forward-looking statement.

Challenge Task B: Edit, format, and proofread the following hand-written letter for all errors; key it correctly. It is a follow-up thank-you letter for the job interview with Ms. Michelle Dowling at Anchor Corporation, Human Resources Department, 55 Pine Street, Edison, NJ 08032–3387.

Thank you for interviewing me on Thursday May 10 for the sales representative position with your firm. The position appears interesting and challenging. I have always admired Anchor Corporation for it's forward looking approach in the field of sales. I am confident that I possess the talent skills and commitment that you require of your employees. You will find me an energetic member of any team effort. I am eager to join your staff and I hope to hear from you soon.

Activity E Writing Practicum Choose Options for Revision of a Cover Letter

Situation: Mrs. Dorothy Frank told her neighbor's daughter, Michelle Yager, a second-year college student, that there are five summer internships available in the city manager's office where she works. Michelle composed the following letter to the human resources director. You have been asked to read the letter and improve the writing.

Directions: Read the entire letter, which consists of a salutation, closing, and numbered sentences. Focus on one sentence at a time and select the best option from the choices given. After completing this task, key the letter.

(1) Dear Mr. Keith Shane:

(2) I am writing to you at the suggestion of Mrs. Dorothy Frank. (3) Dorothy said there are 5 summer-internships available in your office and I am most interested in applying for 1 of them. (4) At Queens college I am majoring in municipal government.

(5) Could you please send an internship application form to the above address and include any requirements you might have for obtaining one of them. (6) Enclosed is a self addressed stamped envelope for your convenience.

(7) If necessary I can provide 3 letters of reference. (8) I am available any day after 2 p.m. for an interview. I look forward to hearing from you. (9) Yours Sincerely,

Revisions

(1) A. Dear Mr. Shane:
   B. Dear Sir:
   C. Dear Keith,
   D. Original salutation
   (1) Choice _____

(2) A. I am writing to you at the suggestion of Dorothy Frank.
   B. I am writing you at the suggestion of my neighbor.
   C. I am writing to you at the suggestion of my neighbor, Mrs. Dorothy Frank, one of your employees.
   D. Original sentence
   (2) Choice _____

(3) A. Dorothy said there are 5 summer internships available and I am most interested in applying for one of them.

B. She informed me that there are five summer internships available in your office, and I am most interested in applying for one of them.

C. She said there are five summer internships available in your office and I am most interested in applying for one of them.

D. Original sentence

    (3) Choice _____

(4) A. I am at Queens College and majoring in municipal government, a field most fascinating.

B. At Queens College, I am majoring in municipal government, a career field that I find fascinating.

C. At Queens College, I am majoring in municipal government. This is fascinating to me.

D. Original sentence

    (4) Choice _____

(5) A. Could you please send an internship-application form to the above address and include any requirements necessary for obtaining one of them?

B. Please send an internship application form to me at the above address and include any other requirements needed in applying for the internship.

C. Please send me an Internship-Application form to the above address and include any suggestions you might have in obtaining one of them.

D. Original sentence

    (5) Choice _____

(6) A. Enclosed is a self addressed stamped-envelope for your convenience.

B. Enclosed is one self addressed stamped envelope for your convenience.

C. I am enclosing a self-addressed, stamped envelope for your convenience.

D. Original sentence

    (6) Choice _____

(7) A. If required I can send three letters-of-reference.

B. If necessary, I can provide three letters of reference.

C. I can get 3 letters of reference if required.

D. Original sentence

    (7) Choice _____

(8) A. I am available any day after 2:00 pm for an interview, and am looking forward to hearing from you.

B. I am available any day after two o'clock for an interview. Thank you for your assistance.

C. I am available any day after 2:00 pm for an interview and thanks for considering my application.

D. Original sentence

    (8) Choice _____

(9) A. Sincerely yours,
Michelle Yager

B. Appreciatively yours,
   Michelle Yager
C. Truly yours,
   Michelle Yager
D. Original closing
   (9) Choice_____

(10) For improved writing, select one of the following options.
   A. Rearrange sentences in the following order: 2, 4, 3, 5, 6, 7, 8.
   B. Combine paragraphs 1 and 2.
   C. Key sentences 5, 7, and 6, in that order, into a second paragraph. Other sentences remain in the same order.
   D. Keep letter in original order.
      (10) Choice_____

Key the letter with the choices and revisions you have made.

Resumes

A **resume** is a marketing tool that outlines a person's skills and experience. It presents an image you want employers to see. The resume should focus on accomplishments, not past job duties. The main goal of a resume is to obtain a job interview. A resume should include the following details.

Contact Information: At the top of the resume, the applicant's full name, address, phone number, and e-mail address should appear.

Objective: The recruiter should get an immediate sense of who the applicant is. Stress what you can do for the company. You can make a general statement if the resume is not targeted for a specific firm or position.

Experience: List job experiences chronologically; your most recent job comes first. Emphasize important responsibilities. Be specific; use action verbs.

Skills: Focus on skills employers want.

Education and Honors (if applicable): The latest academic enrollment information should be written first. This section can appear as the first major category, especially if the individual is a first-time applicant.

Other Activities: Include any activities that may be related to your career or that show involvement in the community or other affiliations.

CATEGORIES OF RESUMES

There are three categories of resumes: **chronological, functional, and combination.** The applicant should use the one that is best suited for the job search. The *chronological* resume outlines the job history of the applicant and starts with the most recent position. This category is popular with candidates who have extensive work experience.

The *functional* resume stresses the skills and educational accomplishments of the applicant and is good for beginning job seekers.

The *combination* resume takes the best from both types, including work experience as well as skills, competencies, and educational information.

Writing Pointers—Resumes

Guidelines to follow when preparing resumes:

- List strongest skills or abilities that make you a good candidate.
- Describe accomplishments emphasizing the results that benefited the past employer.
- Focus on qualifications that reflect the needs of the hiring company.
- Eliminate wordy statements; be specific.
- Avoid spelling errors and poor grammar.
- Omit unrelated personal information.
- Include contact information.
- Include soft skills (team player, flexibility, self-motivated).
- Use an easy, readable format.

ELECTRONIC RESUMES

Resumes are often scanned electronically by companies. Many job search engines, specialty job sites, job-hunting companies, and newspapers have a database tool in which the software reads the resume and stores it in a database. Prospective employers can then peruse the resumes. If the software cannot read the resume, it is rejected. Therefore, a *scannable resume must be modified from the traditional, printed version* into a plain text document that can be scanned by any computer. Make sure you do the following:

- Provide a list of keywords, preferably nouns, that are descriptive of your skills, abilities, education, and job titles. These words are matched with the employer's list. This section follows the heading in the resume.

- Avoid italics, bold face, underlines, bullets.

- Do not use abbreviations and acronyms.

- Use a font that produces a clear, plain text copy.

- Leave white space to separate sections.

- Left-justify the document; eliminate columns.

- Print on high-quality white or light-colored paper.

It is preferable that an **online resume** be incorporated into the text of the e-mail rather than as an attachment. Some human resources departments will not open attachments for fear of computer viruses. For security reasons, you may want to remove the home address and telephone number from the heading; keep only the e-mail address. Some applicants submit a traditional and an on-line resume.

MODEL RESUMES

The three model resumes that appear on pages 307–309 represent a beginning job applicant. The first example, a printed version, is a combination resume. The emphasis, however, is on the educational background and the applicant's skills.

The second version is an example of how the traditional, printed version is adapted to a scannable or e-mail resume.

**Model Resume for Individual with Work Experience
Seeking Higher-Level Position**

Laurie Wheeler

500 River Lane   Riverdale, NY 10471   718-220-7832   lauriew@yahoo.com

Career Objective:
Administrative position that requires leadership skills in the field of marketing for a multinational organization.

Experience:
Built a loyal client base by providing consistent support and product information.
Designed multimedia presentations for clients.
Planned promotional campaigns for new products.
Delivered projects within strict time guidelines.
Established good working relationship with clients, co-workers, and management.

Work Experience:
Project Coordinator, 2005–Present
ABC Electronic Company, New York, NY
Support Vice President of Marketing on projects involving new electronic products, plan promotional campaigns and multimedia presentations for global markets, prepare Web-related marketing plan, and act as liaison with clients.

Administrative Assistant, 2003–2004
Assisted sales manager with the daily office tasks, answering telephone inquiries, preparing correspondence and reports, and coordinating appointments and meetings.

Special Skills:
Detail-oriented, software knowledge, good listener, and team player
Computer: PageMaker, PowerPoint, MS Office Suite, Adobe Photoshop
Bilingual: Competency level in Spanish

Education:
Bronx Community College, Bronx, NY, Associate of Applied Science degree, marketing major, office systems minor.

Pursuing a four-year degree in business administration, Fordham University, New York, NY.

Laurie Wheeler
500 River Lane
Riverdale, NY 10471
(718) 220-7832
lauriew@yahoo.com

Uses general objective

CAREER OBJECTIVE

To obtain a challenging position as an administrative assistant with a multi-national firm that is a leader in its field.

EDUCATION

Emphasizes education and skills; highlights related courses

Bronx Community College of CUNY
Bronx, NY 10453-3101
Associate of Applied Science degree, Office Information Systems Major, GPA 3.5 (2007)

Related courses include:

Accounting	Multimedia Theory
Business Communications	Principles of Interpersonal Communications
Microcomputer Applications	Web Page Design

Skills:
Microsoft XP Professional, Microsoft Office (Word, Excel, PowerPoint, and Access)

Honors:
Dean's List (2005–2007)
J.P. Murphy's Award for Volunteerism

Bold side headings and bullets for clarity

WORK EXPERIENCE

Bronx Community College, Bronx, NY
Student Assistant to Information Systems Department (school session 2005–2007)

Uses action verbs

- Worked closely with faculty with filing, faxing, and copying documents
- Inputted student information into a database
- Assisted faculty in processing course registration
- Interacted with students on departmental matters

Riverdale Realtors, Riverdale, NY (summers and part-time 2004–2005)

- Inputted potential clients' information into a database
- Recorded and forwarded telephone messages to real estate agents
- Greeted customers
- Assumed responsibility for running office when realtors were off-site

Lists activities that show involvement

ACTIVITIES

- Volunteered to tutor lower-grade students in reading skills
- Volunteered to help children with special needs in recreational activities

Online: addresses and telephone numbers may be omitted

Laurie Wheeler
500 River Lane
Riverdale, NY 10471
(718) 220-7832
lauriew@yahoo.com

Lists applicable keywords

KEYWORDS
Administrative Assistant. Microsoft XP Professional. Microsoft Office. Word Excel. PowerPoint. Access Communication Skills. Organizational Skills. Interpersonal Relations. Volunteer. Student Assistant. A.S.S. degree, Bronx Community College. Office Information Systems Major.

Avoids bold headings

CAREER OBJECTIVE
To obtain a challenging position as an administrative assistant with a multinational firm that is a leader in its field.

Write out degree title to avoid confusion

EDUCATION
Bronx Community College of CUNY, Bronx, NY
Associate of Applied Science degree, 2005
Office Information Systems Major. GPA 3.5

Related courses include
Accounting, Business Communications, Microcomputer Applications, Multimedia Theory, Principles of Interpersonal Communications, Web Page Design

Uses white space for clarity

Skills:
Microsoft XP Professional, Microsoft Office, Word, Excel, PowerPoint, Access

Honors:
Dean's List (2005–2007)
J.P. Murphy's Award for Volunteerism

WORK EXPERIENCE
Bronx Community College, Bronx, NY
Student Assistant to Information Systems Department, school session 2005–2007
- Worked closely with faculty with filing, faxing, and copying documents
- Inputted student information into a database
- Assisted faculty in processing course registration
- Interacted with students on departmental matters

Riverdale Realtors, Riverdale, NY, summers and part-time 2004–2005
- Inputted potential clients' information into a database
- Recorded and forwarded telephone messages to real estate agents
- Greeted customers
- Assumed responsibility for running office when realtors were off-site

ACTIVITIES
Volunteered to tutor lower-grade students in reading skills
Volunteered to help children with special needs in recreational activities

Activity F   Writing Power: Composing Correspondence

Case Study 1:   Letter of Application to Business

After reading the case, respond to the questions in "Organize Your Ideas," then compose the letter.

Case: One of your instructors recommended that you send a letter with your resume to the well-known accounting firm Forrest & Smith, 55 Midland Drive, Chicago, IL 60607–8935 for possible employment in an entrylevel position. You are graduating with a two-year degree in accounting from your local community college. You have completed a three-month internship with a local accountant, where you assisted with financial records and payroll. Don't forget to indicate your computer skills.

ORGANIZE YOUR IDEAS

1. What would be a strong opening statement to attract the reader's attention?

    _____

    _____

    _____

2. What important points would you emphasize in the body of the letter regarding your individual strengths?

    _____

    _____

    _____

3. What would you say in the closing statement to get an immediate response?

    _____

    _____

    _____

Case Study 2: Letter of Application in Answer to Newspaper Advertisement

After reading the local newspaper advertisement that follows, which appeared in *The Daily Press,* answer the questions in "Organize Your Ideas" and draft a letter of application to Box MPM, 100 East 43 Street, New York, NY 10017-2001. Use "Ladies and Gentlemen:" as the salutation.

Case:

> ### ADMINISTRATIVE ASST
> ### ENTRY LEVEL OK
> National weekly newspaper seeks a highly organized individual for its Customer Relations Department. Applicant must be good with people. Verbal and typing skills a must. Computer knowledge essential. Good entry-level position for motivated individual.

ORGANIZE YOUR IDEAS

1. What would you write in your opening statement to stimulate the reader's interest in you as a potential candidate for the job?

   _____

   _____

2. What specific details would you highlight in the body of the letter to focus on your strengths in reference to the position?

   _____

   _____

3. What would you say in your closing statement to get a favorable response?

   _____

   _____

Case Study 3 and 4: Cover Letter and Resume of Student

The writing activities in this chapter have focused on the types of correspondence that you will compose during your job search. In this exercise, you will draft a cover letter and resume for a position that you personally would seek. To help you write an effective resume, the model previously shown can serve as a guide when you prepare your own. This sample resume contains the parts that are found in all resumes; however, the format might differ.

Case: Select a job for which you might wish to apply that was advertised in your local newspaper. Write a cover letter and resume based on your qualifications and background.

Challenge Level Case

Case Study 5: Interview Follow-Up Letter

A thank-you note after an interview helps you stand out against other applicants. If you are interested in a position, the follow-up letter will remind the interviewer of your meeting. This is an important final step in the interview process.

Case: Write a follow-up letter after an interview for a position as an administrative assistant that you had with Sandra Alexander, Human Resources representative for Intercontinental Electronics Corporation. This is a highly respected telecommunications company that has a reputation as a global leader in the field. They are located at 10037 Country Road, San Jose, CA 95100–5321.

Activity H   Surfing the Web

Job Searching

As we discussed in this chapter, it is important to obtain job information before you start actively searching for employment. In this assignment, you will be asked to check Web sites that offer career information and job listings. This task will familiarize you with the vast number of resources available to you when you actively are seeking a job or a career change.

Task A:

■ Review *two* Web sites focusing on career planning or job searching.

■ Compare the feature of each of the Web sites.

■ Write a summary of the important features of each Web site.

- State which Web site you would prefer reviewing when searching for career information or job listings; give rationale for your choice.

    You may refer to any Web site, Google, or the sites mentioned in the chapter.

Task B:

- Choose a company or organization that interests you for possible employment.

- Select the company's Web site.*

- Review the company's background, philosophy, and career opportunities.

- After reviewing the information, write a summary stating if you would still consider the company for employment; give reasons for your decision.

* Companies have their own Web sites. Search by company name.

Cultural Communication

Russia:

- It is necessary to deal with key decision-makers when conducting business.

- Bring all documents to a business meeting.

- Presentations should be clear and easy to understand; materials written in Russian are welcomed.

- Exchange of business cards is common practice; print in English and Russian.

- Appointments may be delayed; do not consider discourteous or disinterest.

See www.executiveplanet.com

"Team Player: One who unites others toward a shared destiny through sharing information and ideas, empowering others, and developing trust."

—Dennis Kinalu

Self-Assessment
English Power

Directions: In the following sentences, insert punctuation and correct number usage where needed and proofread. Then key each sentence.

1. The two hour course sponsored by the human resources department will help improve the individual's self esteem.

2. The proposed contract offers employees a 15 day leave policy and a 3 week vacation package.

3. The newly-created advisory board will review the 100 million dollars veterans' memorial.

4. We will use 8 ½ by 11 inch heavy stock paper for the employee manual.

5. The speaker is well-known in the field of conflict resolution.

6. The well spoken applicant is self confident that she will meet the challenges of the job.

7. The fax read Colonial flight fifteen will arrive at Kennedy Airport at 11:10 o'clock in the morning.

8. 100 volunteers raised 25000 dollars for the drive to aid disabled children.

9. We need an up to date report on employee absenteeism.

10. The address of the new 60 story building is 1 Park Drive.

Editing Power

Directions: Edit, format, and proofread the following memorandum; Key it correctly. The memo will be sent to Department Managers from Amy Rosario, Vice President. Subject: Meeting on the Findings of the Outsourcing Report. Use current date.

For the past 5 years, we have been outsourcing our customer relations services. Our main goal was to offer our clients satisfactory assistants at lower costs to our firm. After this period of time we needed to assess the program. I asked Ronald Baker and his staff in Human Resources to complete a survey evaluating the success of this segement of the business; if necessary, modifications would be implemented.

I have received the report from Ronald and I am impressed with the detailed information that is in the document. Surprisingly, the staff found that many of our clients were dissatisfied with the service. Over 50% of those responding to the survey felt that often there was miscommunication between the representative and the customer. This caused frustration on the part of our clients. Since the beginning of our outsourcing our sales have decreased by 500 thousand dollars, a ten percent decline in revenue. This outcome suggests a drop in our loyal client base.

One of the recommendations by the committee is to consider homesourcing. This appears to be trend among some of the firms. We could hire part time employees in the States who are stay home parents, college students or senior citizens. They understand our culture and are familiar with our colloquialisms. The added employee costs would be absorbed by an increase in our business.

We shall meet on Monday, May 1 at 10 o'clock in the morning, to attend a presentation by Ronald and his staff.

Writing Power

Directions: Draft a letter of application to Ms. Mercedes Diaz, Manager of Human Resources at the hotel chain Excelsior. Executive offices are at One Dupont Circle, Las Vegas, NV 89100-2301. This company has a fine reputation worldwide in the hospitality industry. The firm is known for its superior service to clients and fair treatment to its employees. Also, they have excellent employee benefits and opportunities to advance within the organization. You believe that this is the type of company that you would enjoy working for. You are graduating from City Community College with an associate degree in office management; enclose a resume with the letter.

APPENDIX A

Answer Keys by Chapter

Chapter 1: Banking on Good Sentence Structure

ACTIVITY A   BUILDING ENGLISH POWER: SENTENCE STRUCTURE

Exercise 1

C   **1.** Internet <u>banking</u> is <u>replacing</u> traditional banking practices.

I   **2.** Bank mergers throughout the country.

C   **3.** Finance <u>charges</u> <u>do</u> not <u>appear</u> on this month's statement.

C   **4.** To access an ATM, <u>you</u> <u>need</u> the customer's personal identification number.

I   **5.** No annual fee for the first year.

I   **6.** When you use a debit card.

C   **7.** As a valued customer, <u>you</u> <u>have</u> a minimum credit line of $10,000.

C   **8.** The <u>bank</u> <u>requested</u> collateral before issuing the loan.

I   **9.** If you pay your credit card balance in full each month to avoid interest charges.

C   **10.** At the end of the calendar year, the <u>bank</u> <u>will inform</u> you of the total interest accrued on all accounts.

C   **11.** Direct <u>deposit</u> <u>is encouraged.</u>

C   **12.** <u>Banks</u> <u>require</u> that you provide identification when cashing a check.

C   **13.** The local <u>bank</u> <u>offers</u> investment plans to its customers.

I   **14.** The penalty charge for insufficient funds in your checking account.

I   **15.** Because ATMs are available 24 hours a day.

I   **16.** Banking on the Internet.

  C   **17.** The bank credit <u>card</u> <u>can be used</u> as a cash card when making purchases.

  C   **18.** The financial <u>advisor</u> <u>suggested</u> opening an IRA account.

  C   **19.** A popular banking <u>service</u> <u>is</u> direct payments of utility bills.

  C   **20.** Some bank credit <u>cards</u> <u>offer</u> frequent flyer bonus points.

Exercise 2 (Answers may vary.)

2. There are many bank mergers throughout the country.

5. No annual fee is required for the first year.

6. When you use a debit card, the transaction is immediately posted on your checking account.

9. If you pay your credit card balance is full each month, you will avoid interest charges.

14. The penalty charge for insufficient funds in your checking account is high.

15. ATMs are popular because they are available 24 hours a day.

16. Banking on the Internet is a convenient way to perform financial transactions.

BUILDING ENGLISH POWER: CAPITALIZATION

1. Ⓨou must reply by Ⓢeptember 1 to receive the promotional rate for the Ⓒ︎Ⓓ.

2. Ⓣhe monthly newsletter, Ⓣhe Ⓑank Ⓕorum, gives investment advice to the employees.

3. New Ⓨork Ⓑank will be closed on Ⓢaturdays during Ⓙuly and Ⓐugust.

4. Ⓜost savings accounts are insured by the Ⓕ︎Ⓓ︎Ⓘ︎Ⓒ, a government agency known as the Ⓕederal Ⓓeposit Ⓘnsurance Ⓒorporation.

5. Ⓦhat did you think of Ⓜr. Ⓑaker's speech in Ⓢan Ⓕrancisco on banking reforms?

6. Ⓣhe Ⓕederal Ⓗome Ⓛoan Ⓜortgage Ⓒorporation announced that mortgage rates are on the rise.

7. Ⓔastern Ⓣrust offers an Ⓘ︎Ⓡ︎Ⓐ that has no annual fee.

8. Ⓐ Ⓒ︎Ⓓ account offers the investor a higher rate of interest.

9. Ⓣhe new computer software, known as Ⓑank Ⓔxpress, will allow users to keep personal and financial records up to date.

10. Ⓞn Ⓣhursday, Ⓓecember 1, the Ⓡoyal Ⓑank will introduce its new service for investors.

11. Ⓓr. Ⓐlan Ⓢmith will speak on global investments at the Ⓞrlando Ⓒonvention Ⓒenter in Ⓕlorida on Ⓢaturday, Ⓙuly 8.

12. Ⓐ︎Ⓣ︎Ⓜs are located in many shopping malls in the Ⓤnited Ⓢtates.

13. The American Bank will sponsor the next World Cup USA.

14. Pathways to Financial Security has made The New York Times best-seller booklist. ("The" is part of the title.)

15. The European Bank will expand its offices to Singapore and Hong Kong.

16. The Banking Institute of America publishes a Spanish edition of its pamphlet on IRAs.

17. The weekly newspaper, Financial Review, publishes the popular column, "World Banking."

18. Bank savings and IRA accounts are FDIC insured.

19. The bank will be closed on Monday, Presidents' Day.

20. The Union Bank of New York has appointed Jane Pastor chairperson of the Health Benefits Task Force.

ACTIVITY B   BUILDING WORD POWER

1. insufficient funds
2. electronic banking
3. global
4. mortgage
5. authorization
6. transactions
7. specialists
8. accrued
9. co-applicant
10. network
11. IRAs
12. ATM
13. collateral
14. FDIC
15. CDs
16. debit card
17. equity line of credit

ACTIVITY D: EDITING POWER

Task A

Date

Mr. Joseph Robinson
131 Post Road
Duluth, MN 55803-5122

Dear Mr. Robinson:

Thank you for choosing Fidelity Savings Bank for your banking needs. We are confident you will be happy doing business with us.

We are enclosing our latest brochure, *Banking Made Easy for the Consumer,* which describes the many services we offer customers. These services include free checking with interest, direct deposits, IRAs, CDs, and life insurance.

Our bank is open six days a week: Monday to Friday from 9 a.m. – 3 p.m., and on Saturday until noon. For you convenience, we have evening banking hours on Tuesday and Thursday. We are also expanding our Canadian services by opening branches on October 10 in Montreal and Quebec.

You will benefit from the many services offered by Fidelity Savings Bank, a member of the Federal Deposit Insurance Corporation.

Cordially yours,

Peter Gerena
Manager
ri

Enclosure

ACTIVITY E   WRITING PRACTICUM

Exercise 1   Writing in Complete Thoughts (Answers may vary.)

1. When a small Midwestern bank failed, the FDIC assured depositors that their money was insured.

2. Banking online allows depositors to complete transactions through the Internet without visiting a bank.

3. Bank USA, a global bank, offers its clients international financial services.

4. One of the restrictions in a CD account is that there is a penalty for early withdrawal of funds.

5. As interest rates dropped, many customers of the bank chose to invest their money in mutual funds.

6. Loaning money to individuals and firms is one of the ways in which banks make money.

7. The benefit of using an ATM account is easy accessibility to cash.

8. If mortgage rates continue to increase, prospective homeowners will not be able to afford purchasing a home.

9. The letter from Mr. Robinson, the bank president, explained the bank's new policy on personal loans.

10. An IRA is an important way for an individual to save for retirement.

Exercise 2   Combining Sentences

1. ATMs are a convenient way for busy persons to conduct banking transactions 24 hours a day.

2. The bank has a special loan rate of 7 percent on American-made cars.

3. A certificate of deposit is a term savings account that pays a higher rate of interest and carries an early withdrawal penalty.

4. Many depositors have online accounts on the Internet to download statements and to pay their bills.

5. You can open a basic checking account for as little as $250 without a minimum balance.

6. Some individuals choose an equity line of credit to make large purchases or for a down payment on a house.

Exercise 3   Developing Meaningful Paragraphs

1. Banking in America has changed dramatically over the past decade. K

2. Banks have responded to changing needs of the consumer in the local communities. K

3. The electronic age has introduced ATMs, direct deposits, and computer transactions, which improved banking services. K

4. Customers now receive fast and efficient service without long waiting lines. R

5. Also, with electronic banking systems, customers can transact their financial business from any area of the country. K

6. Also, a large number of banks have merged to offer additional services that facilitate handling global transactions. K

7. They are open some evenings, Saturdays, and Sunday mornings. K

8. With these changes, banks are prepared to meet the challenges of the next millennium. R

■ Order of Sentences: 1, 3, 4, 5, 2, 7, 6, 8

Rewritten Paragraph: Banking in America has changed dramatically over the past decade. The electronic age has introduced ATMs, direct deposits, and computer transactions, which improved banking services. Customers now receive fast and efficient service without long waiting lines. Also, with electronic banking systems, customers can transact their financial business from any area of the country.

Banks have responded to changing needs of the consumer in the local communities. They are open some evenings, Saturdays, and

Sunday mornings. Also, a large number of banks have merged to offer additional services that facilitate handling global transactions.

With these changes, banks are prepared to meet the challenges of the next millennium.

Exercise 4   Writing Opening and Closing Sentences in Letters

Opening Sentences

1. B (Question attracts reader's attention.)
2. A (Clear purpose stated)
3. B (Informative)
4. B (Goodwill approach)

Closing Sentences

5. B (Suggests action to be taken)
6. B (Positive forward-looking statement)
7. A (Offers a friendly invitation)
8. A (Maintains goodwill)

Chapter 2: Ensuring Subject-Verb Agreement

ACTIVITY A   BUILDING ENGLISH POWER: SUBJECT-VERB AGREEMENT

1. plan, protects
2. procedures, help
3. club, has been able
4. you, ask
5. union and management disagree
6. industry, faces
7. policy, was
8. contract, includes
9. Michael and friend, pay
10. course, qualifies
11. you, become
12. damage and theft, are covered
13. records, indicate
14. team, has presented
15. insurance and coverage, are
16. you, are
17. faculty, agrees
18. rates, have decreased
19. company, was advised
20. representative and manager, plan

ACTIVITY B   BUILDING WORD POWER

1. catastrophic insurance, umbrella insurance
2. phasing out
3. escalating
4. cafeteria-type medical insurance, option
5. bodily injury insurance
6. property damage insurance
7. deductible
8. premium
9. subsidized
10. accelerated
11. alternative
12. liability insurance

ACTIVITY D: EDITING POWER

Task A

(Current Date)

Mr. William Simms
10 Maple Avenue
Toledo, OH 43692-9987

Dear Mr. Simms:

We are happy to enclose a renewal for your automobile insurance policy for the coming year. Please review your policy carefully so that you are fully protected.

Our brochure, *The ABCs of Auto Insurance,* is enclosed to help you determine whether your present policy is meeting your needs. This brochure lists in detail the features we offer automobile owners. Our policy offers discounts to drivers with good safety records. For full protection, you should have adequate bodily injury and property damage coverage.

If you agree with the limits of liability and coverage included in the enclosed policy, detach the premium statement and mail it with your payment. If you have any questions, our representatives are available 24 hours a day at (800) 841-9000. After doing business with us, you will agree that our reliability and customer services are superior to those of our competitors.

Our firm values policyholders like you, and we sincerely appreciate the opportunity to serve you.

Sincerely yours,

David Knight
Vice President
ri
Enclosures

ACTIVITY E   WRITING PRACTICUM

Exercise 1   Concise Writing (Answers may vary.)

1. The pamphlet on health insurance options explains the benefits.

2. A 10 percent increase in automobile insurance premiums is effective immediately.

3. After the storm, there were hundreds of claims by homeowners.

4. The injured motorist will sue the other driver.

5. The firm will offer its employees a life insurance policy.

6. If you would like to increase your liability insurance, please call me.

7. The study showed that fraudulent claims caused an increase in auto insurance rates.

8. You will receive a gift if you attend our seminar at the Americana Hotel.

9. I believe that there should be a federally funded insurance program for catastrophic disasters.

Exercise 2   Run-On Sentences (Other options may be acceptable.)

1. We offer insurance specifically to small businesses. They often have difficulty finding insurance rates that are affordable.

2. The judge ruled in favor of the plaintiff's lawsuit, and the defendant was found negligent and fined $1,000.

   - or -

   The judge ruled in favor of the plaintiff's lawsuit; the defendant was found negligent and fined $1,000.

3. In most states insurane companies do not offer flood insurance to individual homeowners; they must apply through a federal program.

4. Shana completed the safe driving program; she will receive a discount on her automobile insurance premium.

   - or -

   Shana completed the safe driving program, and she will receive a discount on her automobile insurance premium.

5. Most insurance policies have a deductible clause so that the insured is required to pay a minimum amount before claims will be processed.

   - or -

   Most insurance policies have a deductible clause; the insured is required to pay a a minimum amount before claims will be processed.

6. Because the building was underinsured, the claims of the tenants could not be met.

Exercise 3   Writing Opening and Closing Sentences

Note: Choices should be based on clarity and conciseness.

Opening Sentences

1. A (identifies writer and clearly states purpose of letter)
2. C (clear statement, not wordy)
3. C (to the point)
4. A (concise and clear)
5. B (expresses pleasure in fulfilling request)

Closing Sentences

6. A (brief statement of appreciation)
7. A (concise statement; builds goodwill)
8. B (concise statement encouraging future business)

Exercise 4 Writing for Correct Sentence Structure

Sample Writing (Answers may vary.)
You could save hundreds of dollars by insuring your automobile with us. Our operating expenses are among the lowest in the industry, and we pass our savings on to our customers.

We have additional money-saving discounts for safe drivers, auto security systems, and multi-car coverage. Our quality service includes 24-hour access to our auto insurance specialists.

Use our toll-free number to get a rate quote; there is no obligation.

Chapter 3: Investing in Subject-Verb Agreement

Exercise 1   Review Subject-Verb Agreement

1. C	6. reviews
2. explains	7. C
3. appear	8. C
4. is growing	9. attends
5. C	10. are

ACTIVITY A   BUILDING ENGLISH POWER: SUBJECT-VERB AGREEMENT

Exercise 2   Subject-Verb Agreement

1. Foreign demand for American technology is increasing.
   Plural Form: demands, are increasing

2. The number of stockholders is demanding more communication from corporate executives.
   Plural Form: A number, are

3. Neither the employee nor the manager agrees with the arbitrator's decision.
   Plural Form: employees, managers, agree

4. There is a concern about the company's financial condition.
   Plural Form: are, concerns

5. The report in which we compare multinational corporations appears in several business magazines.
   Plural Form: reports, appear

6. The enclosed pamphlet from the brokerage firm gives information on a variety of mutual funds.
   Plural Form: pamphlets, give

7. Each of the brokers predicts an upswing in the stock market.
   Plural Form: All, predict

8. A seminar on financial planning is offered by the local bank.
   Plural Form: Seminars, are offered

9. There is a tax-free municipal bond that pays a high dividend.
   Plural Form: are, bonds, pay

10. Everyone agrees that individuals should have a savings plan.
    Plural Form: All, agree

11. Either a U.S. savings bond or a treasury note is a secure investment.
    Plural Form: bonds, notes, are

12. Each financial decision impacts your net worth.
    Plural Form: (All) decisions, impact

13. The stock price of the electronic company has increased during the past year.
    Plural Form: prices, have increased

14. The fund, which invests in diversified stocks, has a high rate of performance.
    Plural Form: funds, invest, have

15. Neither the bank nor the investment firm was willing to underwrite the project.
    Plural Form: banks, firms, were willing

ACTIVITY B   BUILDING WORD POWER

1. bonds
2. securities
3. stocks
4. prospectus
5. investments
6. investment portfolio
7. mutual fund
8. stockbroker
9. glossary
10. multinational
11. proxy
12. Web site
13. blue chip stock(s)

ACTIVITY D: EDITING POWER

Task A

```
(Current Date)

Ms. Barbara Simmons
One Park Road
Kansas City, MO 64141-6202

Dear Ms. Simmons:

A growing number of Americans are using financial
planning to manage their money better. Everyone agrees
that investors should be well informed of market trends.
    We invite you to send for a free copy of our
Financial Planning Guide. It is written in an easy,
understandable manner. Ten experts in the investment
field offer suggestions on how to invest money. A
glossary of financial terms appears in the back of the
booklet for reference.
    There are many types of investments. We suggest that
you carefully read what the recognized authorities in
the financial field have to say. Then, you will be able
to make wise decisions.
    Why not send for your copy today?

Sincerely yours,

Suzanne Rudman
Vice President
ri
```

ACTIVITY E   WRITING PRACTICUM

Exercise 1   Rearranging Sentences for Continuity of Ideas

1. a, c, b, d

The use of computers to keep abreast of financial information is becoming increasingly popular.

With the Internet, an investor can communicate with investment specialists, retrieve securities information, and refer to financial databases. Online computer networks are making conventional ways of researching information as obsolete as using a typewriter. All you need are a personal computer, a modem, and Internet access to keep the information superhighway at your fingertips.

2. b, a, c, d

In response to your advertisement placed in the summer job mart at River Community College, I would like to apply for the position.

Last summer, I had experience working as an intern for a small investment firm in my hometown. I was fascinated by the challenges of the brokerage field.

Please send me an application for your management trainee program.

3. d, c, a, b

You will be pleased to know that we are introducing an automatic monthly investment plan.

With this plan, you authorize us to transfer a fixed amount each month from your bank account to your mutual fund account. There are no fees for this service, and you can terminate the plan at any time.

If you have any further questions, please call your account representative.

4. d, c, b, a

Thank you for contacting Investment Services Corporation.

Our firm offers a wide range of investment plans tailored to the needs of our clients. All of our investment consultants are professionals who are knowledgeable in the securities market.

We have enclosed a brochure that explains our services; feel free to contact one of our experienced representatives for further help.

5. b, a, c, d

We have enclosed your free copy of Financial Review.

As an experienced investor, you will find this monthly newsletter an incredible source of information on all types of investments. Each month a prominent business professional writes about a financial topic of interest to our readers.

Please take time to read this valuable pamphlet and don't hesitate to send in your subscription.

Exercise 2   Inappropriate and Outdated Phrases

1. Many	**6.** Because	**11.** Know
2. According to	**7.** Because	**12.** Thank you
3. Now	**8.** Ought not to	**13.** At your request
4. Because	**9.** Must	**14.** Because
5. Should have	**10.** Somewhat	**15.** Should relax

Chapter 4: Telecommunicating with Verbs

ACTIVITY A   BUILDING ENGLISH POWER: VERB TENSE

1. office, introduced, simple past
2. machines, have decreased, present perfect
3. interest, has increased, present perfect
4. corporation, will have introduced, future perfect
5. editor, has used, present perfect
6. subscriber, took, simple past
7. control, has been discussed, present perfect (passive voice)
8. you, have, simple present
9. force, has been organized, present perfect (passive voice)
10. personality, has been invited, present perfect (passive voice)
11. company, had planned, past perfect
12. executives, carry, simple present
13. I, chose, simple past
14. firm, has given, present perfect
15. directors, had discussed, past perfect
16. we, had demonstrated, past perfect
17. bank, has encouraged, present perfect
18. I, wrote, simple past
19. we, will drive, simple future
20. popularity, has risen, present perfect

ACTIVITY B   BUILDING WORD POWER

1. videoconferencing
2. facsimile equipment (fax)
3. modem
4. laptop computers
5. telecommunications
6. electronic mail (e-mail)
7. notebook
8. monitor
9. mouse
10. configuration
11. software
12. Internet
13. protocols
14. networking

ACTIVITY D: EDITING POWER

Task A

(Current Date)

Mr. Edward Burke, Jr.
1100 Broad Street
Cleveland, OH 44190-8030

Dear Mr. Burke:

Thank you for your inquiry about our computer product line. The authorized dealer nearest you is Computer Mart, 5 Metro Office Park, Cleveland, OH 44190-3598.

Computer <u>Mart</u> offe<u>rs</u> a complete line of products from laptop computers to network systems. For businesses, custom configurations and on-<u>site</u> installations are available. You may want to consider Computer Mart's excellent leasing program, which has been popular <u>for</u> many years.

Our dealer has maintain<u>ed</u> <u>its</u> efficient and reliable service for the pas<u>t</u> 20 years. The sales representatives <u>have</u> received training on our equipment. Therefore, they will be able to discuss your needs and recom<u>m</u>end equipment best suited for your business.

Feel free to visit the showroom; you will find everyone most helpful.

Sincerely yours,

Lloyd Pearson
Sales Manager
ri

ACTIVITY E   WRITING PRACTICUM

Exercise 1:   Correct Verb Tense, Subject-Verb Agreement, Correct Word Usage

a. simple present tense

Casual games *are* very popular online. *Sites* on the Internet *offer* hundreds of games free. To test one's knowledge, there <u>are</u> online versions of Scrabble and Jeopardy. Today's cell phones <u>allow</u> individuals to download the games. The future <u>promises</u> to join the mobile phone and personal computer to offer games *in*terchangeably.

b. present perfect tense

The trend in technology *has been* toward easier access and ease of communications for small business and the individual proprietor. Computer networks and online sources *have given* the entrepreneur the opportunity to retrieve valuable information related to a particular industry or market. Reports on consumer trends, product innovations, and sales analyses *have helped* small business compete in the marketplace.

c. simple past tense
Last year, mobile technology <u>expanded</u> rapidly. A number of innovations <u>added</u> new features to cell phones such as built-in cameras and test imaging. Companies <u>offered</u> to download films and music for a small fee. Consumer demand <u>grew</u> for these new phones.

d. simple future tense
A popular online innovation will be the practice of blogging. Web sites on which the writer <u>will post</u> messages for anyone to read *will show up* on the Internet. On such Web sites, individuals <u>will interchange</u> ideas on any subject. The interaction <u>will occur</u> immediately with high-speed Internet access.

Exercise 2   Changing Verb Tense from Present to Past

```
DATE:          (Current Date)

TO:            Branch Offices

               R. J. Tompkins Corporation

FROM:          Ray DeJesus

SUBJECT:       Telenetwork System
```

We <u>wanted</u> to alert all of our branch offices that we <u>converted</u> our telephone lines to a new computerized system on September 5.

This <u>allowed</u> for several improvements over our old system. Each new desk unit <u>consisted of</u> a modular console that <u>included fax</u>, voice mail, and three-way conferencing features. Executive offices <u>had</u> hookups for videoconferencing and taping facilities. We <u>were</u> confident that our interoffice communications <u>benefited</u> from this change.

The plan <u>was</u> to install the system over the Labor Day weekend so that the business day <u>had</u> few interruptions. We <u>appreciated</u> your cooperation in this matter.

Exercise 3   Changing Verb Tense from Present to Present Perfect

The Internet <u>has introduced</u> a new era in communications. Through a computer network, friends, business colleagues, and customers <u>have interacted</u> and <u>have shared</u> information instantly with one another. The Internet <u>has been</u> as popular as using a cellular phone or faxing a message. It <u>has been</u> the focus of the computing world.

Computer networks <u>have changed</u> the way business <u>has handled</u> its transactions. Information <u>has been</u> globalized and resources <u>have been</u> available from all over the world. The following services <u>have been</u> available to the Internet user: online shopping, banking transactions, checking status of orders, researching databases, voice messaging, and exchanging e-mail.

The Internet <u>has grown</u> rapidly. Protocols for this online computer network <u>have not limited</u> the type of users. An increasing number of large corporations, small businesses, and individual subscribers <u>have joined</u> the Internet for their means of communication.

Chapter 5: Lots of Commas in Real Estate

ACTIVITY A BUILDING ENGLISH POWER: COMMA CONJUNCTION

1. The home improvement business has become a major industry, and future trends indicate a growing market.

2. The custom-built homes are designed by a well-known architect, but the prices are moderate.

3. The residential community is located near the highway and is convenient to major shopping malls. (Correct)

4. The five acres of land will be sold to individual buyers or to a real estate developer. (Correct)

5. Mortgage rates have been low during the last year, and that will affect future sales.

6. Office space rents by the square foot and is quite costly in desirable business districts. (Correct)

7. Waterfront property has become increasingly expensive, but buyers are always interested in purchasing such real estate.

8. The tenant owes three months' rent, and that is the reason the landlord will take legal action.

9. Congratulations on your election to the governance committee of the building, and the Board thanks you for your contributions to good management.

10. The architect's design for the neighborhood park has been completed, and construction should begin in two months.

11. The land will be sold by the acre and parceled out in smaller lots. (Correct)

12. The property has easy access to the downtown area, and that site is located right off Exit 23 on the interstate highway.

13. The court ruling prohibits the use of wetlands for commercial development, but the firm will appeal the case.

14. A day-care center will be built in the new corporate park, and it will be available to employees and the community.

15. The Association of Realtors will hold its annual conference in June, and we urge individuals who are interested in the field of real estate to attend the meeting.

16. Tara accepted the position at the real estate firm and will begin next week. (Correct)

17. Either the construction company will build on the old railroad site, or it will move to the new industrial park.

18. Mortgage rates have been low and, that is good news for homeowners.

19. Our company has grown rapidly, but it is not planning to expand in Europe.

20. The community voted for a town park and that the residents would be able to use the new facilities free of charge. (Correct)

ACTIVITY B   BUILDING WORD POWER

1. references
2. town code
3. debris
4. periodically
5. index
6. principal
7. lease
8. security deposit
9. corporate park
10. realtors
11. mortgage
12. condominium
13. cooperative
14. prorating
15. delinquent

ACTIVITY D: EDITING POWER

Task A
(Form Letter)

(Current Date)

Dear Neighbor:

Our company, Capital Realtors, <u>has</u> been engaged in the Westchester real estate industry for over 25 <u>years</u>, and our firm <u>has</u> earned a fine reputation in the community. We take <u>pr</u>ide in analyzing a <u>pr</u>ospective client's need<u>s</u> <u>a</u>nd matching the proper house to the client. Our experienced brokers carefully research each <u>propert</u>y, but the cost is never <u>passed</u> on to the buyer.
  We believe that the market in this area is recovering and that there are many good opportunities to buy real estate. If you are interested in either a new home or a parcel of land for development, visit our office and speak to one of our experienced representatives. Satisfied clients are the best source of <u>references</u>, and a list of repeat clients <u>is</u> available to you.
  We look forward to serving you. Don't hesitate to call Capit<u>a</u>l Realtors at (914)623-1000.

Sincerely yours,

John Costello
Vice President
ri

ACTIVITY E   WRITING PRACTICUM

Exercise 1   Use of Adjectives and Adverbs

1. scheduled (adjective)
2. revised (adjective)

3. interested (adjective)

4. densely (adverb)

5. satisfactorily (adverb)

6. required, revised (adjective, adjective)

7. leased (adjective)

8. newly, renovated (adverb, adjective)

9. recently, acquired (adverb, adjective)

10. experienced, fairly (adjective, adverb)

Exercise 2   Comparative and Superlative Adjective Forms

1. largest		6. more
2. more		7. least
3. higher		8. lower
4. finest		9. earlier
5. most		10. greatest

Exercise 3   Correct Word Choice

1. Most (adjective superlative)	6. An
2. Almost (nearly)	7. A
3. bad (adjective)	8. an
4. badly (adverb)	9. an
5. well (adverb)	10. a

Exercise 4   Converting from Passive to Active Voice

1. The local construction firm will build 50 single-family homes.

2. The city council has proposed an increase in real estate taxes.

3. The builder announced a reduction in the price of the new homes.

4. The engineer submitted the plan for urban development to the town board.

5. Union Bank offers mortgage financing to first-time home buyers.

6. The landlord has submitted a plan to convert the building to co-operative ownership.

7. The Board of Directors vetoed renovations.

8. The bank rejected the mortgage application that the young couple submitted.

9. The speaker mentioned the difficulty in changing the existing building code.

10. The majority of the shareholders attended the annual meeting of the condominium.

Chapter 6: Maintaining Healthy Complex Sentences

ACTIVITY A   BUILDING ENGLISH POWER: INTRODUCTORY CLAUSES, PHRASES, AND PARENTHETICAL EXPRESSIONS

1. For many workers, health care is a major expense.

2. If you wish to continue to participate in the insurance plan, please return the signed form.

3. To include vegetables and fruits in your daily diet is recommended for good health (Correct)

4. Since your last bill, premium rates have increased slightly.

5. You will receive supplemental insurance benefits if you are hospitalized. (Correct)

6. More than ever, you need adequate medical insurance.

7. We cannot process your claim, however, without a detailed statement.

8. In an effort to control costs, we increased the deductible on the dental plan.

9. We have served one million members since we offered our plan. (Correct)

10. To exercise regularly is important for physical fitness. (Correct)

11. As you know, a smoke-free workplace is endorsed by most Americans.

12. DWI laws, without a doubt, have become stricter in the past decade.

13. After the public debate, Congress will address the issue of health insurance.

14. Within the last few years, HMOs have become an alternative approach to medical treatment for patients.

15. Arthritis problems, according to some doctors, can be treated with a proper nutritional diet.

16. You need to make reservations before next week if you plan to attend the health fair. (Correct)

17. There are a number of medical Web sites, such as WebMD.

18. If individuals exercise, they will lower their stress levels.

19. To surf the Web for information can be time-consuming. (Correct)

20. As you know, you are entitled to health and dental insurance.

ACTIVITY B   BUILDING WORD POWER

1. ophthalmologist	8. Metabolism
2. cholesterol	9. nutritionist
3. nutrition	10. comprehensive
4. network	11. Biomedical
5. HMO	12. outpatient
6. orthopedic	13. mammogram
7. transition	14. DWI

ACTIVITY D: EDITING POWER

Task A
(Form Letter)

```
(Current Date)

Dear Participant:

As a result of a comprehensive one-year study on medical
insurance costs, sections of our medical plan have been
restructured.
In an effort to control future costs, the following
changes will become effective immediately:

    1. Your deductible will increase to $200 for an
       individual and $350 for a family.
    2. There will be a 5 percent increase in the premium
       rate.
    3. You will need a second opinion for major surgery.
       If this procedure is not followed, payment will be
       denied.

You may wish, however, to consider our monthly payment
plan if you find that an increase in premiums may be
difficult to absorb. Please feel free to call our
Customer Service Department at (800)336-1000 if you need
assistance.

Sincerely yours,

Cynthia Washington
Director
ri
```

ACTIVITY E   WRITING PRACTICUM

Exercise 1   Using a Thesaurus (may be other options.)

1. inexpensive, low-cost	5. great, extensive
2. connection, link	6. ease, lessen
3. started, initiated	7. increase, elevate
4. choose, select	8. treatments, solutions

Exercise 2 **Replacing Descriptive Words (Answers may vary.)**

1. The National Heart Association states that foods filled with saturated fats are disastrous (poor, detrimental) for your health.

2. Selecting a(n) comprehensive (quality, ideal) medical plan can be one of the most important choices a family can make.

3. Reading numerous health coverage brochures can be confusing (dull).

4. The nurse who administered my blood test was efficient (competent).

5. In addition to improving your health, a well-structured exercise plan can be invigorating (stimulating, exhilarating).

6. Filling out medical forms is a tedious (monotonous, boring) activity.

7. Everyone hopes that medical reimbursement checks are issued promptly (expeditiously, quickly).

8. The choice of a physician is a key (major) factor when selecting a health plan.

9. My yearly physical revealed that I was in excellent (good) health.

10. Recuperating after a surgical procedure can be a gradual process.

Exercise 3 **Choosing Positive Opening Sentences in Letters of Adjustment and Refusal**

A. Topic: Refusing an Invitation

Option: 1. ___X___ 2. _____

Reason: The opening statement should recognize the importance of this organization's activity. Option 2 is curt and shows no interest or appreciation for the opportunity.

B. Topic: Refusing an Invitation

Option: 1. _____ 2. ___X___

Reason: The buffer statement should express the writer's acknowledgment of the invitation in a positive manner and indicate the reason for nonacceptance. Option 1 is unacceptable because it starts with an upbeat remark but then turns negative without providing a reason for nonacceptance.

C. Topic: Refusing a Claim

Option: 1. _____ 2. ___X___

Reason: Option 2 acknowledges the request and tells the reader what has to be done. Option 1 leaves the reader with insufficient information.

D. Topic: Refusing a Claim

Option: 1. ___X___ 2. _____

Reason: Option 1 is empathetic and expresses the reason for declining the claim. Option 2 is cold.

E. Topic: Refusing an Applicant

Option: 1. ___X___ 2. _____

Reason: Statement begins with a positive approach and shows empathy for the applicant. Option 2 conveys a negative attitude.

F. Topic: Refusing an Applicant

Option: 1. _____ 2. ___X___

Reason: Option 2 acknowledges the client's interest and regrets not being able to offer the special package. Option 1 lacks interest in the customer's needs and displays poor goodwill.

G. Topic: Requesting an Adjustment

Option: 1. _____ 2. ___X___

Reason: Option 2 gets to the point in a positive manner. Option 1 is somewhat arrogant.

H. Topic: Requesting an Adjustment

Option: 1. _____ 2. ___X___

Reason: Option 2 uses a positive tone to imply that a billing error was made. Option 1 reflects an argumentative, accusatory tone.

Chapter 7: Retailing Commas in Words, Phrases, and Clauses

ACTIVITY A   BUILDING ENGLISH POWER: COMMA USE IN SERIES, CONSECUTIVE ADJECTIVES, NONRESTRICTIVE/RESTRICTIVE CLAUSES, APPOSITION, DATES, CITIES, AND STATES

1. You, a valued customer, are eligible for our money-saving bonus plan.

2. On May 1, 20xx, our popular, well-known rug sale will take place.

3. Price Cutter, a national chain, will open a store in Huntington, New York, a thriving suburban community.

4. Designer clothing, which appeals to today's shopper, can be purchased at discount stores.

5. Appliances carry a manufacturer's warranty that offers consumers protection against product defects. (Correct)

6. Shoppers who look for affordable quality are joining warehouse price clubs. (Correct)

7. Our electronics store, which is located in the mall, is offering a 10 percent discount on VCRs, camcorders, and CD players.

8. As a valued, respected charge customer, you are invited to our annual two-day sale, which will be held this weekend.

9. If you are interested in discount stores, Chet Edwards' latest guide, *The Popular Discount Malls*, is now available at your bookstore.

10. The seminar speaker discussed today's competitive market, consumer preferences, and new marketing trends.

11. The new, upscale mall that attracted huge crowds on the weekend will extend its shopping hours.

12. The popular home-furnishing store offers free shipping, a convenient layaway plan, and low credit rates.

13. The firm has scheduled Friday, July 31, for its annual physical inventory.

14. Our spring catalog, which was recently mailed to you, illustrates the latest women's fashions.

15. The best seller *Repackaging Your Sales Approach* sells for $19.95 plus shipping. (Correct)

16. The lengthy, informative sales report was distributed to the staff.

17. The semi-annual sale that was scheduled for Wednesday, March 1, has been postponed.

18. The European designer who specializes in women's sportswear will show his line of clothing at the fashion show. (Correct)

19. The retail store that sells organic food is moving to the new shopping mall. (Correct)

20. Individuals can download music, movies, and games on the Internet.

ACTIVITY B   BUILDING WORD POWER

1. warehouse clubs
2. boutiques
3. electronic malls
4. Megamalls
5. upsurge
6. redeemed
7. Innovative
8. backlogged
9. privileged
10. outlet malls
11. upscale
12. physical inventory
13. warranty
14. franchises

ACTIVITY D: EDITING POWER

Task A
(Form Letter)

```
(Current Date)

Dear Customer:

We value you as a customer and want to show our sincere
appreciation for your support and loyalty.
   A special weekend has been reserved for our preferred
customers. This weekend, June 15, 16, and 17, you are
invited to take 10 percent off our entire line of
merchandise, which includes jewelry, clothing, and home
furnishings. To get this extra 10 percent off the
ticketed price, present this letter and use your
Albertson's charge card when making your purchase.
   We are introducing a new service for our busy
customers. The Shopper's Cafe will serve salads,
sandwiches, and gourmet coffees throughout the day.
We look forward to serving you.

Sincerely yours,

Sam Ross
Vice President
ri
```

ACTIVITY E   WRITING PRACTICUM

Exercise: Parallelism

1. The goals of the manufacturer are to mass produce custom-made clothing and to sell directly to the consumer.

2. The antiquated marketing system has been updated by using computer technology and by sending employees for training.

3. In marketing, computers are used for product inventory control, daily sales records, and customer feedback.

4. Suburban malls have replaced downtown shopping areas because they are centralized, diversified, and accessible.

5. Our entire line of merchandise, which includes jewelry, furniture, and new fall fashions, is on sale.

6. This month's sales of winter clothes will be a huge success because of two-day sales and a 20 percent discount.

7. Come to the selling course prepared to take notes, to listen to the guest speaker, and to ask some questions.

8. Your mail-order catalog was received yesterday, and my order for furniture was sent to the purchasing department today.

9. Good salespersons should have knowledge <u>of</u> and familiarity with their stock.

10. The department store, specializing in sporting goods, also features designer clothing, <u>exercise equipment</u>, and <u>travel books</u>.

11. The mall has increased its budget for hiring security personnel and <u>preventing shoplifting</u>.

12. The company sent out direct mailers <u>to advertise</u> the sale and promote new merchandise.

13. When the shopping mall was designed, the architect considered mall motif, <u>store layout</u>, and accessibility to roads.

14. The shopper purchased groceries at the supermarket, <u>cosmetics at the drug store</u>, and <u>a sweater at the boutique</u>.

15. Service, <u>dependability</u>, and <u>product value</u> are the major goals of our firm.

Chapter 8: Check-In with the Semicolon

ACTIVITY A   BUILDING ENGLISH POWER: COMMAS AND SEMICOLONS

1. For hotel reservations, you can call your travel agent; or you can dial our toll-free number.

2. Hotels in major cities offer complimentary features in their weekend packages; for example, continental breakfast, health club, and free parking.

3. Popular vacation resort areas include San Juan, Puerto Rico; Cancun, Mexico; and Hilton Head, South Carolina.

4. A great way to visit new areas is to stay at bed-and-breakfast inns; they are informal and friendly.

5. The conference room has been reserved for our June meeting; plans for the luncheon are incomplete.

6. The convention activities will be held in Scottsdale, Arizona; in addition, local tours will be offered.

7. For your information, a layout of the Conference Center is attached; and a brochure about our facilities is enclosed.

8. Registration for the conference will take place in the hotel lobby; and the exhibit area, which is rather large, will be held on the mezzanine floor.

9. We, unfortunately, cannot accommodate your group during the week of May 15; but our facilities are available the following week.

10. The members of the Executive Board, after visiting several hotels, met to discuss future convention sites; but they were unable to reach a decision.

11. Reservations must be guaranteed with a credit card; otherwise, rooms are held only until 4 p.m.

12. Our hotel chain combines quality accommodations, fine service, and good value; moreover, these hotels are highly rated by travel agents.

13. A block of 20 rooms has been held for your company conference; you are reminded of our 48-hour cancellation policy.

14. We offer a special weekend rate; however, reservations must be made two weeks in advance.

15. Our hotels are located at the following airports: London, England; Milan, Italy; and Tokyo, Japan.

16. We will fly to Atlanta on Thursday morning; therefore, you can schedule an afternoon meeting.

17. The article appeared in the July 10, 2007, issue of *Leisure Living*; and it was distributed to our travel agents.

18. The hotel chain is expanding into the vacation market; namely, timesharing ownership, resort living, and cruises.

19. The new suburban trains are fast and efficient; they will be popular with the commuters.

20. The general manager will visit the hotel locations in Memphis, Tennessee; New Orleans, Louisiana; and Jacksonville, Florida.

ACTIVITY B BUILDING WORD POWER

1. consolidation
2. amenities
3. Gourmet
4. projections
5. implemented
6. complimentary
7. partition
8. directories
9. continental breakfast
10. concierge

ACTIVITY D: EDITING POWER

Task A

(Current Date)

Mr. Stuart Hall
105 Los Gatos Boulevard
Sacramento, CA 95813-3223

Dear Mr. Hall:

SUBJECT: FACILITIES FOR ANNUAL CONVENTION

We have rec<u>ei</u>ved your inquiry about holding an annual convention at Royale Americana Hotel. We are pleased that we will be able to accom<u>mo</u>date your group.

Concerning our facilitie<u>s</u>, they are the finest in the are<u>a</u>; and our convention rates are competitive. We have 10 meeting rooms that hold a maximum of 50 people each and have noi<u>se-p</u>roof partitions that allow for expansion. For the conference room<u>s</u>, the latest sound equipment is available. Our guest rooms are spacious and well furnished. The three gourmet restaurants that we have on the premises cater to different taste<u>s</u>; however, light snacks are served at our Oak Bar. We also offer our guests recreation amenitie<u>s</u>; namel<u>y</u>, an indoor poo<u>l</u>, health sp<u>a</u>, and free movies. A walkway connects our hotel to a major shopping mall with boutique shops and wel<u>l-k</u>nown retail stores.

A computerized check-in system is use<u>d</u>, and our guests are greeted in the lobby with "smart-card" keys and a conference packet. A brochur<u>e</u>, price lis<u>t</u>, and layout of our facilities <u>are</u> enclosed for your review.

I am sure you will find Roy<u>ale</u> Americana Hotel the ideal <u>site</u> for your convention.

Sincerely yours,

Carlos Ramirez
Convention Manager
ri
Enclosures

ACTIVITY E WRITING PRACTICUM

Exercise 1 Misplaced Modifiers (Answers may vary.)

1. The hotel visitors riding the jitney saw the golf course.

2. Mr. Smith left his briefcase containing his wallet, his passport, and his important papers in the hotel room.

3. Ms. Garcia met a relative in the hotel lobby whom she hadn't seen since childhood.

4. The new hotel that was managed by Mr. Bright was built by Gutierrez Construction Co. in 1996 at a cost of $2 million.

5. The office clerk made a reservation for a room with double beds and a private bath for Mr. and Mrs. Robert Jiminez.

6. For the convenience of its guests, the Belle Convention Center has excellent facilities, good restaurants, and shuttle service to and from the airport.

7. Telephone reservations are accepted on a space-available basis for prospective guests.

8. For dinner, the dress code for men is formal with jackets.

9. Picture Waterfront Inn as a vacation spot with its landscaped beachfront and its rocky shoreline.

10. Business travelers use our deluxe hotels at two airports; namely, Chicago O'Hare and Los Angeles International.

11. The small hotel, a charming place, is within walking distance of the shopping district.

12. Spas are ideal for stressed individuals.

13. The concierge recommended to the guests a restaurant which is a short distance from the hotel.

14. The beach resort gave its guests a complimentary night.

15. The resort, nestled in the mountains, offers its guests a relaxed vacation.

Exercise 2   Dangling Modifiers

1. I saw a spectacular view of the countryside while riding in the hot-air balloon.

2. While she was traveling in the Southwest, her family was touring Europe.

3. The owner decided to sell the sculpture, which was hidden in the basement for the last 40 years.

4. The president arrived in town while I was a guest at the hotel.

5. After visiting the seaside village many times, I drew plans for a summer cottage.

6. After three days of rain, the visitors left the national park.

7. My assistant completed the report while I was getting ready for the staff meeting.

8. After my 10-hour flight, I was fatigued.

9. The people of New Zealand welcome visitors to see the breathtaking scenery.

10. Since we prefer the beaches to the mountains, the Caribbean was our choice.

Exercise 3   Modifier Errors (Answers may vary.)

(1) Anyone who has studied at the Acme School of Hotel Management can learn to make quick decisions in the field of hotel management in a matter of minutes. (2) Located in a thriving and bustling downtown metropolitan area, our campus offers students the benefits of internships at nearby hotels. (3) Our workshops and seminars are led by well-trained, professional leaders in the hotel industry. (4) Our brochure, which includes itemized costs and course descriptions, will be sent free of charge on request.

Exercise 4   Modifier Errors (Answers may vary.)

(1) Arriving at our hotel, we found that members of a Bird Watchers' Convention had been checked into our room. (2) Apologizing, the desk clerk led us to another room on the first floor. (3) The dining room was crowded with people wearing binoculars, eating, and discussing the local migrating bird population. (4) There were other guests among the bird watchers, but they were hard to spot. (5) Rising early to spot the

birds, the devotees woke us up each morning. (6) Eventually giving in, we were intrigued by the bird-watching excursions and decided to join in on the fun.

Chapter 9: Marketing Possessives

ACTIVITY A   BUILDING ENGLISH POWER: POSSESSIVES

Exercise 1   Possessive Nouns

Phrase	Singular Possessive	Plural Possessive
Policy of the firm	firm's policy	firms' policies
1. bonus of the employee	employee's bonus	employee's bonuses
2. report of the committee	committee's report	committees' reports
3. representative of the company	company's representative	companies' representatives
4. profit of the business	business's profit	businesses' profits
5. gift of the mother-in-law	mother-in-law's gift	mothers-in-law's gifts
6. export policy of a country	country's export policy	countries' export policies
7. testimony of the eyewitness	eyewitness's testimony	eyewitnesses' testimonies
8. toy of the child	child's toy	children's toys
9. fee of the attorney	attorney's fee	attorneys' fees
10. salary of the executive	executive's salary	executives' salaries

Exercise 2   Contractions

1. It is
2. cannot
3. Who is
4. have not
5. will not

Exercise 3   Review of Possessives

1. The firm's decision to introduce video disks in its marketing plan will affect the advertising department.

2. Management met to discuss the use of telemarketing to increase the businesses' sales.

3. A multimedia approach provides opportunities to meet many readers' and listeners' needs.

4. David and Emily's proposal to study the advantages of direct mailing was given to the marketing research group.

5. The applicant with five years' experience in fashion display was offered the department manager's position.

6. Franchises offer an individual the opportunity to be one's own boss.

7. The Jones's and Burns's companies are merging to increase their productivity.

8. Salespersons' attitudes often determine customers' decisions to purchase merchandise.

9. Competitors' prices are influencing the sales policies of the firm and its subsidiaries.

10. The women's and men's departments are being reorganized to include designer clothing.

11. We bought three similar CDs for our brothers-in-law's birthdays.

12. The store is offering a 10 percent discount off the manufacturer's suggested retail price.

13. Trucks are a popular means of transporting goods because merchandise can go directly from the shipper's place to the customer's business.

14. The library's new electronic information center will offer access to business periodicals.

15. Although Jared has the advantage of better locations for his shops than Eric, each of Jared's and Eric's repair shops has a good reputation for fast and satisfactory service.

16. It was not **anyone's** fault that the shipment was delayed.

17. Subscribers will be able to visit the **newspaper's** Web site to read **its** editorial page.

18. The **HMO's** ruling affected the **patient's** insurance coverage.

19. I sat in my **boss's** seat at the **men's** basketball game.

20. **Lori and Donna's** presentation on e-marketing was well received by the **firm's** sales staff.

Activity B   Building Word Power

1. franchise
2. franchisee
3. commission
4. standalone
5. subsidiary
6. supplement
7. Telemarketing
8. Network marketing
9. entrepreneur
10. franchiser
11. feasibility
12. rebate

ACTIVITY D: EDITING POWER

Task A

```
TO:        Sales Representatives

FROM:      Eric Choy
           Vice President

DATE:      (Current Date)

SUBJECT:   FAX SOFTWARE
```

Because of complaints from sales representatives, we are
now considering alternative procedures to eliminate time
wasted while waiting to use a standalone fax machine.

One suggestion is the feasibility of using fax
software to transmit documents directly from the desktop
PCs. Studies show that users of this type of software
have increased their productivity; sales representatives
can save an hour of each workday. You no longer waste
valuable time that could be spent contacting a
prospective client.

General Computer Company will present its software at
a meeting scheduled for Monday, June 19. Please clear
your calendar to attend. After this session, we shall
expect the sales force's reaction before a decision
is made.

ri

ACTIVITY E WRITING PRACTICUM (Answers may vary.)

Exercise 1 Rewrite Concisely

1. Because of bad weather, our plane arrived at midnight.

2. In three days, we shipped 1000 lbs. of food.

3. If we have another bad hurricane season, we shall be forced to raise the insurance rates.

4. Even though we cut the budget by 20 percent, we still face a deficit.

5. We request that you refer to last month's statement and check the purchases.

6. We received your check to cover the $100 balance.

7. Please repeat the instructions.

8. You must call a meeting to get a consensus on the proposed advertising compaign.

Exercise 2 Sentence Rewrite for Clarity

(1) Most people strongly emphasize personal health and appearance in their daily living. (2) However, very busy schedules don't always enable individuals to get needed nutrients.

(3) The Indigo Vitamin System is a nutritionally balanced combination of vitamins and minerals essential for a healthy body. (4) Furthermore, the Indigo Vitamin System encourages a weight management program that includes daily exercise, proper diet, and stress control.

(5) After following it for one year, I am so strongly committed to the Indigo Vitamin System that I have become an independent distributor of its nutritional line. (6) If you are impressed by the enclosed brochure and wish to order any of the exceptional products, please contact me. (7) You also can become an independent distributor after using the products for a trial period.

(8) As an independent distributor, you will represent an outstanding product line, which will give you a good income. (9) You will receive a discount on all items you purchase. (10) Whether you are a beginner or a veteran salesperson, you will receive the training support needed to provide your customers with superior service.

(11) Good health is the key to a successful and productive life.

(12) Accept our invitation to try the Indigo Vitamin System, which will give you a healthier, more active lifestyle.

Chapter 10: Traveling with Colons and Pronouns

ACTIVITY A   BUILDING ENGLISH POWER: PRONOUNS AND COLONS

Exercise 1   Pronouns

1. he
2. their
3. them
4. him
5. us
6. He and I
7. her
8. they
9. her and me
10. She and I

Exercise 2   Who, Whom, That, Which

1. who
2. whom
3. who
4. whom
5. whom
6. Whomever, who
7. Whom
8. which
9. whom
10. whomever
11. whom
12. whom
13. who
14. who
15. who
16. that
17. who
18. whomever
19. that
20. whoever

1. We plan to leave for the airport at <u>3:10 p.m.</u> with <u>whoever</u> is available at that time.

2. <u>Who</u> is interested in touring the following cities_: London_, Milan_, and Athens?

3. Tourists <u>who</u> are planning to travel by car should review the following checklist<u>:</u> get car tuneup_, obtain roadmaps_, get sightseeing information_, and carry emergency supplies.

4. The manufacturing executives will visit their plants as follows_: Bangkok_, Thailand_; Jakarta_, Indonesia_; and Kobe_, Japan.

5. <u>Who</u> has scheduled the afternoon tour for <u>1:15 p.m.</u>?

ACTIVITY B   BUILDING WORD POWER

1. emerging	9. instantaneously
2. itinerary	10. diversified
3. budget	11. Globalization
4. cost conscious	12. liaison
5. nominal	13. accrues
6. segments	14. strategies
7. preliminary	15. no-frills
8. priority	16. extended-stay hotels

ACTIVITY D: EDITING POWER

Task A
(Form Letter)

```
(Current Date)

Dear Customer:

SUBJECT: ADDITIONAL TRAVEL PRIVILEGES
```

In an effort to offer our customers additional travel <u>privileges,</u> we are pleased to announce our new frequent flyer plan with Executive Airlines.
    Whenever you arrange a tour or make plane reservations through <u>us,</u> you will rec<u>ei</u>ve bonus air miles based on the number of miles flown and type of land arrangements. Anyone <u>who</u> accrues 25,000 miles can apply for a free <u>round-trip</u> ticket in business class to any U.S. city served by <u>E</u>xecutive Airlines. If you have a minimum of 10,000 <u>miles,</u> you will be able to get a cash <u>discount</u> on one of our regularly priced tickets. This new policy offers our customers a greater <u>incentive</u> to take more vacations.

An added amenity for our customers is our new priority reservations system. This <u>computerized</u> service allows you to call our to<u>ll-f</u>ree number for reservations. Our representatives are on call seven days a week for vacation information and suggested travel packages.

<u>Whoever</u> wishes to take advantage of this frequent flyer plan needs only to fill out the enclosed application form. There is no charge to enroll in the frequent flyer plan. Why not join the thousands <u>who</u> have already taken advantage of this offer.

Sincerely yours,

Edward Lawson
General Manager
ri
Enclosure

ACTIVITY E   WRITING PRACTICUM

Exercise 1   Pointing and Limiting Adjectives

1. Those <u>kinds</u> of package tours are inexpensive.

2. <u>That</u> tour guide was well informed.

3. <u>Those</u> cruises cater to senior citizens.

4. Please ask <u>those</u> travel agents to come to the tourism convention.

5. Are these <u>types</u> of flights eligible for frequent flier miles?

6. <u>This</u> brochure describes a very exciting trip to the Galapagos Islands.

7. I can't decide between <u>these</u> accommodations and <u>those</u> luxury rooms.

8. <u>Those</u> countries <u>that</u> are in the news because of terrorism show a sudden drop in tourism.

9. <u>That</u> bellhop took such good care of my luggage that I gave him a big tip.

10. These <u>kinds</u> of side trips are available for nominal fees after you pay for the total package.

Exercise 2   Writing Sentences for Conciseness and Clarity

1. People now prefer shorter vacations.

2. We decided to take an auto trip because of the increase in airfare.

3. If a strike occurs, the passengers will receive a refund.

4. Usually, individuals still prefer to discuss vacation plans with a travel agent.

5. At your request, we mailed you the travel brochure for Alaska.

6. Thank you for payment for your European vacation tour.

7. I am unable to attend next week's seminar.

8. Thank you for your support and help.

9. Although we have sent you numerous reminders, we have not received your check for the overdue balance of $500.

10. We are sending you our check for $100 to reserve the meeting room.

Exercise 3   Writing Paragraphs for Conciseness and Clarity (Answers may vary.)

Paragraph 1

Are you planning a trip this summer? A fast, efficient way to do this is to use TripSaver, a computer software package to help you plan your vacation. This package will map out a route, suggest side trips, and give you estimated driving time. This program also will list overnight accommodations. For a quick, scenic way to travel, use TripSaver.

Paragraph 2

Join our Five Star Travel Club to get a low-priced vacation of $199 for each member of your family. Members receive reduced rates on airfare, hotel accommodations, and car rentals. You may travel to exotic Hawaiian resorts or to cosmopolitan U.S. cities.

To be eligible for these inexpensive vacations, join our club today. Mail the enclosed card; we will bill you for the $25 membership fee.

Chapter 11: Governing Quotations

ACTIVITY A   BUILDING ENGLISH POWER: QUOTATION MARKS

1. The town supervisor stated, "If you have any suggestions on ways in which we can improve the town, please contact my office."

2. "Property taxes will increase by 10 percent," stated the controller, "unless we reduce spending."

3. "Are you interested in the newly formed civic association?" asked my neighbor.

4. The judge suggested that a community service program could be an alternative means of punishment for minor offenses. (reported speech)

5. The notice read as follows: "A public hearing to discuss housing will be held on April 15, 2007, at Town Hall."

6. "You, an active civic leader, are invited to attend the meeting on Thursday," stated the council president.

7. I asked, "Have you seen the article titled 'Federal Budget' that appeared in the *Tribune Herald* last week?"

8. Did the community leader say, "We need to have greater recreation facilities for our youth"?

9. Do you plan to attend the program called "Multicultural Interaction" that is being sponsored by the Community Development Department? (reported speech)

10. "As you know," commented the congresswoman, "we are introducing legislation to give financial assistance to college students."

11. My friend asked, "Have you read the article 'The Role of Government in the 1990s'?"

12. "With the changes in traffic patterns," announced the legislator, "we need to revise our noise ordinance."

13. "Is it possible that the trial will be postponed?" asked the lawyer.

14. In honoring the town resident Jim O'Connor, the mayor said, "Jim's dedication to his neighbors has helped our quality of life."

15. The civic association member asked, "Why were the beautification plans for Main Street postponed until the spring?"

16. The chapter, "Ensuring Clean Water," in the newly published book *Save Our Environment* reviews a number of suggestions to improve our drinking water.

17. Mr. Ryan said, "Government works better in cooperation with its citizens."

18. The student said, "I cannot find the article entitled 'Protecting Open Space.'"

19. The committee chairperson asked, "What progress has the task force made on evacuation plans for the town?"

20. The governor commented, "We need to abolish the state sales tax"; however, some of the legislators disagreed with the suggestion.

ACTIVITY B   BUILDING WORD POWER

1. fiscal	8. town council
2. multicultural	9. municipal
3. legislation	10. alternative
4. stalled	11. bulk
5. diminished	12. ordinance
6. budget	13. commissioner
7. legislator	14. assessment

ACTIVITY D: EDITING POWER

Task A

```
TO:         Civic Association Leaders

FROM:       Paul Turner

DATE:       (Current Date)

SUBJECT:    BUDGET HEARINGS
```

You are cordially invited to participate in the 200x___
budget process. There will be two public meetings to
discuss the budget proposal.

The first meeting will be held o<u>n</u> Thursday, October
1<u>5,</u> 20_<u>,</u> at 7 p.m., at City <u>H</u>all. The following
departments will make their presentation<u>s:</u> Department of
<u>Public Works,</u> Parks and Recreation<u>,</u> and Planning and
Zoning. The second meeting that will be held on <u>N</u>ovember
1 at 7 p.m. will include the following department<u>s:</u>
<u>P</u>olice,<u> Fire,</u> and<u> P</u>urchasing.

At these meeting<u>s,</u> the public will have an
opportunity to ask questions on any item of the budget.
In the <u>past,</u> people frequently have aske<u>d,</u> <u>"</u>How come we
were never informed about local issue<u>s?"</u> I firmly
believe that local residents must be knowledgeable about
<u>their</u> community. As I have stated previousl<u>y,</u> <u>"</u>Public
involvement is vital to effective functioning of
government.<u>"</u>

I look forward to working with you as we begin to
prepare for the next fiscal year.

ri

ACTIVITY E   WRITING PRACTICUM

Exercise 1   Using Prepositions Correctly

1. of	**9.** for
2. between	**10.** about
3. with	**11.** about
4. to	**12.** among
5. from	**13.** by
6. in	**14.** at
7. to	**15.** during
8. on	

Exercise 2   Puzzling Words

1. fewer	**12.** Sometime	**23.** quit, quiet
2. less	**13.** some time	**24.** stationary
3. may	**14.** They're	**25.** stationery
4. can	**15.** their	**26.** council
5. set	**16.** Anyone	**27.** counsel
6. sit	**17.** Any one	**28.** capitol
7. lose	**18.** everyone	**29.** capital
8. loose	**19.** Every one	**30.** angry
9. allot	**20.** Regardless	**31.** did
10. between	**21.** lay	**32.** doesn't
11. among	**22.** lie	

Chapter 12: Help Wanted: Applying Hyphens and Numbers Correctly

ACTIVITY A   BUILDING ENGLISH POWER:HYPHENS AND NUMBER USAGE

1. Employers are interested in self-motivated individuals who are well informed about the firm's products.

2. The regular conference fee is **$20**; members have a 10 **percent** discount.

3. Applicants should send a follow-up letter to thank the interviewer.

4. The well-known speaker Dr. Robert Reed will present a two-day workshop on self-assertiveness.

5. The applicant's interview was scheduled for **2** p.m. at the company's headquarters at **One** Park Row.

6. The firm budgeted **$1.2 million** for renovation of its 50-story building.

7. At the conference, the vice president of the firm remarked that the sales force will be reduced by one-third by mid-April.

8. The new contract includes a three-week vacation for employees who have been in the company for **five** years.

9. Home-based work is a good option for part-time employment.

10. The 12-page manual will give you detailed, step-by-step instructions for the new computer software.

11. Seventeen- and eighteen-year-olds are encouraged to find volunteer internships to gain hands-on experience.

12. Entry-level jobs have become more demanding with the need for higher technical skills.

13. The president of the company is <u>well known</u> in the electric utility industry.

14. Some individuals prefer the freedom of a freelance job rather than a traditional 8-hour position.

15. **Twenty** applicants were interviewed for the **three** positions as paralegals.

16. We are voting for either a **one- or two-year** contract. (12.2)

17. The human resources director **commented,** "Only **one-third** of the applicants qualified for the **position.**" (12.8, 11.1, 11.6)

18. We asked all supervisors to submit a **3-year** plan for their departments by Friday at **5** p.m. (12.10)

19. The **$3 million** grant was <u>**well received**</u> by the <u>**newly elected**</u> chairperson. (12.9, 12.4, 12.1)

20. Please fax me **five** copies of the plan which proposes a **35-h**our workweek. (12.9, 12.10)

ACTIVITY B   BUILDING WORD POWER

1. modulated
2. teleconferencing
3. human resources
4. commitment
5. assertiveness
6. assess
7. internship
8. preliminary
9. crucial
10. prospective
11. perusal

ACTIVITY D: EDITING POWER

Task A


```
(Current Date)

Attention Human Resources Department
Anchor Corporation
55 Pine Street
Edison NJ 08032-3387

Ladies and Gentlemen:
```

Please consider me as an applicant for the position of sales representative <u>that</u> you advertised in the *New York Times* on Sunday, May 16. I have chosen your company because it is a well-respected organization with a reputation for supporting employees in their professional development.

As shown in my enclosed resume, you will find that my educational background has provided me with an excellent foundation for the position for which I am applying. I am skilled in the use of Microsoft Office software, including Word, Excel, and PowerPoint. My present position as an administrative assistant has enabled me to develop my interpersonal and communication skills, which are essential in a sales position. I will bring to the job a willingness to work and an eagerness to learn.

May I have the opportunity to discuss employment possibilities with you? I would like to schedule an interview at your convenience. My telephone number is (student's telephone number).

Sincerely yours,

(Student's Name)
Enclosure

ACTIVITY E   WRITING PRACTICUM

Revisions

1. A (correct format)

2. C (clear explanation of job source)

3. B (grammatically correct)

4. B (clear and complete statement)

5. B (a comprehensive and well-written statement)

6. C (complete, punctuated correctly)

7. B (correct grammar and number usage)

8. D (concise and correctly written)

9. A (correct format)

10. C

REKEYED LETTER

Dear Mr. Shane:

I am writing to you at the suggestion of my neighbor, Mrs. Dorothy Frank, one of your employees. She informed me that there are five summer internships available in your office, and I am most interested in applying for one of them. At Queens College, I am majoring in municipal government, a career field that I find fascinating.

Please send an internship application form to me at the above address and include any other requirements needed in applying for the internship. If necessary,

I can provide three letters of reference. I am enclosing a self-addressed, stamped envelope for your convenience.

I am available any day after 2 p.m. for an interview. I look forward to hearing from you.

Sincerely yours,

Michelle Yager

Enclosure

Model Documents

MODEL LETTER
FULL BLOCK FORMAT
SPECIAL NOTATION AND ENUMERATION

Date

CONFIDENTIAL

MS. ADAM BRIGHT
COMPANY NAME
STREET ADDRESS
CITY STATE ZIP
Dear Ms. Bright:

1.

2.

Sincerely yours,

Dictator's Name
Title

PS:

Document Coding
Option

MODEL LETTER
FULL BLOCK FORMAT
ATTENTION LINE/SUBJECT LINE/COPY NOTATION

Date

ATTENTION MR. JOHN SANCHEZ
COMPANY NAME
STREET ADDRESS
CITY STATE ZIP
Ladies and Gentlemen:
SUBJECT: COMMUNICATIONS SEMINAR

Sincerely yours,

Dictator's Name
Title

Enclosure

c: Mr. Rocco

Document Coding
Option

MODEL FORM LETTER

Current Date

Dear Customer:

Sincerely,

Dictator's Name
Title

Enclosure

Document Coding
Option

MODEL LETTER
MODIFIED BLOCK FORMAT

Date

MR. JOSEPH ROBERTS
111 POST ROAD
DULUTH MN 55801-9123
Dear Mr. Roberts:

Sincerely yours,

Dictator's Name
Title

Enclosure

Document Coding
Option

Date

Attention: Mr. John Sanchez
Davis Electronics Corp.
105 Cove Drive
Sacramento, CA 95813-3223

(*double space*)
Ladies and Gentlemen:
(*double space*)
SUBJECT: COMMUNICATIONS SEMINAR
(*double space*)

_____

_____

_____.

(*double space*)

_____

_____

_____.

(*double space*)

_____

_____.

(*double space*)

_____

_____.

(*double space*)

Sincerely yours,

(3 blank lines)
Dictator's Name
Title
(*double space*)
ri (*reference initials of secretary*)
(*double space*)
Enclosure (*An item is enclosed with letter.*)
(*double space*)
c Mr. Ramon Nogueras (*Copy of document is being sent to Mr. Nogueras.*)

Note: For explanation of ATTENTION line see chapter 5, pg. 111

REGISTERED

ATTENTION MR JOHN SANCHEZ
DAVIS ELECTRONICS CORP
105 COVE DRIVE
SACRAMENTO CA 95813-3223

Document Coding
Option

Date

CONFIDENTIAL

Ms. Joan Bright
Vice President
ABC Company
10 Executive Drive
Orlando, Fl 32766-1008

(*double space*)
Dear Ms. Bright:
(*double space*)

_____

_____

(*double space*)
1.   _____

     _____.

(*double space*)
2.   _____

     _____

     _____.

(*double space*)

     _____

     _____.

(*double space*)
Sincerely yours,

(*3 blank lines*)

Dictator's Name
Title

(*double space*)
ri

(*double space*)
PS: _____.
(*Postcript is an afterthought.*)

```
┌─────────────────────┐
│   Document Coding    │
│       Option         │
│                      │
└─────────────────────┘
```

Envelope notation:

```
┌──────────────────────────────────────────┐
│  ─────────                    ┌────────┐  │
│  ─────────                    │        │  │
│                               └────────┘  │
│  CONFIDENTIAL            REGISTERED        │
│                                            │
│         MS JOAN BRIGHT                     │
│         VICE PRESIDENT                     │
│         ABC COMPANY                        │
│         10 EXECUTIVE DRIVE                 │
│         ORLANDO FL 32766-1008              │
│                                            │
└──────────────────────────────────────────┘
```

Date

Mr. Joseph Robison
131 Post Road
Duluth, MN 55803-5122

Dear Mr. Robison:
(*double space*)

_____
_____
_____ .

(*double space*)

_____
_____
_____.

(*double space*)

_____
_____.

(*double space*)

_____
_____
_____.

(*double space*)

_____
_____
_____.

_____.

(*double space*)

                                  Mr. Joseph Robison
                                  131 Post Road
                                  Duluth, MN 55803-5122

Sincerely yours,
(*3 blank lines*)

Dictator's Name
Title

(*double space*)
ri

Enclosure

Document Coding
Option

Current Date

(*Individualized names, and addresses may be merged in this space.*)
(*Approximately 10X*)

Dear Customer:
(*double space*)

_____

_____

_____.

(*double space*)

_____

_____

_____.

(*double space*)

_____

_____

_____.

(*double space*)

_____

_____

_____.

(*double space*)
Sincerely,

(*3 blank lines*)

Dictator's Name
Title
(*double space*)
ri

Enclosure

Document Coding Option

SECOND-PAGE HEADING

Use a second-page heading whenever there is a continuation of a letter. Some companies have their own letterhead; otherwise, the following information should appear on the continuing pages of the correspondence. Suggested formats are shown below:

Individual's name, Date, Page number

-or-

Individual's name

Date
Page number

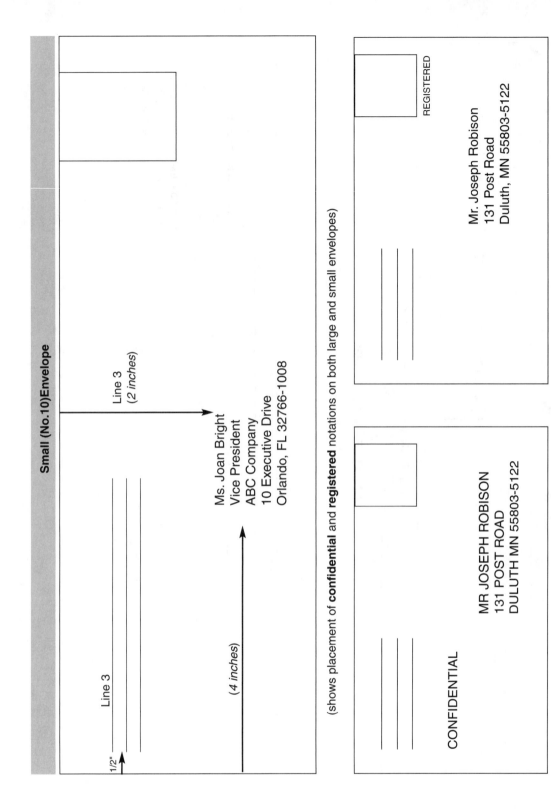

Small (No.10) Envelope

Line 3

1/2"

(4 inches)

Line 3
(2 inches)

Ms. Joan Bright
Vice President
ABC Company
10 Executive Drive
Orlando, FL 32766-1008

(shows placement of **confidential** and **registered** notations on both large and small envelopes)

REGISTERED

Mr. Joseph Robison
131 Post Road
Duluth, MN 55803-5122

CONFIDENTIAL

MR JOSEPH ROBISON
131 POST ROAD
DULUTH MN 55803-5122

Small (No.6,3/4)Envelope

Line 3

1/2"

(2½ inches)

(line 12)

ATTENTION MR JOHN SANCHEZ
BRYANT OFFICE EQUIPMENT
982 PENN AVENUE
NASHVILLE TN 37200—4233

Ms. Joan Bright
Vice President
Apex Data Corporation
One Park Row
New York, NY 10021–3541

Note: When using the envelope template of a word processing program, accept the default positions for the mailing and return addresses. In a window envelope, the placement of the inside address should have a 1/4 in. space around the edge of the window.

To: _____
(*double space*)
FROM: _____
(*double space*)
DATE: _____
(*double space*)
SUBJECT: _____
(*triple space*)

_____

_____.

(*double space*)

_____

_____

_____

_____.

(*double space*)

_____

_____

_____

_____.

(*double space*)

Enumeratedite
ms using
bullets

• _____

_____.

(*double space*)

• _____.

(*double space*)

• _____.

_____

(*double space*)
ri

Enclosure
(*double space*)
c Carla Green, Director

┌─────────────────────┐
│ Document Coding   │
│   Option   │
└─────────────────────┘

E-Mail Correspondence

Subject of E-mail

File	Edit	View	Tools	Message	Help

Reply	Reply All	Forward	Print	Delete	Previous	Next

Receiver's e-mail address

Purpose of message

To: cruz@aol.com
Cc:
Subject: Subscription Renewal
Attachments: none

Salutation included; message sent outside company

Dear Ms. Cruz:

We acknowledge your subscription renewal to Money Matters. Every Friday online you will receive a weekly update of financial news.

Message is concise and clear

Thank you for renewing.

Contact information

Laura Crawford
Subscription Manager
lcrawford@aol.com

E-Mail Memorandums (Internal Companies Memo)

Subject of E-mail

File	Edit	View	Tools	Message	Help

Reply	Reply All	Forward	Print	Delete	Previous	Next

To: O'Brien.sue@packards.com
Cc:
Subject: Meeting for Sales Staff
Attachments: none

Informal style

Salutation and closing optional

Just a reminder that Wednesday's meeting to discuss the sales promotional campaign for the Notethink laptop is scheduled for 10 a.m. See you then. Larry

(*2 inches*)

TITLE
(*triple space*)

_____

_____

_____.

(*triple space*)

SIDE HEADING
(*double space*)

_____

_____

_____.

(*triple space*)

SIDE HEADING
(*double space*)

_____

_____

_____.

(*triple space*)

SIDE HEADING
(*double space*)

_____

_____

_____.

Note: Spacing may vary when keying on computer. If keyed as a single-spaced business report, do not indent first line of paragraph.

APPENDIX C

Addressing Government Officials

PRESIDENT OF THE UNITED STATES

THE PRESIDENT
THE WHITE HOUSE
WASHINGTON DC 20500–0000

Dear Mr. President:

UNITED STATES SENATOR

THE HONORABLE (FULL NAME)
UNITED STATES SENATE
WASHINGTON DC 20510–0000

Dear Senator (Surname):

GOVERNOR

THE HONORABLE (FULL NAME)
GOVERNOR OF (STATE)
CAPITAL CITY STATE ZIP CODE

Dear Governor (Surname):

MEMBER OF STATE LEGISLATURE

THE HONORABLE (FULL NAME)
THE STATE SENATE OR THE HOUSE
    OF REPRESENTATIVES
CAPITAL CITY STATE ZIP

Dear Mr./Ms. (Surname):

UNITED STATES CONGRESSMAN/ CONGRESSWOMAN

THE HONORABLE (FULL NAME)
HOUSE OF REPRESENTATIVES
WASHINGTON DC 20515–0000

Dear Mr./Mrs. (Surname):

MAYOR

THE HONORABLE (FULL NAME)
MAYOR OF (CITY)
CITY STATE ZIP CODE

Dear Mayor (Surname):

APPENDIX D

Postal Abbreviations

State	Abbreviation	State	Abbreviation
Alabama	AL	Montana	MT
Alaska	AK	Nebraska	NE
Arizona	AZ	Nevada	NV
Arkansas	AR	New Hampshire	NH
California	CA	New Jersey	NJ
Colorado	CO	New Mexico	NM
Connecticut	CT	New York	NY
Delaware	DE	North Carolina	NC
District of Columbia	DC	North Dakota	ND
Florida	FL	Ohio	OH
Georgia	GA	Oklahoma	OK
Hawaii	HI	Oregon	OR
Idaho	ID	Pennsylvania	PA
Illinois	IL	Puerto Rico	PR
Indiana	IN	Rhode Island	RI
Iowa	IA	South Carolina	SC
Kansas	KS	South Dakota	SD
Kentucky	KY	Tennessee	TN
Louisiana	LA	Utah	UT
Maine	ME	Vermont	VT
Maryland	MD	Virgin Islands	VI
Massachusetts	MA	Virginia	VA
Michigan	MI	Washington	WA
Minnesota	MN	West Virginia	WV
Mississippi	MS	Wisconsin	WI
Missouri	MO	Wyoming	WY

Proofreader's Marks

Mark	Meaning	Draft Copy	Corrected Copy
～	delete	I will not attend.	I will attend.
∧	insert	inspect for breakage *(and test)*	inspect and test for breakage
STET ...	leave it in	role of key persons	role of key persons
¶	new paragraph	The check cleared. ¶Your statement	The check cleared. Your statement
～	transpose	sturdy and durable equimpent	durable and sturdy equipment
↰	move copy as shown	well known. The speaker was	The speaker was well known.
≡	Capitalize	The World of Bytes	THE WORLD OF BYTES
/	make lowercase	The Local branch	The local branch
#	space	Hemay be	He may be
◯	spell out	⑤CDs	five CDs
‖	align copy	TO: John Woods FROM: Rosa Bell	TO: John Woods FROM: Rosa Bell
◡	close up	how ever	however
⊙	insert colon	the list below	the list below: pens,
∧	insert comma	pens paper clips, and disks	paper clips, and disks
⊙	insert period	I saw Mr Smith.	I saw Mr. Smith.

APPENDIX F

Personal Dictionary

The words in this Appendix appear in Activity B, "Building Word Power," in each chapter.

accelerate   (*v.*; 2)—to progress faster

accrues   (*v.*; 10)—to be added or increased periodically

alternative   (*n.*; 2, 11)—choice between two or more things

amenities   (*n.*; 8)—extra services offered to customers

ASAP   (adv.; 9)—abbreviation for "as soon as possible"

assertiveness   (*n.*; 12)—the quality of being self-confident or forceful

assess   (*v.*; 12)—to evaluate

assessment   (*n.*; 11)—an official evaluation of taxable property

ATM   (*n.*; 1)—automated teller machine

authorization   (*n.*; 1)—legal power to complete a transaction for another person

backlogged   (*adj.*; 7)—refers to tasks or materials accumulated and unperformed

biomedical   (*adj.*; 6)—term describing medical science that deals with the relationship between body chemistry and function

blue chip stocks   (*n.*; 3)—stocks of corporations that are leaders in their fields and have demonstrated consistent growth

bodily injury insurance   (*n.*; 2)—physical damage coverage

bonds   (*n.*; 3)—interest-bearing certificates issued by government or business to raise money

boutique   (*n.*; 7)—small retail shop selling current, trendy clothing

budget   (*n.*; 10, 11)—plan of income and projected expenses

bulk   (*n.*; 11)—large quantity

cafeteria-type medical insurance   (*n.*; 2)—type of insurance for which the individual chooses portions of coverage related to his or her needs

catastrophic insurance (*n.*; 2)—insurance covering expenses from a major accident or disaster not covered by other insurance

certificate of deposit (CD) (*n.*; 1)—savings account for a specific period of time that offers a higher rate of interest and carries a penalty for early withdrawal

cholesterol (*n.*; 6)—a fatty substance found in the body

co-applicant (*n.*; 1)—a person who files a joint request in which both individuals are financially responsible

collateral (*n.*; 1)—item of value, such as stocks or property, used to secure a loan

commission (*n.*; 9)—additional pay added to a salary based on total sales

commissioner (*n.*; 11)—individual who is the head of a department or division of a governmental agency

commitment (*n.*; 12)—pledge to do something, dedication

complimentary (*adj.*; 8)—free of charge

comprehensive (*adj.*; 6)—inclusive; of broad scope

concierge (*n.*; 8)—an individual who arranges special services for hotel guests

condominium (*n.*; 5)—building complex in which units are individually owned

configuration (*n.*; 4)—arrangement of parts making up the whole

consolidation (*n.*; 8)—grouping or merging together

continental breakfast (*n.*; 8)—breakfast consisting of a beverage and bread or light pastry

cooperative (*n.*; 5)—building complex in which owners of an apartment are shareholders of the building

corporate park (*n.*; 5)—cluster of office buildings in a park-like setting

cost conscious (*adj.*; 10)—sensitivity to costs of products or services

crucial (*adj.*; 12)—important; significant

debit card (*n.*; 1)—card used to authorize transactions deducted directly from the checking account

debris (*n.*; 5)—rubbish or the remains of something destroyed

deductible (*n.*; 2)—amount of insured's liability for a claim

delinquent (*adj.*; 5)—business term describing a past-due account

diminished (*v.*; 11)—reduced, lessened

directories (*n.*; 8)—lists of names, places, and items

diversified (*adj.*; 10)—varied

DWI (*n.*; 6)—acronym for "driving while intoxicated"

electronic banking (*n.*; 1)—banking transactions completed through electronic machines

electronic mail (e-mail) (*n.*; 4)—system through which messages are transmitted via computer networks

electronic malls (*n.*; 7)—system on the Internet through which merchandise can be purchased via the computer

emerging (*v.*; 10)—evolving into something new or improved

entrepreneur (*n.*; 9)—individual who initiates, organizes, and manages a business

equity line of credit (*n.*; 1)—loan account for a specified amount of money secured against value of property

escalate (*v.*; 2)—to grow or increase

excess (*n.*; 1)—extra

extended-stay hotels (*n.*; 10)—accommodations that offer home-like suites with kitchen facilities; rates are based on longer stays

facsimile equipment (fax) (*n.*; 4)—telephone and electronic equipment through which an exact copy of information is transmitted

FDIC (*n.*; 1)—Federal Deposit Insurance Corporation, a federal agency that insures savings deposits up to $100,000

feasibility (*n.*; 9)—capability or practicality of completing an activity

fiscal (*adj.*; 11)—pertaining to financial matters

franchise (*n.*; 7, 9)—licensing right to run a business or service for a well-known company according to set operating procedures; e.g., McDonald's™ franchise

franchisee (*n.*; 9)—individual or firm that has been granted a franchise

franchiser (*n.*; 9)—company or manufacturer that grants licensing rights to individuals to run a business

global (*adj.*; 1)—worldwide

globalization (*n.*; 10)—interaction of institutions or governments on a worldwide basis

glossary (*n.*; 3)—list of terms in a special subject with definitions

gourmet (*adj.*; 8)—term describing specialized, fancy foods

home equity line of credit —see equity line of credit

HMO (*n.*; 6)—health maintenance organization; group offering medical services to its subscribers

human resources (*adj.*; 12)—term used to identify personnel departments in companies

implemented (*v.*; 8)—put into effect

index (*n.*; 5)—guide used to measure items such as prices or wages

innovative (*adj.*; 7)—term used to describe new ideas or methods

instantaneously (adv.; 10)—immediately

insufficient funds (*n.*; 1)—not enough money in an account to clear checks for payment

Internet (*n.*; 4)—system that allows users to communicate with others throughout the world via computers

internship (*n.*; 12)—voluntary work assignment without pay

investment (*n.*; 3)—the use of money for the purpose of receiving profit

investment portfolio (*n.*; 3)—list of stocks and bonds owned by an individual, bank, or business

IRA (*n.*; 1)—individual retirement account; a savings plan that allows individuals to put aside money that is not taxed until retirement

itinerary (*n.*; 10)—schedule of travel dates, accommodations, and events

laptop computer (*n.*; 4)—compact, lightweight computer that is easy to carry

lease (*n.*; 5)—contract between landlord and tenant specifying terms of agreement (e.g., length of contract, monetary deposit on apartment)

legislation (*n.*; 11)—laws proposed by local, state, and federal government

legislator (*n.*; 11)—individual elected or appointed to a law-making body

liability insurance (*n.*; 2)—protection against injury and property damages of another person

liaison (*n.*; 10)—a person who acts as a connection between individuals or organizations

mammogram (*n.*; 6)—x-ray examination to detect breast cancer

megamall (*n.*; 7)—large building or site in which retail stores, restaurants, entertainment, and accommodations are located

metabolism (*n.*; 6)—process by which the body converts food and oxygen into energy

modem (*n.*; 4)—electronic device used to convert and transmit data to or from a computer over telephone lines

modulate (*v.*; 12)—to regulate

monitor (*n.*; 4)—a computer screen

mortgage (*n.*; 1, 5)—a loan given by a bank to finance the cost of property, which is security for repayment of the loan

mouse (*n.*; 4)—small, hand-held device that moves the cursor on the computer screen

multicultural (*adj.*; 11)—of diversified ethnic backgrounds

multinational (*adj.*; 3)—referring to many nations

municipal (*adj.*; 11)—pertaining to the local government of a town or city

mutual fund (*n.*; 3)—group formed to invest money obtained from shareholders; investments include stocks and bonds

network (*n.*; 1, 6)—system of interconnecting equipment used for communications; group of individuals who cooperate on a project

network marketing (*n.*; 9)—selling approach in which individuals use personal contacts to make sales

networking (*n.*; *adj.*; 4)—systems of computers linked together to transmit data

no-frills (*adj.*; 10)—no extra amenities; basic services

nominal (*adj.*; 10)—very small amount in proportion to the value of the whole; for example, *nominal* fee for shipping and handling

notebook (*n.*; 4)—a portable, lightweight computer

nutrition (*n.*; 6)—nourishment that promotes good health

nutritionist (*n.*; 6)—individual specializing in nutrition

ophthalmologist (*n.*; 6)—medical doctor specializing in functions and diseases of the eyes

option (*n.*; 2)—right to choose

ordinance (*n.*; 11)—local law or rule

orthopedic (*adj.*; 6)—dealing with treatment, disease, and injuries of the spine, bones, joints, and muscles

outlet mall (*n.*; 7)—mall with discount retail stores

outpatient (*n.*; 6)—person receiving medical treatment or care but not requiring an overnight hospital stay

partition (*n.*; 8)—wall separating two areas

periodically (adv.; 5)—recurring from time to time

perusal (*n.*; 12)—act of reading or examining

phasing out (*v.*; 2)—gradually bringing to an end

physical inventory (*n.*; 7)—manual handcount of merchandise

potpourri (*n.*; 8)—combination, collection, mixed

preliminary (*adj.*; 10, 12)—introductory

premium (*n.*; 2)—the amount paid for an insurance policy

principal (*n.*; 5)—when used as a financial term, refers to the amount of money owed, not including interest

priority (*n.*; 10)—importance

privileged (*adj.*; 7)—entitled to a special advantage

projections (*n.*; 8)—studies predicting future trends

property damage insurance (*n.*; 2)—insurance against claims if the insured's car damages someone's property or land

prorate (*v.*; 5)—to divide proportionately

prospective (*adj.*; 12)—potential, expect to happen

prospectus (*n.*; 3)—report reviewing the financial condition, terms of ownership, and organizational plan of a new business

protocol (*n.*; 4)—set of standards or procedures that allow computers to interact

proxy (*n.*; 3)—stockholders who cannot attend an annual meeting give another person permission to vote on issues on their behalf

realtor (*n.*; 5)—individual who is licensed by the National Association of Real Estate Boards to deal in real estate

rebate (*n.*; 9)—deduction off the original price of an item

redeem (*v.*; 7)—to pay off or buy back

reference (*n.*; 5)—person who can offer personal or employment information on an individual; recommendation

securities (*n.*; 3)—stocks and bonds

security deposit (*n.*; 5)—sum of money given as protection against losses resulting from damages or failure to pay rent

segment (*n.*; 10)—portion or section

software (*n.*; 4)—programs used on a computer (e.g., Microsoft® *Word, Excel*)

specialist (*n.*; 1)—individual devoted to a particular field of study

stalled (*v.*; 11)—delayed or put off

standalone (*adj.*; 9)—term used to describe a computer that operates independently of a network system

stockbroker (*n.*; 3)—agent who buys and sells stocks and bonds for a client

stocks (*n.*; 3)—certificates that show ownership in a corporation

strategies (*n.*; 10)—skills or plans used to reach a goal

subsidiary (*adj.*; 9)—providing secondary or support service to the main organization

subsidized (*v.*; 2)—supported with financial help

supplement (*v.*; 9)—to add to

telecommunications (*n.*; 4)—communications using telephone and video equipment

teleconferencing (*n.*; 12)—use of telephone and video equipment to conduct a joint meeting from two or more office sites

telemarketing (*n.*; 9)—use of the telephone to sell goods or services

town code   (*n.*; 5)—body of laws passed by town regulating various procedures (e.g., building, environmental, and fire codes)

town council   (*n.*; 11)—group of elected officials who run local government

transaction   (*n.*; 1)—business deal or agreement

transition   (*n.*; 6)—change from one stage of activity to another

umbrella insurance   (*n.*; 2)—type of insurance that protects the insured against losses not covered by regular insurance

upscale   (*adj.*; 7)—above the average

upsurge   (*n.*; 7)—upward movement or increase

videoconferencing   (*n.*; 4)—system that uses computer terminals and communications equipment to display data and images

warehouse club   (*n.*; 7)—large retail store selling items in large quantities at discounted prices for its members

warranty   (*n.*; 7)—guarantee by manufacturer that quality and service of product are satisfactory

Web site   (*n.*; 3)—a group of "pages" on the Internet made available by a business, organization, or individual that gives specific information

INDEX

Invitation letters, 111, 113–114
irregardless/regardless, 273
Irregular verbs, 74
Italics, for titles, 34, 155, 263
Items, series of, 292
its/it's, 78, 205

J

Job interview, 299–300
Job interview follow-up letters, 302
Job offer, 300
Job search, 298–299
Job snapshot
Insurance, 29
Finance/Investments, 51
Telecommunications, 73
real estate, 97
health care, 122
retail sales, 149
hospitality, 176
marketing, 204
travel, 230
government, 262
human resources, 289

L

lay/laid/lie, 273
less/fewer, 273
Letters
of apology, 85, 86
attention line, 111
bad news, 216–218
claims, 245, 246–247
claims, response to, 245, 247
closing sentences, 17
collection, 110–111, models, 112–213
community public relations, 276–277
cover, 300–301
cultural communication tips, 49
customer complaint, 85–86

customer complaint, response to, 161–162
e-mail, 90–92
format, 64
guidelines, 17–18
informational, 19
of inquiry, 188–189
of inquiry, response to, 189, 190
interview follow-up, 302
invitation, 111, 113–114
notification, 42, 43, 245, 246
opening sentences, 16
promotional, 19, 20, 216
of refusal, 135–136
of request, 63, 64
of request, response to, 63–64, 65, 245
sales, 42
salutation, 64, 216, 231
subject line, 111
transmittal, 221, 222
lie/lay/laid, 273
Loan officers, 2
lose/loose, 273

M

mad/angry, 273
Marketing, 203–228
corporate snapshot, 203
job snapshot, 204
Marketing analysts, 204
may/can, 273
Measurements, 206, 291
Medical assistants, 122
Medical office managers, 122
Medical records technicians, 122
Memorandums
bad news, 217
defined, 63
e-mail, 90–91, 92
internal business proposals, 194–196
model, 65
writing pointers, 63, 64
Memo reports, 140–142, 166–168
Mexico, 285

Millions, amounts of money in, 34, 291
Minutes of meetings, 282–284
Misplaced modifiers, 184
MLA Style Manual, 252
Modifiers
dangling, 186–187
misplaced, 184
one-thought, 128, 180, 238, 267, 289–290
Money amounts, 34, 128, 238, 291, 292
most, 107
Municipal clerks, 262

N

neither/nor, 51–52
News releases, 281
Nonrestrictive clauses, 149
Notification letters, 42, 43, 245, 246
Nouns
collective, 30
compound, 205
plural, 204–205
proper, 4
singular, 204–205
number, 52
Numbers
house, 291
hyphen usage, 290
joining prefix to, 290
money, 34, 292
page, 291
percentages, 79, 155, 291
plural, 155, 206
usage, 291–292
writing as numbers, 291–292
writing as words, 180, 291

O

Objective pronouns, 231
Occupational Outlook Handbook, 2006-2007, 298

of/off, 102
One-thought modifiers, 128, 180, 238, 267, 289–290
Online resumes, 306–307, 309
on-site, 155
or, 51–52
Outdated words and phrases, 62
Outlines, 253–254
Ownership, and possessive case, 205

P

Page numbers, 291
Paragraphs, 103
Parallelism, 158–159
Paraphrasing, 262
Parenthetical expressions, 123
Passive voice, 74, 109
past/passed, 78
Past perfect tense, 74
Past tense, simple, 73
patient/patience/patients, 128
Percentages, 79, 155, 291
Perfect tense, 73–74
Periodic memo reports, 166–168
Periods
to end sentence, 9
and quotation marks, 155, 263
personal/personnel, 57
Personal pronouns, 205
perspective/prospective, 102
Phrases
defined, 123
inappropriate/outdated, 62
introductory, 123
prepositional, 271
Plagiarism, 251
Plural nouns, 204, 205
Plural numbers, 155, 206
Plural subjects, 29
p.m., 267
Possessive case, 204–206
joint ownership, 205
separate ownership, 205
Possessive pronouns, 231

Underlining, of
titles, 263

V

Verbs
defined, 29
irregular, 74
subject-verb
agreement, 29–30,
51–52
tense, 73–74

Voice
active, 74, 108
passive, 74, 109

W

well-, words beginning
with, 180, 290
well/badly, 106
which/that, 233, 234
who/whom, 233

Wordiness, 18, 37
Word processing
programs, 131–132
Words
inappropriate/outdated,
62
puzzling, 272–274
repetitive, 214
self-, 128, 290
well-, 180, 290
Writing, six Cs of, 18

Y

you, 30

Z

Zeros, in dollar amounts,
238, 292